Research Methodology in Social Sciences

Research Methodology in Social Sciences

Asit Kumar Patnaik

Commonwealth

Research Methodology in Social Sciences

ISBN : 81-7169-664-3

Edition - 2026

Published by :
COMMONWEALTH PUBLISHERS (P) LTD.
4831/24, Govind Lane,
Ansari Road, Darya Ganj,
New Delhi - 110002
Ph. : 23272541, 23242541
e-mail : commonwealthpublishers2016@gmail.com

Distributed by :
ARJUN PUBLISHING HOUSE
4831/24, Govind Lane,
Ansari Road, Darya Ganj,
New Delhi - 110002
Ph. : 23272541, 23242541
e-mail : arjunbooks2001@gmail.com

Laser Typesetting by :
Dimple Computers
Delhi

Printed at :
Balaji Offset
Delhi

Preface

Research is a scientific and systematic search for pertinent information on a specific topic. Some people consider research as a movement from known to unknown. We all possess the vital instinct of inquisitiveness for, when the unknown confront us, we wonder our inquisitiveness makes us probe and attain full and fuller understanding of the unknown. This inquisitiveness is the mother of all knowledge and the method, which man employs for obtaining the knowledge of whatever the unknown, can be termed as research. Research is thus an original contribution to the existing stock of knowledge making for its advancement.

Research methodology is a way to systematically solve the research problem. It may be understood as a science of studying how research is done scientifically. It is necessary for the researcher to know not only the research methods, but also the methodology. It is necessary for a researcher to design his methodology for his problem as the same may differ from problem to problem. Research methodology has many dimensions and research methods do continue a part of the research methodology.

The scope of research methodology is wider than that of research methods. Thus, when we talk of research methodology we not only talk of the research methods but also consider the logic behind the methods we use in the context of our research study and explain why we are using a particular method or technique and why we are not using others so that research results are capable of being evaluated either by the researcher himself or by others.

The present book will enable the researchers, irrespective of their discipline, in developing the most appropriate methodology for their research studies, and to make them familiar with the art of using different research methods and techniques. It is hoped that the humble effort made in the form of this book will assist in the accomplishment of explanatory as well as result-oriented research studies. The book is primarily intended to serve as a textbook for graduate students of research methodology in all disciplines. It is hoped that the book shall provide guidelines to all interested in research studies of one sort or the other.

Editor

Contents

1

Research Methodology Formation

Theories are sets of verbal statements that synthesize the behaviour of empirical systems. Depending upon one's point of view, theories either describe the behaviour of empirical systems or provide sufficient explanation to allow us to understand "why" those systems behave as they do. Wherever one stands on this matter, the adequacy of either description or explanation involves the ability to make successful predictions. The classical logical-positivist view on this matter assumed that, in principle, theories could be completely explicated by discovering a series of covering laws and then pursuing all the logical entailments. This paradigm, which appears to have tenuous links to the construction and exploitation of theories in the natural sciences, seems completely foreign to the social sciences.

Despite those efforts, there is little legacy of any substantive importance in the literature on social theory. Perhaps the lack of true axioms or social laws has been the greatest stumbling block; perhaps it is other factors. Regardless, the nomological-deductivist approach has not borne a great deal of fruit. Instead of covering laws and hegemonic propositional systems, most working theories are loose affairs that consist of a series of models of varying degrees of complexity and explication, with several auxiliary hypotheses called in when needed.

Furthermore, most working scientists, who should have a natural affinity to the axiomatic approach, find the logical algebra of linear equations a far more adaptable research tool than the axiomatic approach borne in the textbooks of symbolic logic.

Based on this view, we are probably well served by Giere's definition of a theory:

> My preferred suggestion, then, is that we understand a theory as comprising two elements: (1) a population of models, and (2) various hypotheses linking those models with systems in the real world.

The author elaborates his second point as follows:

> The links between models and the real world below are nothing like correspondence rules linking terms with the things or terms with other terms. Rather, they are again relations of similarity between a whole model and some real system. A real system is *identified* as being similar to one of the models.

What, then, can we conclude regarding the status of theories in the social sciences? First, it is evident that the general concept encompasses a variety of explanatory forms—some of which are so divergent that they appear to have little in common at first glance. Second, the only apparent consensus on the ontological status of theories is that they should be internally consistent and potentially open to refutation. Third, excruciating difficulties exist With the linkage between our theory language and attempts to operationalize it. It is for these reasons that many social scientists, and especially quantitatively oriented researchers, have opted for a much narrower (some would say arbitrary) definition of theory, while others have abandoned the term entirely. Instead, these people have generally opted for the term *model* to describe their theory statements, and they speak of model construction or model formalization when referring to their attempts at theory construction. The switch in terminology may be more political than substantive, although commentators of all stripes do seem to acknowledge that "model" is a distinct and far less encompassing term than "theory." Whether we speak of theories or models, however, several issues need to be addressed. A primary one is that some association needs to be made between the ideational world and the empirical world.

The English philosopher Hume, for example, made a fundamental distinction between the world of ideas and the world of facts. This practice of viewing two realms-that of ideas and that of facts-remains with us today and is a fundamental issue within the philosophy of science. It is generally accepted that some form of "truth" can be determined within each realm. Thus, for example, statements of relations among ideas are assumed to be true if they follow certain rules of semantic logic. To repeat an example presented by Quine both the following statements are deemed to be true:

— No unmarried man is married.

— No bachelor is married.

The first statement is true by logical necessity, since one cannot be in some state A and not A simultaneously (i.e., married and not married). The second statement is analytically true if we assume that the term *bachelor* and the implied concept'. *Unmarried man,* are synonymous. The important point here is that both sentences are true independent of the state of the world. This class of truths is variously identified as "linguistic" or "analytic" truth. On the other hand, the statement "The median age in Canada in 1985 was 31.1 years" is a statement of purported fact. Its truth value is not based on its logical or semantical veracity; rather, its truth value is based on its empirical veracity.

What is the nature of the relationship between semantic relationships (statements) and empirical facts? In other words, how closely linked do those ideas we call theories need to be to their empirical referents to be considered valid or invalid? This is a central issue for scientific theories. One extreme view is that a perfect relationship between a concept and its empirical referent must exist. This position is termed *radical reductionism*. As Quine points out, however, this position is "unnecessary and intolerably restrictive." To follow the radical reductionist argument to its logical conclusion would require our theories to be as complex as the reality they purport to describe and explain. In essence, nothing is to be gained by generating theory, for it is only by allowing for a parsimony in our theory language that theory becomes worthwhile.

Theories become useful to us when linguistic terms and relations cover classes of empirical events and relationships. To follow Quine, then, "more reasonably ... we may take full statements as our significant units—thus demanding that our statements as wholes be translatable into sense-datum language, but not that they be translatable term by term". Within this framework, the problems facing scientists as they attempt to test theory become more complex. Not only is there still the issue of linking some semantic concepts to empirical phenomena, there is now the issue of deciding which are the essential semantic elements that need to be linked and which can be omitted.

Put in a more pragmatic framework, let us assume that we have a reasonably complex theory. Is the theory necessarily disconfirmed if a complete correspondence appears neither between the concepts of the theory and their empirical referents, nor between the semantic relations of the concepts and factual relations among the empirical referents? Since we do not require a direct correspondence between the semantical and the empirical worlds, some slippage is to be expected. These are critical questions for which no definitive answer currently exists, or probably ever will. How critically one views this problem is likely related to whether one supports a, realist or nonrealist (instrumentalist) stance.

One might expect realists to be those seeking a closer correspondence between their theory statements and the empirical world. From an extreme instrumentalist perspective, it might be argued that one should care only about the degree to which a theory makes successful predictions, no matter how well individual theory components correspond to their empirical counterparts. We can develop a better appreciation for the role of theory in methods, however, by looking more closely at the constituent components of theories intended for empirical assessment.

The language of science

Substantive science consists of statements of relationships among concepts and, as with all linguistic statements, statements in science are composed of nouns (things, concepts) and verbs (relations between things). The *things* we talk about are concepts, which may themselves be verblike gerunds (e.g., "coping"). As Kaplan tells us, "The process by which a term is introduced into discourse or by which the meaning of a term already in use is more exactly specified, may be called *specification of meaning*.

This process is ordinarily explicated by the concept of definition—a logical equivalence between the term defined as an expression whose meaning has already been specified." A central question for understanding the research enterprise is: How are concepts formulated? Interestingly, researchers have conducted little formal empirical research on this issue although considerable anecdotal material exists. Further, much of the discussion surrounding this issue has been prescriptive rather than descriptive. Without formal evidence, therefore, Greer's assertion that "the natural history of psychological meaning is from sense data to symbol to the individual's system of meaning to the resulting interpretation of the experience" seems reasonable. If this is the situation, then it appears that concepts arise initially for labelling and identifying observables.

Thus, the task is one of generating a symbolic (usually linguistic) referent for the sense datum and providing a definition for the symbol that denotes the essential and unique characteristics of the sense datum. Concepts so generated are often defined as first-order concepts. We can link those first-order concepts to other concepts to form second- or higher-order concepts. When we join or linked those lower order concepts to form complex concepts (as in sentences), their meanings often change so that we formulate a different view or understanding of the symbols' original referents.

Thus, our definitions may start as referents to sense data, but over time they are modified and infused with meanings that can affect how we view the sense data. Instead of simply reflecting the sense data, the symbols then become a mechanism for organizing the sense data. Ultimately, this iterative process can result in concepts changing how we draw boundaries around the sense data. Experience also teaches us that when lower-order concepts are embedded in a metatheoretical framework, or linked to form a model or theory, higher-order concepts can be generated.

Establishing whether those higher-order concepts are valid requires us to conduct further empirical investigation. As Bierstedt asserts: "It is necessary to rely upon the investigation itself in order to determine whether or not properties the definition ascribes to the concept actually do belong to it, whether, to put it bluntly, the *definiens* does in fact define the *definiendum*, whether, in short, the definition is 'true.'" Because of this process, some concepts will arise and be linked to their empirical referents in a "bottom up" format while others will be linked to their referents in, a "top down" fashion.

That is to say, sometimes we start with an observable or sense datum and then seek an adequate construct to act as its referent, while in other instances we will start with a concept or construct and attempt to find an adequate empirical referent.' In either instance, it is necessary ultimately to specify and link the concepts to their observational referents and vice versa. Concepts must be clearly defined in order for us to understand them.

The drafting of such definitions can be pedantic but useful exercise, since a great impediment to the generation and transmission of knowledge is a lack of common understanding of what basic concepts stand for. Thus, trying to determine what we mean by *anomie*, or *locus of control*, or *alienation* is not necessarily an exercise in navel gazing. Consider the latter term-alienation. If used outside a specific context, most social scientists will quickly raise the question about whether it is meant in a Marxist, Durkheimian, or psychiatric sense.

The sophomoric exercise of defining one's terms is often overlooked in everyday 'Science, but it is essential to the full development of any working theory. Comparisons of supposedly "like" studies in reviews of literature often show that contrary results are a consequence of different modes of conceptualization rather than truly contradictory empirical results. As John Madge notes in his discussion of the differences between American and British understandings of the term "billion":

> It is undeniable that any such discrepancy is a nuisance, a barrier to perfect communication. In this case there may not be any very compelling reason to choose one meaning rather than the other, but one doubts that in the long run, two peoples who want to share the instrument of language will have to agree between themselves which usage to adopt.

A typical hierarchy of definition consists of three levels, referred to as *real definitions, nominal definitions,* and *operational definitions.* A real definition is usually considered to be the underlying or true meaning of a concept. For example, the real definition of a chair is assumed to be the quintessential or prototypical concept of the entity that exists in the mind of the observer. Nominal definitions are linguistic representations of real concepts. Practically speaking, nominal definitions are akin to dictionary definitions.

Thus, for example, Webster's dictionary defines a chair as "a seat with four legs and a back rest, for one person." This may be distinguished from a stool (which has no back rest), or a bench (which has room for more than one person). It is current vogue in some circles to deny real definitions and assume the semantic basis of nominal definitions as the starting point for defining concepts. That is, some people assume that whatever cannot be verbalized, cannot be conceived. Clearly, they do not share the frame of mind of former U.S. Supreme Court Justice Potter Stewart, who declared that while he might not be able to define pornography, he knew it when he saw it. Finally, operational definitions are the empirical referents to which real and nominal definitions are applied. As Gwynne Nettler notes in his book *Explanations:* "For scientists, the experiential reference of operational definitions is an advantage. Such definitions tend to be clear and certain.

The clarity and certainty gained by this mode of

definition are a result of both its empirical base and its referential restriction: *The term shall be used to refer to what this test tests and nothing more."* A continuing weakness of the logical-positivist framework is the difficulty in identifying linkages between levels of definition-especially between nominal and operational definitions. Formally, definitions are supposed to be linked by rules of correspondence, but we have very little to say about them except that ultimately they rely on intuition. More than 30 years ago, Nagel noted in *The Structure of Science* that:

> It is pertinent to observe, however, that no one has yet successfully constructed such definitions. Moreover, there are good reasons for believing that the rules of correspondence in actual use do not constitute explicit definitions for theoretical notions in terms of experimental concepts.

The difficulty inherent in specifying rules of correspondence undoubtedly contributed to the rise of behaviourism in psychology and radical operationalism in other fields. We might note that radical empiricism is often seen as a safe refuge by many, especially after they have spent considerable time trying to decipher some obtuse, and illogical theory. Undoubtedly, there are few sociology graduate students who have not thrown their arms up in the air with the utterance of "Who cares what Durkheim or Marx 'really meant' anyway?".

Theory in measurement

It is often pointed out by critics of mainstream social science that the process of measurement (i.e., the relating of facts to concepts) is itself a theory-laden enterprise. Essentially, we are told, science is not objective because the scientist observes only what she or he wishes to observe. Undoubtedly, this is true—one tends to "see" only what one looks for, and what one looks for is a theoretical imperative. That observation and measurement are theory guided, however, does not undermine the "objectivity" of the scientific method, which is to find ways of rejecting the null hypothesis. A more important criticism revolves around the comment that theories cannot be tested with observations defined, or constructed, or conceived by that same theory. Inherently, this situation creates a tautology, since the validity of a theory is being tested by the observations the theory defines as valid.

Again, we can avoid the problem by taking a step back and separating the substantive aspects of a theory from the theoretical aspects of measurement. As Ray Pawson notes,' "There is, however, no circularity involved in the use of theory-laden measurement provided that theories drawn upon in the construction of the instrument are not the same as those tested it' the application of the instrument".

Levels of analysis

Some sociologists spend a great deal of time considering whether "social reality" is a phenomenon sui generis. Ultimately, this question reduces itself to the individualist/group debate. Durkheim and his intellectual predecessor, Comte, would argue that a group is more than the sum of its parts. Others, such as George Homans *(The Nature of Social Science),* would argue that a group is merely the aggregate of the individual egos-nothing more, nothing less. In the resulting ideological slugfest, the followers of Durkheim suggest that Homans is guilty of reductionism; Homans and his followers argue that the Durkheimians are guilty of reification. We cannot propose to solve this debate here; however, as every economist and demographer knows, making certain predictions at the micro level but not at the micro level is possible, and vice versa. For example, we can make fairly accurate predictions about the rate of mortality for a given population in the coming year. Much more unpredictable, however, is the identification of individuals in that population who are likely to die in that year. Clearly, the population at risk consists of an aggregate of individuals.

On the other hand, our understanding of behaviour (as defined by our ability to explain and to predict) is obviously related to the unit of analysis. Once we have achieved some consensus on the meaning of concepts, the next step is to examine the manner in which concepts might be related. The assertion of a relationship between two or more concepts is called a proposition. Thus, to state that "poverty causes crime" is to present a proposition.

A *hypothesis,* on the other hand, is a conjectural statement relating two or more variables. Our proposition that "poverty causes crime" can be phrased as a hypothesis by converting the terms "poverty" anti "crime" into variables. The statement "The propensity to commit a criminal act is inversely related to level of income" is a hypothesis. Scientific hypotheses also require the statement of facts and not values. Thus, the statement: "John is a good person" does not qualify as a hypothesis since the term "a good person" is a question of values, not fact.

Some apparent value statements can be posed as statements of fact, however. To state "The more one gives to charity, the more likely one is to be perceived as a good person" is a hypothesis, since it involves a question of fact: to wit, Do people think others who donate to charity are good people? Hypotheses must also be open to refutation. The statement that "poor people have less money than rich people" is true by definition. It is a tautology in that being poor necessarily implies the condition of having less money than "the rich." Tautological statements cannot be refuted because they are true by logical necessity. To summarize then, the following factors distinguish hypotheses from propositions or more general assertions: a) the subjects and objects of hypothesis statements are variables, b) hypotheses are conjectures of fact and not values, and c) hypotheses must be subject to possible refutation; that is, they must be "vulnerable," to use Popper's term. So far, we have discussed the noun parts of hypotheses and some general characteristics of hypotheses.

Scientific hypotheses can also be characterized by several logical relationships, that is, different linking characteristics. While constructing many typologies of relational characteristics is possible, the following five dimensions are either those most often alluded to, or those explicitly identified in the research literature. Variations along these dimensions determine how one variable affects another. Later we will discuss the issue of causality.

Traditional notions of causality required that the relationship between two variables be characterized as sequential, sufficient, and necessary. Not examining the nature of the relationships implied in many hypotheses has led to substantial confusion and wasted debate over the years. If we return to our "poverty causes crime" example, abundant cross-sectional evidence shows that poverty and crime do indeed coincide. Since the nineteenth century, however, the debate has followed a pattern. First, it was proposed that "poverty caused crime" either through some mechanism of necessity or by reason of a more ephemeral concept such as relative deprivation. Labelling theorists later pointed out that "crime causes poverty," since being labelled a criminal limits one's life opportunities.

The more sophisticated among us then quickly came to the conclusion that the relationship was reversible, so that "poverty can cause crime and crime can cause poverty." Thus, the relationship is perhaps best viewed as reversible as opposed to irreversible. Few social scientists view relationships as deterministic, therefore, it is almost axiomatic these days that the poverty—crime relationship should be characterized as stochastic.

Similarly, since we often think in "causal" terms where asymmetry is necessary, it is unlikely that the relationship would be identified simply as coextensive. Asymmetry within causal models often implies temporal precedence; therefore, we may wish to assert that this particular relationship requires sequentiality. Poverty is clearly only a contingent condition for crime, since the overwhelming majority of "the poor" never become official criminals. Clearly an intervening or contingent factor is required to produce the phenomenon.

Similarly, crime has more causes than mere poverty. In fact, many factors might be reasonable substitutes. Thus, the apparently simple proposition that "poverty causes crime" takes on greater substantive meaning when we define it as likely to be all of the following:

— reversible
— stochastic
— sequential
— contingent
— substitutable

The process of generating good propositions and translating them into unambiguous, testable hypotheses is not easy, especially when several interrelated linkages are involved. Still, it is upon this base that the methodological edifice rests and, as suggested earlier, no amount of methodological wizardry can improve faulty theorizing.

Formalizing propositions

A great difficulty facing social scientists is the problem of converting verbal explanations of propositions to some type of symbolic or mathematical form that can adequately express the intended relationship. For many students of the social sciences, going from a verbal statement to a structural equation involves a level of magic that would put Houdini to shame. Even those who have a "handle" on the matter often become frustrated at their inability to express the "full intent" of the relationship in symbolic form.

Some of these frustrations result because any attempt to define systematically a relationship in symbolic form, or metalanguage, generally involves a higher order of specificity than we are willing to provide. Other frustrations result from the inherent limitations of the symbolic system (calculus) we choose to use, while others result from personal lack of familiarity with thinking in such a fashion. While we cannot provide a complete exploration of all possible approaches to this problem, some guidelines and examples can make the task less daunting. We will start with simple bivariate relationships and expand that discussion to include the multivariate situation.

Bivariate relationships

Perhaps the best starting point is to generate a graphical representation of what it is that we mean to say. While classical path analysis has fallen out of favour in recent years (for valid statistical reasons), the graphic framework afforded by this approach does provide a useful start. Let us assume that we start with a simple hypothetical proposition: "There is an inverse relationship between aggregate income levels and rates of crime." 'We may diagram this relationship as follows:

$\uparrow$ Propensity to crime $\leftarrow \downarrow$ Level of income

Current practice in most of the social sciences is to transform discursive statements into the symbolic form of linear algebra. This need not be the case but it is convenient, since most assessments of the validity of theoretical propositions rest on the use of conventional statistical analysis (which uses either scalar or linear algebra as its symbolic language). Thus, a typical first step in formalizing this relationship is to construct a linear equation of the following form:

$$Y = \beta_0 - \beta_1 X + \varepsilon$$

Where Y is the dependent (left-hand side) variable "crime rate" and X is the independent (right-hand side) variable "level of income." Following most criminologists, we have substituted "crime rate" for "propensity to crime," since measuring outcomes is much easier than measuring tendencies. This small change, however, introduces some slippage at the outset. Whether we can live with it is the first of a series of important decisions that must be made. This model can be estimated using standard regression procedures, thereby providing an expected value of β_1.

The intercept in this instance is usually of little value and is simply considered a scaling or "nuisance" parameter. Once β_1 has been estimated, its interpretation is that for every one unit increase in X, there is a corresponding β_1 increase in Y, and this increase is constant over the entire range of X. Some students rail at the simple "linearity" assumption implicit in this model and suggest that few, if any, social relations follow a straight line. That is, few relations have a constant rate of increase in Y along all values of X. This is likely true for this relationship.

Intuitively, it seems (at least to me) that crime rates ought to be more sensitive to changes in X as X tends toward extreme values. This change in meaning of the fundamental relationship can be had simply by changing what we call the "functional form" of the relationship.

Thus, for example, we might write:

$$Y = \beta_0 X^{\beta_1} \exp(\varepsilon)$$

or, to simplify estimation,

$$\ln Y = \ln \beta_0 + \beta_1 \ln X + \varepsilon$$

We have produced a model commonly known as the log-linear model. This model really has two components of interest. First the relationship is a power function, where Y is related to X through the exponential β_1. When X is exponentiated, Y is related to X through a simple β_1 multiple of the power result of X. Ultimately, the function is one of geometric growth. A model that straddles the traditional linear model and the log-linear model is the semilog model, often used to define exponential growth curves. This variant is very similar to the one just discussed but is defined as follows:

$$Y = \exp(\beta_0 + \beta_1 X + \varepsilon)$$

or

$$Y = \ln \beta_0 + \beta_1 X + \varepsilon$$

Commonly, X is some measure of time, in which case, the slope, β_i can be interpreted as the average rate of growth in Y per unit time.

More çomplex "two-variable" models can be developed. For example, it is possible to specify a quadratic from such as:

$$Y = \beta_0 + \beta_1 X + \beta_2 X^2 + \varepsilon$$

Depending upon the signs associated with the βs, the curve may be either concave or convex. Although this model is substantively a bivariate, or "two-variable" model, the change in specification leads to the realm of multivariate models, since more than one slope is being estimated. Further extensions of "two-variable" multivariate relationships lead us into the realm of time series or ARIMA (autoregressive integrated moving average) models. These models allow for estimating models involving autocorrelation. Without entering a time dimension into our models, we are assuming that the process being investigated either is static or has achieved equilibrium.

For example, if we collect data on crime rates and poverty rates across 100 randomly selected cities, it might be possible to detect a simple linear relationship of the form: $Y = \beta_0 + \beta_1 X + \varepsilon$. The inherent equilibrium assumption here is that the parameters in the model, β_0 and β_1, are time invariant. That is, within the range of sampling variation, those values will be consistent, say, from year to year. Now, each of these different functional forms has a different substantive interpretation of the nature of the relationship between crime and labour force participation—a substantive meaning that is not captured by the simple graphic presentation defined by our original statement (Propensity to crime ← Level of income). Even the incorporation of up and down arrows (↑and ↓) into the schema does little to advance the cause.

Decisions about functional form can be rationalized by asking ourselves a series of questions.

1. Is the function continuous or discrete? If it is discrete, does it consist of several discontinuities (steps) or just one?
2. Is the function monotonic or segmented?
3. Is the function linear or nonlinear?
4. Is the function intrinsically nonlinear or nonintrinsically nonlinear (i.e., transformable to linear)?

Table 1 presents some commonly used functional forms. Some are intrinsically linear in that they are additive in the parameters; others are nonlinear in that the parameters are not additive. While theoretically relevant, nonlinear models often pose practical problems for parameter estimation.

Most modern statistical packages, however, include nonlinear estimation procedures. Often, those procedures are time-consuming and are sensitive to initial, or starting values, thus making them less popular than more direct estimation procedures such as ordinary least squares (OLS). In some situations, however, it is possible to "linearize" the equation through a suitable transformation, thereby allowing standard generalized least squares approaches to be used. For those nonintrinsically nonlinear (i.e., transformable-to-linear) functions in Table 1, a linearized form is presented. Procedures for estimating and transforming non intrinsically nonlinear functions into ones that are additive in the parameters are presented in several sources.

Table 1.

Some linear and transformable-to linear models

Model	*Structural equation*	*Linearized Model*
Line through origin	$Y = \beta X$	NA
Straight line	$Y = \beta_0 + \beta_1 X$	NA
Parabola	$Y = \beta_0 + \beta_1 X + \beta_2 X^2$	NA
Polynomial of kth order	$Y = \beta_0 + \beta_1 X + \beta_2 X^2 + ... + \beta_k X^k$	NA
Power function	$Y = \beta_0 X \beta_1$	$\log Y = \beta_0 + \beta_1 \log X$
Exponential decay or growth model asymptotic to zero	$Y = \beta_0 \exp(-\beta_1 X)$	$\log Y = \beta_0 + \beta_1 X$
General exponential decay or growth	$Y = \beta_0 \exp(-\beta_1 X) + \beta_2$	$\log (Y - \beta_2) = \beta_0 + \beta_1 X$

We will now examine three pieces of research to explore the issues surrounding theory formalization in more detail.

Returns to education

The economic theory behind this is relatively straightforward. Classical human capital theory notes that education entails an opportunity cost to the individual due to forgone earnings and the direct costs involved in acquiring the education. To encourage workers to undertake further schooling, there must be a likelihood of higher lifetime earnings as compensation.

Those higher lifetime earnings are justified, however, only if more schooled workers are more productive than less schooled workers. Ultimately, a long-term equilibrium will be achieved between lifetime earnings and schooling such that expected earnings will encourage enough people to pursue the amount of higher education required to fulfill market demand. The basic income—education relationship put forward in the economics literature is that of Mincer. Mincer's model suggests that income = *f* (schooling, experience) In other words, income is related to how much schooling one obtains, and how much experience one has in the labour market. Thus the three terms that need defining are *income, schooling,* and *experience.*

Definitions

Income. For income, Mincer uses the U.S. Bureau of the Census definition of earnings: that is, income obtained through wages and salaries.

Schooling. The operational definition for schooling used in most of the literature consists of "years of formal education." This is usually estimated by summing the highest number of years of elementary school achieved (grade level), the highest number of secondary school years achieved, and the number of years of postsecondary education acquired. The normal range is between 0 (for no formal education) to 18+ for those with postgraduate university degrees. While this operationalization clearly has the advantage of simplicity (both for conceptual and data analytic purposes), no element of *quality is* included regarding either the type of education (training) received, or how much is actually learned.

Experience. Usually this term is operationalized as the number of years in the labour force. Functionally, Mincer defined experience as current age minus years of schooling minus 6. Again this formulation has the advantage of simplicity. However, it does not consider periods outside the labour force (which may be especially important for women), nor again, the *quality* of the experience. For example, some workers receive substantial on-the-job training and others do not. For some workers, experience is enhanced by staying in the same industry as long as possible; for others, the quality of their experience is enhanced through an exposure to a variety of work environments.

Whatever its theoretical limitations, Mincer's model is explicit in its relationships and captures much of the empirical variation in earnings. Written as a regression equation, Mincer's model is defined as:

$$\log(\text{earnings}) = \beta_0 + \beta_1 \text{ schooling} + \beta_2 \text{ experience} + b_3 \text{ experience}$$

The dependent variable log-income is regressed on the independent variables, since this transformation addresses a large portion of the heterosckedasticity problem often encountered with income data. Income also appears to have decreasing marginal utility, such that the perceived value of incremental units decreases as one's total income increases. Mincer estimated this equation based on the annual earnings of American, white. Based on the available data, the following results were obtained:

$$\log(\text{income}) = 6.20 + .107 \text{ schooling} + .081 \text{ experience} \\ —.0012 \text{ experience}$$

Since the model is represented in only three dimensions, graphing Mincer's results to obtain a visual representation of the model is easy. The implications underlying Mincer's functional form are quite evident. Each incremental year of education represents a constant log-dollar increase in income, while experience shows a decelerating rate of return as one heads toward one's retirement years. For those not practiced in thinking in terms of log-income, it is possible to convert the relationship back into original dollar units by exponentiating the entire right-hand side of the equation. Clearly, in raw dollar terms, the incremental impact of schooling and experience becomes much more exaggerated.

The professionalization of psychology

We will focus on a far more complex study than Mincer's. Frank, Meyer, and Miyahara put forward a thesis that the prevalence of "professionalized psychology" depends on the sociocultural configuration of a society. Specifically, they argue, societies that have strong sociocultural norms regarding individualism are more likely to give rise to and to support the development of professionalized psychology than do "other polities." They argue that this is so even when other key social and economic factors are considered.

Since the authors use a linear structural equation approach to testing the model, they outline the essential model using a type of path diagram. In the path diagram, the linkages between the structural factors are identified along with the relationships between the structural factors and their empirical referents (operational definitions). As in the preceding example, we will start with a definition of key terms.

Definitions

Dependent variable-professionalized psychology. The term "professionalized psychology" appears to rest on conventional interpretations of the terms, since it is not defined directly in the article, There are, however, a couple of sentences that help to clarify the meaning of the term as used in the study. Specifically, we are told that:

> our indicators describe only professionalized aspects of the field, rather than, for instance, its prominence in mass culture.

and

> Because we are concerned with the scientific and professional' field of psychology *in general,* not with psychology as used in the treatment of individuals, we exclude specialized medical applications like psychiatry and counselling psychology.

This article is inconsistent in its use of nomenclature or terminology regarding the dependent variable. That is, in the title the authors refer to the *prevalence* 'of professionalized psychology, while other places (including the path diagram) cite the *prominence* of professionalized psychology. Undoubtedly, this confusion is the result of sloppy editing; however, the difference is important. Prevalence refers to a measure of occurrence, of tallies or counts. Prominence refers to a quality of distinction or eminence. Since all the operational indicators used are reflections of quantity, we will assume that the titular nomenclature is correct and that references to prominence are mere editorial slips.

Independent variables—individualism. The concept of an individualist polity is clearly less intuitive to the professional audience than is the dependent variable. Thus, the authors provide a clearer description of the term. They write:

> Individualism refers only partly to sociocultural arrangements encouraging individuals to be completely autonomous and uncontrolled. More importantly, it encompasses the rise and legitimation of' model,., of society in which the individual is seen as it central constitutive element: the sovereign source of public life. . . .

Further,

> We use indicators to determine the degree to which the status of individuals is especially central in national societies.

Economic development. The second independent variable, which is considered a key control variable, is economic development. This variable is not defined outside its operational indicators and is assumed to be self-evident.

It is clear from the path diagram and various references that the model is strictly linear in its functional form. "National economic development" and "political-cultural individualism" are considered causally prior to the "prevalence of professionalized psychology." The two independent variables are assumed to be correlated but not in any causal sense.

Controls. A strength of this study is the emphasis placed on identifying causality and spuriousness. The authors controlled for several variables that might have a confounding impact upon the primary relationships, although these were not incorporated. Among the variables considered by the authors were:

— English-language bias

— national population size

— government revenue as a proportion of GDP

— social disorder and economic development

— expansion of tertiary education

— volume of general scientific activity

The graphic imagery of the path model fits well with the mathematical formalization of structural equation models to produce both a succinct model and an intuitively appealing imagery.

2

Interpretation of Data

A varied data collected with the help of various methods like questionnaire, schedule, interview, observation, etc. collected through any one of the above sources may be of simple or complex in nature. Simple nature data can be organised very easily while the complex nature data requires proper processing because which may contain errors wither in recording or transcription or, the informants may deliberately or unconsciously supply information which makes the data to be unreliable. These errors that should be detected and corrective steps are to be taken. This can be done by means of editing. Where the research necessitates to maintain secrecy of the information supplied by the informants that should be done by coding and decoding process.

All this process is often called processing' which refers to recasting and dealing with the data making ready for analysis. Then the data is to be put into some definite form because raw data is a most Jumbled form with which one cannot use to render this haphazard, complex, unintelligible mass of data into some significant and understandable form. 'They are called classification and tabulation respectively. The term analysis refers to a closely-related operations that are performed with the purpose of summarizing the collected data and organizing in such a manner yielding answer to the question. In simple words, it means studying the tabulated material in order to determine inherent facts or meanings. In the words of Selltiz, Jahoda et al., the term analysis refers to such process facilitating the data for the operations designed to draw conclusions or test hypotheses.

Explaining the figures what they mean in the context of the theory on which the study is based, is often termed 'interpretation'. Analysis involves organizing the data in a manner and interpretation that explains facts or figures. Thus, interpretation proceeds to knowledge and the analysis is hardly complete without interpretation coming into play. The problem of analysis and interpretation vary from one study to another. Several steps involved in the 'integrated operations' that are called the 'analysis and interpretation' of data. They are:

— Classification of data

— Tabulation of data

— Statistical analysis of data

— Interpretation of data

Classification of data

Classification is the process of arranging the data in related facts into classes say, according to similarity or dissimilarity. Facts with one class differ those of another class with reference to some characteristic called 'basis of classification'. Sorting out facts on one basis of classification and afterwards, on another basis is called 'cross-classification'. While taking decision about the category that are to be instituted, the researcher must select appropriate principle of classification to provide a good logical basis.

Objectives

The principal objectives of classification are:

1. It facilitates comparison
2. It condenses the mass of data into classes which can be readily apprehended
3. It identifies the most significant features of the data at a glance
4. It makes possible the statistical application

Types of classification

Broadly, classification is divided into four types, viz. (a) qualitative classification, (b) quantitative classification, (c) geographical classification, and (d) Chronological classification.

Qualitative classification

In this category the basis for classification is quality or attribute such as sex, colour, beauty, literary, religion, etc. Qualitative classification is studied under

(i) simple classification-when only one attribute, i.e. presence or absence of attributes is studied two classes are formed, one possessing the attribute and the other not possessing attribute. This type of classification is known as 'simple classification'.

(ii) Dichotomous classification under this method, two classes of attributes say sex into males and females are formed, is called 'two-fold or dichotomous classification'.

(iii) Multiple classification—a number of groups are formed on the basis of quality or attributes say sex into males and females, each category again into literates and illiterates, and each sub-category again into employed and unemployed, is called 'multiple classification'.

(iv) Attributes can be classified indicating high, medium and low intensity of them (attributes) either on their presence or absence. Identifying the location of an absolute zero point in order of weightage given to the scale is called 'serial scale'.

A particular score is assigned to the varying degrees of responses. The way in which the scale is formulated and the method of scoring employed will determine the score relevant to the issue. Some issues form a gradation method that the individual agrees with only one or two of these, and disagrees with the remaining issues on either side of the scale. In other words, the informants are asked to each of proposition in terms of degrees of' agreement or disagreement. Such scales in which an individual's response fixes his position are called 'summated scales'.

In some scales, the individual indicates his agreement or disagreement with each proposition and his total score is computed by additing scores assigned to his responses to each of the propositions comprising the scale. Such scale may be called 'cummated scale' An individual whose attitude is at a certain point on the dimension being measured will answer favourably all the items on one side of the point and answer unfavourably all those on the other side of the point. This scale called 'cumulative scale'.

Quantitative classification

Classification is done not on the basis of attributes but on the variables. A variable refers to quantitative data while an attribute refers to qualitative data. Examples for quantitative, classification are height, weight, etc.

Geographical classification

Classification is made on the basis of location. Examples are villages, wards, cities, etc.

Chronological classification

A period of time is the basis to made classification under this method. Examples are weekly, monthly, yearly, etc.

Statistical series

Arrangement of classification in [the tabular form is termed as 'statistical series'. The statistical series are of four types namely

— array,

— discrete series,

— continuous series, and

— inclusive and exclusive series.

Arrangement of the measurements of an individual item either ascending or descending order is called array'. This array is made based on the scientific order. Example, alphabetical, geographical, etc. The table which contains only one measurement or size is known as 'discrete series'. In other words, data do not progress from one class to the next without a break.

Example, children in each family. In discrete series, there are two columns representing size of measurement in the first column and frequency or number of cases Which occur to a size in the second column. Instead of being measuring the size in digit form, the measurement is in a continuous flow say, the age of persons may be any period, a few minutes, days. It is known as 'continuous series'. In other words, the measurement or size is in the form of we continued flow rather than independent integers.

For example, eight students got marks between 50 and 60; and live students got marks between 60 and 70. The marks are technically known as size or measurement. Two limits of size or measurement are known as lower and upper class limits. Thus, in the second category, 60 is the lower class limit while the same is the upper limit in the first category. The difference between lower and upper class limits or range of a class is known as 'class interval' or 'magnitude of class'. The number of students would be called as 'frequency'. When the upper class limit of one class in the lower limit of the next class, it is known as the 'exclusive' method of classification. In the above example, eight students whose marks are between 50 and 59.99.

A student whose marks are 60, it would be included in the class of 60 and 70. This method is widely in practice. Under the inclusive method of classification the upper class limit of one class is included in that class itself. For example, ten persons income varies between 100 and 199; and another five persons income varies between 199 and 299. The persons whose income varies between 100 and 199 is included in the class itself.

Coding

Coding may be regarded as the classification-process necessary for tabulation. It consists of symbols, usually numerical to each answer that falls in a predetermined class. It is defined as "an operation by which data are organised into classes and a number or a symbol is given to each item, according to the call class in which it falls. The raw data are transformed into symbols through coding that may be tabulated and counted. This process is done by one person officially titled him as 'coder'. Coding will be adopted where complex cross-tabulation occur. It is done at any of three stages.

(a) The informant himself may be asked to codify his own reaction or situation; e.g. poll-type and multiple choice answers

(b) The interviewer may codify informants' reactions while recording them

(c) The codification may be done in the office after the interviews are over based on the 'code book'.

A book containing codes under which what type of responses should fit into one definite category is called 'code book'. In preparing codes for various types of answers, it is necessary in the first instance to note down all the answers received on a separate -sheet of paper. This can be done by checking each schedule. After this, the responses are categorised into a relatively small number of groups. This classification of items should be made in such a way that all possible responses can be distributed in them. Coding of such data must fulfil the following requirements.

1. The category must be exhaustive
2. The category should be exclusive
3. For supplementary responses separate codes should be provided
4. The categories selected must be related to the subject of study
5. The category of 'no response' must be made in order to find out the persons who did not answer that particular question.

Design of coding

The design of coding may be different for manual tabulation and for machine tabulation. In the former, numericals, letters are more preferable. If the letters are used we can code at least twenty-six possible responses in one column. Of course, there is no bar in using numbers. In the latters, coding is usually done on punch cards. A punch card contains 80 columns and 12 rows thus, providing a field for (80 × 12) 960 boxes. Coding on punch cards can be done in two ways namely (a) multiple punches and (b) single puch. For the computer programming, single punch cards are to be used. In case of sorter, multiple punch cards can be used. However, single punch cards are preferred. The cards shall be provided with well written instructions and should be instructed not to deviate. But during coding we may got certain responses which have not been included. To code such responses, it is necessary to take the decision, jointly by all the coders or if the decision has been by the Director of project all the coders should be instructed accordingly.

Checking the coding operation

It is obvious to test or verify a sample of the schedules or all the schedules by a person other than the coder according to the instructions. If the coding by the two differs, then reliability of the code book requires to be tested. Errors may also be caused by the incompetent or irresponsible coders.

Editing

The process of scrutinizing the data to improve its (data) quality for coding is known as 'editing'. When the data-collector is submitted material to the project-officer, the possibility of eliminating many potential coding difficulties still exist. A careful and diligent examination of the data as soon as they are collected and if necessary, a systematic questioning of the interviewers or observers helps to avert many coding problems.

In other words, editing not only helps to avoid later coding problems but also improves substantially quality of data-collection by pointing out where the interviewers or observers might have misunderstood instructions or might not have recorded data in sufficient detail. Editing is defined as "the process by which errors and omissions in the filled in questionnaires or in the observation, noted inadequate, wrong or false entries are detected". Editing aims at to ensure that the data are:

1. As accurate and reliable as possible
2. Consistent with other facts secured
3. Uniformity entered
4. As complete as possible
5. Arranged so as to facilitate coding, the tabulation

Tabulation of data

Tabulation is a part of the technical process in the statistical analysis of the data. The technique of presenting data, either qualitative or quantitative in the columns and rows is called tabulation. Prof Neiswanger defined it as "a systematic organization of data in columns and rows".

Objectives of tabulation: The following aye the main objectives of the tabulation. They are:

(a) To make the purpose or enquiry clear

(b) To make the significance of enquiry clear

(c) To express the data in least space

(d) To make comparison easy

The data in the table form represent in least possible space, making the information clear to the view. When two sets of figures are given side by side it is easier to form a comparative idea of their tables.

Types of tables

There are two types of tables.

— simple table or frequency distribution and

— complex table or cross table.

Simple table: Different qualities of an attribute are written left-hand and the frequency occurrances of the each class are written in another column. This type of arrangement is known as simple table or frequency distribution. In constructing a frequency distribution three things are essential. They are: (a) the classes made must be mutually exclusive, (b) the tabulation must have internal logic and order, and (c) the class intervals must be carefully and reasonably selected.

Complex table: In preparing complex table, the concept of property space is used. The concept of property space in social science research is used to locate the errors according to their abilities or characteristic features. The dimensions on which we locate people in property space can be of different kinds.

Preparation of table

Preparation of table is an art and requires an expert handing of data. The preparation of table depends upon the size and nature of data, number of classes and nature of comparison to be sought, space available and purpose of tabulation. The contents of a table are given below.

1. *Title of the table:* The first part of a table is its heading. Every table is provided a suitable heading. It should be short, clear and convey the purpose of the table. It may contain four types of information which are as:

(a) What is the subject matter of the table ?

(b) What is the time to which it belongs ?

(c) What has been the basis of classification ?

(d) What is the source from which the table has been extracted ?

The heading should be preferably a clause Dot a full sentence and should be given at the centre of the table.

2. *Stubs and captions:* The headings of the different columns and rows are known as 'stubs and captions' respectively. Captions generally give the basis of classification, e.g. sex, education, etc.

3. *Size of column:* Proper size of column is not only facilitates proper centering the figure but also gives a smart and nice appearance to the whole table.

4. *Arrangement of items in* Rows: Several schemes of arrangement of items in the rows (horizontal lines) can be adopted. The following are the most commonly followed methods:

(a) Alphabetical arrangement according to which the items are arranged in alphabetical order

(b) Geographical arrangement in which the items are arranged according to geographical location

(c) Historical arrangement according to which the items are placed in a chronological order

(d) Numerical arrangement according to which the items are arranged to the number of group

(c) According to magnitude in which the highest number is placed at the top and the other items arc arranged in descending order

5. *Arrangement of columns: As* in the case of rows, so also in the case of columns (vertical lines) different arrangements may be followed. They are:

(a) Thc first column is generally descriptive in nature and gives the names of groups

(b) The movement of eyes in reading is from left to right, so more important information should be given in left side

(c) The figures to be compared should always be given side by side

(d) The percentage, average or ratio have computed if any should be given side by or in parenthesis below the figure

6. *Totals:* The totals for different columns and rows have to be given separately. This affords a comparison of total to total and cross checking of the grand total.

7. *Demarcation of columns:* If the columns have been divided into a number of groups and sub-groups, some arrangement is necessary to -distinguish a group from a subgroup or ordinary column.

8. *Footnote:* If there is anything special about the figures or the whole table to which the attention has to be specially drawn, the same may be done by giving footnote below the table.

Essential of a good table

1. Attractive
2. Manageable size
3. Comparable
4. Clear
5. Suitable for the purpose
6. Scientifically prepared

Significance of table

The table is of very much importance in social *science research* which is given below:

1. Table conserves space and reduce explanatory and descriptive statements to a minimum
2. The visualization of relatings and the process of comparison is greatly facilitated by table
3. The tabulated data can be more easily remembered than the data which are not tabulated
4. Table gives a significant form to classification

5. Tabulation helps to present a clear cut picture of the complex mass of data and thus, make it easy to understand
6. Table provides a basis for computation
7. A tabular arrangement facilitates the summarization of items and the detection of errors and omissions

Statistical analysis of data

Tabulation is a part of description or summarizing the information about the study-problem that have obtained on the sample thereof. In order to estimate the reliability of generalization, statistical analysis is very much needed. Statistics is a branch of applied mathematics that helps to get a precision of the data relevant to the complex social phenomena. In statistical analysis, a clear and practical differentiation is made between descriptive statistics and statistical inferences.

The descriptive statistics emphasises description of the data with the help of measures of central tendency, measures of dispersion, correlation, etc. It is a simple and from a scientific point of view less refined than inductive statistics. However, it is very important indispensable tool for any research problem. Getting generalization is concerned with the statistical inference.

A sample is studied for the sake of phenomena that the investigator is interested (a) to get some hypothesis about the parent population from which the sample is drawn (problem testing) and (b) to know Population parameters based on statistics (problem estimation). The values derived by using central tendency, correlation, etc. for the sample observation are called 'statistics'.

The values derived by using central tendency, correlation, etc. for population observation are called 'parameters'. Thus, the mean of sample data is a statistic while the mean of a population is a parameter. The important step in research is that of testing hypothesis and determining whether the hypothesis is consistent with the facts. A hypothesis which is tested for possible rejection is known as 'null hypothesis'.

Null hypothesis is very much useful in testing the significance difference between assumed and observed values. As against the null hypothesis, alternative hypothesis is specified the value that the investigator believes as true. Every alternative hypothesis is paired with the null hypothesis. The test of hypothesis included the calculation of statistics and its standard error. Standard error is used as an instrument in testing hypothesis. If the difference between observed and expected results is more than 1.96 and 2.58 times the standard error, the result of experiment does not support the hypothesis at five per cent and one per cent level of significance respectively.

The hypothesis, in question, is accepted at five per cent and one per cent level of significance means the investigator is running the risk allowing wrong decision in five and one out of hundred occasions respectively. . Thus, the smaller the difference between the observed and the expected results the greater the reliability of the estimate. In social science research most commonly used statistical tool are:

1 *Rank: A* rank is merely the relative position of a case that occupies in a group. Often it is more significance than measurement itself.

2. *Measures of relationship:* Correlation coefficient is commonly used type statistical analysis particularly in critical study of tests. It uses for prediction. The higher the degree of correlation, the greater the accuracy with which one can predict a score. The

correlation of test results with a criterion is called 'the coefficient of validity'.

3. *Measures of variability:* Variability means dispersion. The measures of variability is the most common corrective measure for concept of average. The measures of variability are (a) the range, (b) the quartile deviation, (c) the average deviation, and (d) the standard deviation.

4. *Measures of central tendency:* The term central tendency connotes the average. The forms of average are many, the most common being the mean. The median and mode are other common forms of average. The mean is mathematically more significant average and is used extensively in advanced statistical analysis.

Interpretation of results

The investigator proceeds the next and important step of ;interpreting the results. Results interpretation may be occurred at two stages. At the beginning, the investigator may summarize and bring together the various numerical values to fore-front which will enable easy comparison and comprehension. The readers generally do not likely to probe into the details of calculations but they like to see the final results. This means summarizing the calculations properly in feasible manner.

After this, interpretation part, which means explaining the figures and facts in the context of theory on which the study is based, is used. In other words, accepting or rejecting the null hypothesis is ended with statistics. And the investigator has to draw the real cause for accepting or rejecting the hypothesis based on the methodology, approach, conditions of study and so or. This interpretative writing is a core step where a beginner of research needs guidance.

The investigator should approach with an open mind and keeps off ideological and personal biases from polluting the research. Being continually conscious of these shortcomings is the way of improving the quality of interpretative writing.

3

Collection of Data

Data originally collected for an investigation are known as primary data. Such data are original (raw) in character and have no statistical analysis. Data which have already been obtained and given statistical appearance to them are known as secondary data. In other words, the primary data have been made use of, it loses its original character and becomes secondary data. A distinction between primary and secondary sources of data, thus, is the only degree of statistical analysis. The above two sources of data may be labelled simply as 'the people' and 'the paper'.

Choice between primary and secondary data

The researcher has to decide at the very beginning whether he will use primary data or secondary data in carrying out investigation. The choice between the two depends upon the following consideration.

- The nature and scope of enquiry
- The purpose of enquiry
- The availability of financial resources
- The availability of time
- The degree of accuracy desired
- The collecting agency, i.e. an institution, or an individual or a government body

The secondary data are increasingly used, the reasons being that it covers diverse field so that an investigator finds required data readily available to him in many instances. Where the secondary data do not provide an adequate basis for analysis, primary data are generally used. However, primary data have prepared to make use of, for the following reasons:

1. The primary source often established a description of procedure use in selecting sample and in collecting data
2. The primary source includes the operational concepts and terms
3. The primary source shows data in greater detail
4. The primary data can conveniently befitted to the, study and therefrom sufficiently accurate results
5, The primary data is original in character so that investigator at a glance apprehend validity of it with sufficient detail and in depth.

Sources of data

The primary source in social science data forms observation directly from the field but more particularly and primarily, the interview, schedule and questionnaire are the techniques for collecting data from the source. The source or field for observation may be personal documents, autobiographies, diaries, letters, visits, etc.

The field for the secondary data are the official documents (newspaper, public records and statistics, biographies) and historical documents. In the words of John Madge the distinction between primary and secondary sources is of 'record' and 'report'. Record is primarily concerned with a translation taking place now, whereas the report is written after the event has taken place. It is observed the process of assembling primary data is called 'collection' of data, is different from the process of 'compiling data from published sources. To quote Crum, Patton and Tebbute, " collection means the assembling, for the purpose of a particular investigation of entirely new data, presumably not already available in publishing sources". Thus, the term 'collection' refers to primary data while 'compilation' to secondary data.

Methods of collecting primary data

The nature, purpose and scope of a research study greatly determines the choice of method to be adopted for collecting data. Secondly, availability of time and finance also governs the choice of method for collecting data. Usually, primary data may be collected with the help of any one of the following methods.

1. Observation method
2. Interview method
3. Schedule/and questionnaire method

Observation method

One of the most important and extensively used method in social science research is observation method. Indeed, it is a primary research instrument of gathering data in a more natural way. The validity and reliability of data are 'core' to research, for which the exactitude and any social science scientific temper avoiding bias may be possible through means of observation.

A social scientist always vigour to adopt more scientific method and quantitative technique in research. As it is known that social sciences deal with society in its totality—social, economic, cultural, political, etc. In fact, it is not always possible to use only quantitative techniques. "Some times quantitative data are difficult, almost impossible" (Dean and others). In all such cases quantitative scientific methods may not be of much avail in research and observation may be the best method or atleast best alternative. Observation technique is adopted for testing hypothesis where structured methods cannot be employed and, pilot enquiries into new problem areas where the purpose is production of hypothesis rather their verification. In physical sciences too, observation is the only method for new experiment. Thus, observation is a perfect method of investigation and probably most popular one in gaining knowledge of research. "Observation is deliberate study through an eye, may be used as one of the methods for scrutinizing collective behaviour and complex of institutions as well as separate units comparing of totality".

Observation is a careful and systematic watching of facts as they occur in nature with regard to the cause and effect mutual relations. In every act of observation, there are two components—the object or what is observed and the subject or the observer. If one may observe one's own immediate experience, it would be subjective observation or introspection. If the observer becomes an entity apart from the thing observed, it would be objective observation or extrospection. In recording psychological information and social information, the introspection and extrospection respectively are appropriate methods. An observer may be are visiting stranger, a participant observer an attentive listene and an eager learner.

Characteristics of observation

1. The use of senses-either to see or to hear-is involved. In collecting things that fall within an act of focussed on them. Thus, two acts-physical and mental elements are in every act of observation.

2. The observer cannot observe anything and everything but can only certain things that fall within an act of observation. Example is the traffic police inspector looking out may observe only of

those vehicle-drivers who are driving too fast, or are sounding their horns except nothing. In the same way, the scientific observer may see many kind of things but he takes notice only of those which are objects of his scientific study. Thus, observation is systematic and relative.

3. Research aims at certain specified objectives which are to be attained by the researcher. In other words, he should notice those facts or activities that relate to the enquiry. On the other hand, he should not notice of anything and everything that comes in his way. For this reason, observation is objective.

4. Observation is direct outcome of dominant interests which serve in the course of investigation.

5. Watching the course of action is embodied with scientific temper. This means observation is efficient from the point of view of drawing conclusions qualitatively based on properly standardized tools. This quality should be converted into quantity.

Types of observation

Observation may take place in the natural or real life setting or in a laboratory. The procedure adopted in observation may vary 'from one study to another depending upon the nature of data and purpose of study under investigation. However, the investigator must sure and secure the answers to the questions like (a) what should be observed, (b) how the observation should be recorded, (c) how to insure accuracy of observation (d) what relationship should be obtained between the observer and the observed.

The classification of scientific observation broadly is as:

1. Participant/non -participant observation
2. Controlled/Uncontrolled observation
3. Structured/Unstructured observation

Participant observation

Participant observation means an activity or a group or activities of group in which the observer himself participate under investigation. He freely mixes with the activities of the group not as a outsider trying to have a critical study of what they do, but as a willing member trying to participate in what they do, not as a total alien but as a full fledged member of the group.

In other words, he lives and shares in lives of the group which is observing. For example, an investigator observing rural and urban conditions in India may be able to gain if he merely stood-by and watched what is going on. Linderman is of the opinion that if one wished to know what the subject is really doing, one should watch him and not ask him. An important point that the observer keep in mind is that be should desist from acquiring any special status but disguised in the group so that the members of the group are unaware of the presence of him. This helps him access to the information otherwise is not possible to obtain. The actual behaviour of the group can be observed by participant observation which cannot be gained either the questionnaires or schedule.

Merits

1. The observer by becoming as one of the members in the group gain insight into the behaviour of the group in the natural settings. The tremendous insight which Nels Anderson developed through participant observation is amply evidenced in his study entitled 'The Hobo'.

2. The observer can gather more information with real and correct as a member of the group than an outsider. Arid certain phenomena and behaviour are not open to observation from outside or from a distance. In such cases the participant observation is the only method of investigation to collect information.

Demerits

1. The main limitation of the participant observation is that the observer may identify himself with the group and may develop emotional attachment. Such emotion identification may loose impartiability as well as objectivity thereby not possibility of real phenomena for analysis under investigation.
2. Certain phenomena cannot be observed in a short time available to the observer.
3. The observer cannot cover wider area through participant and as such the velocity of the conclusion reached from the observation of the small group or place may become doubtful.

Non-participant observation

In non-participant observation, in contradiction to the above, is characterized by a relative lack of participation by the observer in the life of the group that he is observing. In other words, the researcher either observes the phenomena from a distance or while being present in the group never participate in its activities. Here it should be observed that the observer is present in the group since he cannot remain a distance observer always. Therefore, Goode and Hatt called it, quasi-participant observation than non-participant observation. The difference between participant observation and non-participant observation is that in the former the observer becomes a member of the group and behaves as a member of the group and actively partake in all activities. And in the latter, though the observer associates himself with the group physically, he keeps aloof in its activities and observes the phenomena as it occur passively.

Merits

1. In non-participant observation the observer is unattached with the activities of the group so that he impartially and objectively can be maintained.
2. As he maintaines cordial relations with the member of the group and will have access to the entire information.
3. The observer being a stranger is less involved emotionally which likely results in the ideals of objectivity and the real phenomena for analysis.
4. He does not remain a mere alien but keeps himself aloof. This helps him to carry on research more smoothly.

Demerits

1. The observer fails to appreciate the significance of actions and activities as he cannot view them by merely a member. This lack of appreciation may make sonic of his findings biased in the background of his own understanding.
2. The observer may not have access to the informal organizations and such he cannot understand the whole of the phenomena.
3. The behaviour of the members of the group may get altered during the presence of the observer. Prof Wirth says that the presence of an observer even merely as one extra person in the interacting situation, will lead to distortion.

Thus, the non-participant observation may not really gain real insights into the phenomena.

Controlled observation

For a systematic collection of data, and for verification of hypothesis, control is imposed on the observer or on the object. As it, is difficulty to impose control on the object, in social sciences, generally continuous the imposed on the observer. Such controls increase precision, reduce bias, ensure reliability, systematise procedure and increase objectivity. And observation is carried according to a plan. Sometimes controls are imposed both on the phenomena and on the observer. The former are laboratory type of experiments which Elton Mayo called 'clinical method'. In the latter when it is difficult to impose control on the object, the observer can control himself.

The following are a few control devices used for the purpose.

1. Preparation of a detailed observational plan which helps the observer to observe systematically making it more standardised and identical conditions.
2. The use of observational schedule helps in objectivity device for observation.
3. The use of mechanical appliances like photos, films, type-recorders, etc. aids to proper observation and objectivity.
4. The use of socio-economic methods render qualitative observations to mathematically precise and thus produce greater objectivity in the observation as well as analysis.
5. The control over the bias of the observer may be exercised through team observation. The individual observation likely to commit errors of observation

and interpretation. But a team of persons can never be wrong.

Uncontrolled observation

Observation is made in the natural environments without being influenced by outside controls or external forces. P.V. Young calls this type of observation as unaided type of observation. The observer does not plan his study in advance. Most of our life situations are studied in some uncontrolled setting as they occur rather than in artificial surroundings created through controls. Uncontrolled observation enables first hand acquisition of knowledge about the social phenomena which means this technique is mostly applicable to the socio-cultural problems.

Structured observation

In this method of observation, a careful definition of categories under which the information is to be recorded. Structured observation is used greatly in Studies designed to provide systematic description or to test casual hypothesis.

Unstructured observation

The unstructured observation is diametrically opposed to the structured observation in its ideal type of formation. The unstructured observation represents the ideal contrast to structured observation characteristics such a careful, definition of the units to be observed, information to be recorded, the selection of pertinent data for observation and standardization of conditions for observation.

In observation method of data collection, the observer can ease himself into the field at an appropriate pace and thereby avoid rebuff by blundering into delicate situation.

Validity of observation

For ensuring the validity of observation, the following points must be fulfilled. They are:

1. The actual observations should be made of the on-the job activity
2. The aims and objectives of activity must be known to the observer
3. The point on which the judgment to be made by the observer must be defined clearly
4. Reporting the observed information should be accurate

In order to make the observation more and more reliable and valuable for the investigation, the observer must qualify himself as an expert. Symonds states the essentials of good observation which are: (a) good eyesight, (b) alertness, (c) the ability to estimate, (d) the ability to discriminate, (e) good physical condition, (f) an immediate record, (g) good perception, (h) freedom from preconceptions, (i) emotional disinterest. To be an expert, the observer should possess the following requirements.

1. The observer should possess efficient sense organs
2. He must be able to estimate quickly and accurately
3. He must alert to observe several things in detail simultaneously
4. He must control the effects of his emotional attitude
5. He must be able to record immediately and accurately the results of his observation.

Interview method

An important and power tool for the data collection specially in the field of research with the social and economic problems is the 'interview'. It implies personal interview in which the interviewer and the interviewee carry on conversation face to face and discuss problems thereto. It may be noted that an interview is more than a conversation. It is not only the words spoken but also the gesture, glances, facial expressions, pauses, intimation, rate of speech, etc. which also matter a lot. In the words of Brown and Ghiselli, "the term interview stands for a generic concept which includes a variety of procedure adopted in collecting data through person to person contact between an interviewer and a respondent." Most field research or empirical social survey is adopted the procedure of interviewing for the purpose of collecting relevant data. This method is to be used as a scientific tool.

The interview method is not be called scientific, if it results would not be useful and reliable. It is unplanned if it is carried on with variable purposes and questioning procedures, and the biases of interviewer enter into the selection, recording and analysis of the data, etc. In other words, the interview, as a tool of collecting data, should be used with caution and adequate carefulness as well as in a scientific manner, and a scientific instrument as well. Interview may be said to be one of the most commonly used technique of data collection in studies of human behaviour. Thus, the interview method is quite effective technique in collecting data in social science research.

Importance of interview

Interview is adopted as a method to offset the drawbacks of questionnaire. The subjects (people) are usually more willing to talk than to write. The interview is often superior to other data-collection devices. The interviewer possesses a skill and talent of carrying interview. Interview is tin important to other methods because of the following factors.

1. The casual factors are being probed by the

interviewer and determine their attitudes and also the origin of the problem

2. It is more appropriate to deal with children, illiterates and others who face the difficulty in understanding the language
3. It is as close to the researcher's vital problem as the interview
4. It is in fact essential in diagnosis
5. It helps for stimulating the interviewee for eliciting vital, valid and reliable response
6. It permits, if necessary small clues in complex material where the development is likely to proceed in any direction
7. It helps to make cross-questioning
8. It provides an opportunity for the interviewer to explain information and to develop certain attitudes on the part of interviewee such an opportunity is indispensable in the interview
9. On the spot improvements, explanations, adjustments or variation can be possible in collecting data because of its flexibility in character
10. The subjects are more willing and less hesitant to talk than to write particularly on delicate, confidential matters, etc. In such context the interview method is more appropriate.

Types of interview

Interview may be classified as structural interview and nonstructural interview. In the former a detailed preplanned schedule is used. The responses may simply be 'yes' or 'no'. This type of interview may involve the use of open-ended question with predetermind order.

The interviewer is free to repeat the questions if the reply is not to the point. In the latter, interview is conducted with no predetermined questions but which proceed on the basis of an interview guide.

The interviewer has much freedom to ask the supplementary questions, if he feels and has much freedom to record the responses according to convenience. In other words, structural interview and nonstructural interview respectively called as controlled, *guided or* direct interview: and uncontrolled, unguided or indirect interview. Non -structural interview again divided into (a) focussed interview (b) non-directive interview, (c) depth interview, and (d) repetitive interview. To study the focus of attention on a given experience and its effects is termed as focussed interview. For example, the reaction of a film-show or TV programme on social behaviour.

The behaviour has been analysed prior to interview. The interviewer tries to focus his attention to the aspect of a film seen or TV programme heard and tries to know the expressions and attitude, regarding the behaviour under study. In non-directive interview, the interviewer's function is to encourage the respondent to talk freely about a given topic under a direct questioning or guidance. He should create a completely progressive atmosphere in which the subject feels free to express himself without fear of dispute and without advice from the interviewer. For example, a psychotherapy in which the patient is encouraged to express his feelings without any directive questions or suggestions from the rapist. In implicit sense, non-directive is most interviewing.

The non-directive is interviewer's function is primarily to serve as a catalyst to a comprehensive expression of the subject's feelings and beliefs. The depth interview is intensive. It can be used in social science research requiring full and detailed expression of social attitudes, emotions. Often there is, a need for repetitive interview specially when the researcher wants to study the gradual influence or changc in the attitude or behaviour of the respondents under varying conditions. This type of interview is particularly useful to trace the specific developments of a social actions to know their reacting influence upon the people.

For example, suppose, a village is linked with town. Naturally it will have its own influence upon the life of villagers. Of course, the influence would not be sudden. A gradual change in economic status, standard of living, opinions etc. of the villagers will occur. To study these influences or changes in time sequence a study has to be conducted at a regular intervals to know the gradual change taking place. The non-structural interviews are more applicable than the structural interviews. But the former requires so much skill on the part of the interviewer in order to frame and ask questions on the basis of interview guide during the interview for obtaining good and relevant responses.

Interview guide

The interview guide is to be prepared after thorough study of the subject concerned and the respondent's behaviour and nature. It would be required detailed thinking and planning about the interview and preparing in a proper sequence the way the questions have to be asked the interviewee. In this context it is always advisable to prepare an interview guide and use the same at the time of interview. Interview guide is a brief written document giving an outline of the different aspects to be studied. It forces the Interviewer to think and plan the interview properly. It is said the President Abraham Lincon used to spend about one-third of his time thinking about the questions he would pose and remaining time on as to what the interview would say. Thus, the interview guide facilitates to gather information fully.

Technique of interview

Conducting an interview is a technical matter and requires a thorough knowledge of the methods and the principles underlying it. The entire process of interview may be broadly studied in five divisions, viz. (a) preparing thinking, (b) developing rapport with the respondent, (c) carrying the interview forward, (d) recording the interview, and (e) closing the interview.

Preparing thinking

The first step before the interview actually taken is to think over the problem properly. This would involve thinking in detail and indepth about the subject and classify it in several in a proper sequence. In this process all the relevant matters have to be chalked out duly and given the shape of questions. The arrangement of questions in a proper way is highly appreciable. After the preparatory plan is ready, the, interviewer has to resume and locate the various respondents who may have to be interviewed In selecting a sample of population in scientific manner which is very essential in social science research. A random sampling should be adopted for the purpose. Practicability is one of the characteristics of research which has to be kept in mind by the interviewer while covering the area under study, The cost factor should not be forgotten.

Developing rapport with the interviewee

Developing rapport with the interviewee is second important step in the interview technique. Once the plan and the interview guide are ready, the interviewer will have to find out the address of the informants with their residential address. After locating the residence, the persons concerned would have to be contacted. For smooth conduct of interview and thereupon getting more useful information may be well appreciate if the interviewer will have a little intimacy with the interviewee. This would also facilitate in chosing time and place of the interview suitably. It should be noted that in the interview the convenience is of very much essential. The first approach to the interviewee should be made carefully so as to get his confidence and cooperation. Generally, he may be greeted with a smile, and 'how do you do'.

The interviewer after getting, so much confidence regarding the desired respondent, the time of introduction is quite a crucial one. If the interviewee is not convinced about the authenticity he may refuse to oblige the interviewer. The correct answers and the facts have to be obtained if due cooperation of the interviewee is secured. For the means of due cooperation the backdoor approaches should be duly avoided. Thus, the basic key to the successful interviewing is to establish rapport with the interviewee to create friendly atmosphere for wealthy responses.

The interviewer could be required to carry the interview forward with the help of interview guide and task the questions to the interviewee with sufficient belief after the rapport of the latter has been established. He should not interfere too much while he is at the receiving end. But he should intervene to bring the interviewee back to the question if he is diverting from the object. However, he will have to handle the situation carefully and apply his own judgment and expertise to carry through the interview and draw facts from the interviewee. The interview is not a mere conversation but is more than that with every effort to gain the correct and desired information.

The interviewer's manner should be friendly and courteous throughout the interview. Listening patiently with self-restraint, of course, is a difficult job but this has to be born to get right information. He should be quite listener but at the same time he should be an analytic listener. The idea should be to put the interviewee at ease so that he will talk freely and fully. Prof Fordynand Zweig found through his experience that "the success of his interview with London Labourers depended primarily in his insight, friendliness, willingness to safeguard the interests and on what he calls 'flow of energy'. To this proper conscious and attention are to be paid otherwise the very purpose of interview would be jeopardised. The interviewer may remain more engrossed in understanding to the replies and forget to record them. And often his admiration may forget to ask questions from, the respondent as well.

The other point which makes more important function of recording the interview is that oftenly the interviewer himself is not received to analyse the data so obtained. Under the conditions mentioned above, it will be a problem indeed for the analyst to tabulate and analyse the data if that is incomplete or something is missing. Even the results obtained may not correct. The only means to avoid it is to sit down with paper and pen to write them immediately just completion of the interview at that time he may afresh in is mind. If he does not act promptly, he may forget to record the relevant and some important information also. An alert student without an extraordinary memory can reproduce some 15 to 20 pages of material from an interview lasting one-and-half hours-if he goes immediately from the interview to the typewriter or to sit down with his notes while the experience is still vivid.

Closing the interview

Closing the interview is the last step in the process of

interview. It is a fact that often closing the interview is a difficult job than starting it. It may be ended by saying good-bye. If it is simple interview with a few questions only, one may leave simply by saying 'thank you very much for the trouble'. 'The interviewer has to see that he should not antagonise the interview and should not abruptly break the friendliness which he has developed during the time of interview.

To make a good departure he should select right time for closing the interview and then he should assemble his file and papers ask certain questions casually, put the papers in file, clip his pen in his pocket and indicate that it is a time for him to leave. He should, thus, make it quite natural to depart. In the light of the above discussian covering some of the major types of the interviews, each one has its own strong points as well as weaknesses that each is suited to a particular kind of situation. The overall merits and demerits of interview method is given below:

Merits

1. The personal interview compared to, especially to questionnaire yields good response.
2. The interview method yields perfect sample because practically everyone can be reached by and can respond to the approach.
3. By the interview method selecting information is likely to be more correct compared to other type of techniques used for securing information. This is because the interviewer presence on the spot clears up irrelevant answers by explaining the questions to the informant.
4. A supplementary information can be collected about the environment which is often of great value in interpreting results. Flexibility is a character of

interview which means new questions may be posed if needed. Because of flexibility the interview is a superior technique for exploration of areas for investigation.

5. In as much as interviewer is present on the spot he can observe facial expressions, gestures, etc. of the informant as also the surrounding pressures of the subject. This facility helps the interviewer to evaluate the meaning of the verbal replies given by the informant. For example, hesitation may give rise to doubt about reliability of repondent and interviewer may then ask indirect questions to verify doubts.
6. Visual stimuli to which the informant may react can be presented.
7. As an experimental the interviewer can be used scoring and test devices.
8. The interview method ensures qualitative as well as quantitative returns compared to other methods.
9. The interview may make and recall of relevant information under the study investigation.
10. The interviewer presence is a double headed-weapon. To merit aspect of it being that face-to-face contact provides enough stimulation to the respondent to probe deeper and detailed. Thus, interviewer acts as a catalyst.
11. Adaptation to the level of education and ability of the person interviewed is possible. Therefore, it avoids misleading questions.
12. The interview is right technique for collecting information about complex, emotionally laden subjects.
13. On the spot adjustment facility may be possible that ensure rich material.

Demerits

1. In terms of cost, energy and time, the interview approach poses a heavy demand.
2. Collecting information both in qualitatively and quantitatively requires a thorough training and skill of interviewers and as also rigorous supervision over them, failing which data may be inaccurate
3. If the interviewer has bias, the collected information may contain the background understanding of the situation by him. In other words, it is said the human equation may distart the returns.
4. Many actions of human beings carry, out are net easily visualized but easily observed.

Schedule and questionnaire

Next to the interview method, the schedule and the questionnaire methods are the popular and widely used ones in collecting data in social science research. In fact, they may be assumed as 'heart of the survey operation'. The preparation of a schedule or questionnaire is much more subtle and frustrating task. The preparation of them would be required full preparations properly worded, arranged, codified and duly pretested and approved by the experts in the area. In quite a few books, the terms schedule and questionnaire are treated as synonymos to research methodology.

Technically, it is desirable to differentiate between them. A questionnaire consists of a set of questions printed or typed in a order on a form. It is despatched through the mail to the respondents who have to give in writing the answers in relevant spaces provided for the purpose on said form. The researcher or the sender does not assist the respondent at all in any manner in filling the form of questionnaire. A schedule also refers to a form containing a set of questions as in the questionnaire.

The schedule is generally filled in with the answers by the enumerator or the researcher or the interviewer himself. He sits with the informant face to face; and puts to the latter the questions from the proforma and records replies to them. Thus, there is a sufficient room for flexibility in it while it is not so in the questionnaire. The difference between the questionnaire and the schedule, in fact, lies in the method of filling the form containing a set of question's.

A questionnaire is self-administered whereas a schedule is not. Otherwise there is not much of difference between the two. In both cases, the wording used for setting the questions may be same. Both of them are used for the purpose of collecting the quantitative cross-sectional data. The questionnaire as well as the schedule are increasingly used techniques for collecting of variety of data in socioeconomic surveys or investigation. They are being recognised as important and popular tools for the purpose.

The reason is being the growing emphasis on the part of social scientists on quantitative measurement of qualitative social behaviour. They also serve as a supplementary devices for personal observation and interview, used for the purpose of collecting information. They assist in standardizing the observed information.

Purpose of a schedule/questionnaire

The form of questionnaire or schedule deals with a variety of questions for the purpose of having a reliable and valuable .data. The questions are aimed at:

1. Ascertaining facts
2. Ascertaining belief about what the facts are
3. Ascertaining feelings
4. Discovering standards of action

5. Exploring present or past behaviour
6. Knowing the conscious reasons for beliefs, feelings, policies or behaviour.

Ascertaining

Some of the above purposes will discuss briefly. The phrasing of questions will need to logically harmonise with purpose. Asking questions must relate to the facts which are in possession of. The reported fact must be checked for its credibility. The usual line of evidence must be followed to this end. The questionnaire be more useful and also economical when tshe respondents are widely dispersed geographically. Further, it leaves the respondent from external influences. In other words, the respondent feels free to provide information or his view according to his knowledge, view and attitude in an unbiased manner.

Data so obtained may be more valid and reliable. The response obtained through the schedule is much higher the questionnaire. Firstly, the field worker remove any doubt or suggestion regarding the meaning of any question or term used with which the answers are not biased. Secondly, the presence of field worker may create emotional feelings in the mind of interviewee. This does encourage him to stimulate either his ability or willings to give the desired and detailed answers. In other words, the subject is remain neutral and may give answers casually or in a perfunctory manner.

Thirdly, there is possibility of putting supplementary questions which may be put to enliven the whole discussion. Fourth, the lifeless questionnaire howsoever cleverly and clearly drafted, attractively printed can be no match to the living field worker who is personally present to enliven the whole atmosphere with interesting discussion, act as an active counterpart to the interviewee, share his emotions and feelings and encourage him to express his views freely and frankly. Last, the schedule can be used effectively for a representative sample of population which cannot do in case of questionnaire as every respondent may not be literate enough to respondent to the questions properly. Because of the meritorious points which have had in the schedule in comparison to the questionnaire, the former has been widely in practice.

The schedule is to be very needed in those areas of research where intensive nature of information required. The discussion made so far is similar to both the schedule and the questionnaire. Now, with regards to types, design characteristics of schedule as well as questionnaire are discussed hereunder.

Schedule

The schedule in social science research may be classified into (a) observation schedule, (b) rating schedule, (c) document schedule, and (d) interview schedule.

Observation schedule: This schedule contains specific topics upon which the observer has to deal with the nature of information that has to record. So this schedule is used for observation purpose:

Rating schedule: To measure the attitude or opinion, the rating schedule is to be used. It is used generally in sociological or psychological , researches. Different ranks or rates or scales are constructed for this purpose.

Document schedule: Document schedule means schedule used for recording data from written documents like autobiography, diaries or official records maintaining by the Government. In preparing the source list of collecting preliminary information about the population, document schedule is used.

Interview schedule: This schedule is used for interview purpose. It contains standard questions to be asked to interviewee for getting information from him.

Aspects to be covered

The form of a schedule or a questionnaire covers the aspects of problem which should, first of all, be split up into various aspects. Understanding properly and clearly the problem under study is for point in framing a schedule or questionnaire. Suppose a researcher selects the problem, "Effect of employment of women upon family life", it should be split into the different aspects of care of the children, household work, material relations, health as well as general attitude. These aspects are to be studied in complete detail. After analysing the problem, the type of information necessary for a valid generalizations is to be decided. To this reference, each aspect has again divided into a number of sub-parts.

These sub-parts should be quite exhaustive to give a full and complete picture of the aspect under the study. Thus, in the above illustration, care of children may further be divided into a care in respect of food, clothing, study, health, character etc. Framing questions keeping in view the splitted and sub-splitted aspects, as above, for eliciting information is the third step. In order to get complete information more and more questions may be asked. Care should be taken in constructing questions so as to give exact sense. The schedule may be utilised for interview or observation. The discussion made under the heading interview is more concerned to the schedule.

Questionnaire

Questionnaire may be classified into structured questionnaire, and non-structured questionnaire. In the former contains definite and direct questions, if necessary additional questions, to get a more detail responses. The latter often called interview guide which is used for depth and non-directive interview. The organization of an enquiry through means of questionnaire differs from the one used in the method of schedule. A large sample may be selected in this method.

The sample has to be large because of large percentage of non-responding people. If it is ready for dispatch, a proper record is to be kept for dispatching with which a comparison can be made on their arrival. If the rate of arrival is fallen considerably a reminder is sent; and a second reminder is sent if necessary. This process generally goes on till the required percentage of responses is to be collected. When the questionnaires have, been received, then they are sorted out and edited. Incomplete, illegible or mutilate ones are not taken into account for analysis and interpretation of data. The remaining are tabulated, analysed and used for drawing generalizations.

Merits of schedule

1. The reliability and validity is more
2. Being personally present the interviewer, there is possibility of gathering unbiased response clarifying the misunderstandings
3. It helps to collect additional information
4. It helps to have an idea about the attitude or subjects

Demerits

1. It is costly affair
2. It creates administrative problems
3. The presence of interviewer may prove a source of bias in the interviewee

Merits of questionnaire

1. Questionnaire is economical in getting information. It

is economical both for the sender and for the respondent in time, effort and cost

2. It covers so large universe which could not otherwise be any other tool
3. It is easy to plan, construct and administer
4. The questionnaire has been constructed skilfully, the researcher may ask anybody to administer it on his behalf
5. It places no pressure on the subject for immediate response which means, he can answer to question at leisure
6. It may be used as a preliminary tool for conducting a depth study later on by any other method

Demerits

1. It gives a biased sample
2. The matter of non-response is always a big question mark
3. Its reliability and validity is low
4. It forms a basis of pooling ignorance as respondent simply tick the point without knowing exactly what it is
5. It cannot be used with illiterate subjects and children
6. It may permit the subject to alter his answers to earlier questions when he finds that he is contradicting while answering some later questions. Thus, his responses may not remain true, factual, honest and original.

4

Social Survey

According to Mark Abrams "a social survey is a process by which quantitative facts are collected about the social aspects of community's composition and activities." From the above definitions it may be drawn the characteristic features of a social survey. It is a study of immediate and burning problems of the society (poverty, unemployment, crime, etc.) and constructive programme of social research for removing the social evils. The scope of it is limited and localised geographically. And it may form the basis of for further social research on the matter. In brief, the social survey is designed to investigate some cause effect relationship on the some aspect of human life.

A social survey is to perceive the information with the aims given below.

1. As we know that the survey will become a basis for further investigation, supply of information to needy one is its main objective. The needy one may be an institution or an individual. Thus, survey is utilitarian in nature and is meant to provide information regarding the practical problems of the society. A researcher for himself may carry on survey but there are some agencies that carry on surveys for others.
2. Survey describes the phenomenon. To a social scientist a survey may have a descriptive as a way of

studying social conditions, relationships and behaviour. For example, survey communities, socio-economic survey describe the living conditions of people of a geographical area. This description of a phenomena would be accurate as well as 'complete if we came face to face with it. Further the purpose of social survey is to get information and it is not meant to test an hypothesis but simply describe the things. Therefore, survey may be started without any hypothesis. The description of data so collected may serve as a basis for a hypothesis later on.

3. Alongside of the description, the social survey explains the determinants for the state affair of a particular situation under study which is to be taken for survey. And thereby a survey may so be specific and purposive.

Social survey has intensive usage and is widely used in a number of disciplines. In social sciences, it can be used for variety of purposes. Availability of nature of information is the main source for undertaking a survey. Broadly the subject matter for social surveys are divided into (a) demographic features, (b) social conditions, (c) social activities, and (d) opinion and attitudes. Demographic features come under the purview of organization and working of family regarding such information as household compositions, marital status, age, family planning programme, etc.

The social conditions to which people are subjective. This includes occupation, income, housing amenities. Many of social actions are conditioned by the social conditions, i.e. social environment in which people live. So, social conditions are helpful to get the full information and thereupon to establish the causal relationship. To study the family relations one would require information on the location, the extent of relationship with elders, etc. A survey of delinquents would be incomplete unless full knowledge of their home and family environment is available. Social activities such as expenditure pattern, radio listening, newspapers reading, social mobility and others may be termed as behavioural information.

For example, to know the expenditure pattern of a group of family houses, it requires to the surveyor full knowledge on expenditure habit say, expenditure towards family, clothing, education, cigarettes, cinema and others. Opinion attitude service includes information regarding opinion and attitudes of the people towards various social factors, and the motives and the expectations of them. This information may be necessary as the basis of nature of questions that may safely be asked for eliciting rich response. For example, the opinion or attitude of a person towards social, economic or political incident survey.

Types of surveys

Surveys are of four types, viz. (a) general or specific survey, (b) regular and ad hoc survey, (c) preliminary and final survey, and (d) census and sample survey. The general survey concerns with collecting general information about population, institutions or phenomena without any specific object or hypothesis. This type of surveys are mostly taken tip by the Government for providing regular data on many socio-economic problems.

A good example for this survey is census of population once in a decade. Any survey is undertaken with the specific motive for testing and validity of some theory or hypothesis, it is termed as specific survey. Information collected through the specific survey is generally of very little value outside the problem under study. For example, marketing survey on a particular issue say, people attitude about the use of television.

Regular survey is regular in nature and repeated after regular intervals. To this, a permanent machinery for collecting information is to be set up. Many of such surveys are mainly economic surveys. For example, a study of family budget can be cited as example. Another example is the Rural Credit Survey of the Reserve Bank of India which collects data regarding the rural credit conditions annually.

Ad hoc survey is undertaken once for all. It may be conducted in phases if the area of investigation is large. Because of completion of survey in phases due to its largeness, it never entails as regular or repetitive survey. A preliminary survey is one which is to be undertaken well in advance to get the first hand knowledge of the universe to be surveyed. Further, it helps the surveyor to get acquaint himself with the nature of the problem so that he can be able to get rich response.

After conducting the preliminary survey only, the construction of schedule or questionnaire may be taken into picture. And it also guides the way of planning as well as organizing the survey on proper lines. The preliminary -survey may also be called 'pilot study'. A pilot study is one which is to be conducted well before taking a detailed study about the main work. After the pilot study has been completed, the final survey is made. Every unit in the universe is to be contacted and data collected from it is called 'census survey' while a few units of the universe covered, it refers to 'sample survey'.

Planning of a social survey

The quality of survey results to a considerable degree depends on the preparations made before the survey is conducted. So, planning a survey is paramount importance in social sciences. The surveyor has to give careful and conducive thought at the planning of a social survey. Planning of social research programme is must for its successful execution. Parton remarked that "only by carefully planning the survey from start to finish can reliance- be placed upon results and in many cases will the findings ever reach the publication stage." Therefore, it is pertinent to think twice properly at the planning of social survey with regards to the following points.

Purpose of the survey

The purpose of the social survey should be specified clearly at the very beginning. A clear objective of the problem indicating the interest in determining the type of information is to be needed.

Scope of the survey

Next to the purpose of survey, scope of it is an important step regarding to the type of information, subject matter, geographical area. For instance, an enquiry may relate to India or a particular State or an industrial town or a particular industry in particular location. The small coverage of the survey the less representative are likely to be the results. The purpose of survey, however, will determine the scope of survey. Apart from the above the object of enquiry, availability of time, and availability of resources are exert great influence on scope.

The method of study

In selecting a particular method for a survey, the surveyor should take the consideration of its suitability and his own knowledge of it.

Unit of data collection

The unit or units of universe must be clearly defined for the purpose of an enquiry before taking the task of collecting information. However, defining the unit is not as simple as it appears to be. For example, to study the size of a mill, we have different criteria of measuring the size of mill such as capital employed, number of employees, production, etc. For efficient collection of information the unit of data collection should have the characteristics which are as under:

(a) The purpose of enquiry being studied must be suited to the unit

(b) The unit should be specific

(c) The units should be stable in character

(d) The unit should be uniform throughout the report

Sources of data

After the purpose, scope and methodology have been defined clearly and properly, the investigator has to plan about the sources of data. The sources of data may be either primary or secondary. Either the two devices or only one device to be used in the investigation may be depended upon the objective and purpose of the survey. Quite often in social sciences investigation both sources may be used.

Mode of data collection

Social phenomena is very complex and influenced by a number of variables. Therefore, it is essential to decide before hand what type of information is to be collected adopting the questionnaire or schedule.

Organization

Organization of survey is very Much important from the point of getting quantitative as well as qualitative data. A number of field workers may be required and training must be given to them if necessary. Arrangements with regard to checking and supervision should be made so as to avoid giving false information. Editing and coding if needed have to be undertaken. Following it classification and analysis of data has to be carried out. All this organizational work should be pre-planned.

Report

After the data have been classified and analysed the next part of a survey is to start drafting. The report of the survey to whom it meant determines the style of presenting the report. In a survey utmost care and cautiousness at each phase of the activity is to be given; poor plan or poor work in one phase may ruin a survey in which everything else is done well. It is noted that social survey and social research is identical in nature in many respects.

Social phenomena is the area for investigation in both cases. Both in social survey and social research, the method and technique use is similar. The other point which is identified in respect of social survey and social research is both are interdependent and are influenced by each other. However, there are some fundamental differences existed between them which are as under:

Social Survey	Social Research
It is concerned with specific problem	It is concerned with general problem
To fulfil immediate needs is the main objective. Thus, it is practical in nature	To develop theories and accurate procedures. Thus, its primary aim is theoretical in nature
Improving lot of men is the purpose. Thus, it is utilitarian in nature	Increasing knowledge o r improving techniques is the Purpose. Thus, it is scientific in nature
It results in a remedial Measures for removing immediate ills	It results in formulation of new theories or discovery of new techniques of study or modification of old concepts
Hypothesis may be developed based on this	Hypothesis is being developed and thus evolves a theory
Hypothesis is not necessary	Hypothesis is essential. The social research Mainly concentrates with the testing of hypothesis
It may be conducted on professional basis	Thirst for knowledge is the incentive and its ultimate satisfaction is the reward for a research scientist

Advantages

The following advantages have with the survey method in comparison to other methods. They are:

1. The surveyor comes in contact with the people whom he wants study. And with this, fie can observe things personally with realities and thereupon his inferences are not based upon any theory or dogma but upon the facts of life.
2. The survey method leads in greater objectivity. Many fold workers use in the survey remove possible personal bias and collect correct information like the operation or Law of Inertia. Because of having this merit with survey method, which has been used for testing the validity of the work before undertaking the main work.
3. Survey may very well lead to the introduction of new theory. For example, poverty was regarded as the cause of crime for fairly long time but increasing crime in advanced countries have falsified this theory.
4. Survey method enables to have full knowledge of social situations. The actual experience with the situation amounts none to any amount of investigation.

Disadvantages

1. For carrying the survey field workers are to be recruited and training is to be given to them. All this needs more money.
2. It is prolonged and time consuming process.
3. The reliability and validity of the data collected through survey is not always without doubt. Honesty and efficiency of the field workers, the cooperation of the respondents, the suitability of

schedules, etc. paramount for collecting valuable data. But all these requirements, are very seldom and the data collected may contain invalid data.

4. Survey is conducted on sample basis, and therefore it is subject to the sampling error.

Research design

A research design is a plan of the proposed research work. It is a blue-print and therefore at its best only tentative. Changes in the design are permitted and are dictated by considerations during the operations of the project. In other words, a research design is not highly specific plan to be followed without deviation but rather a series of guide-posts to keep one headed in the right direction.

A research design is a catalogue of the various phases and facts relating to the formulation of a research efforts. As Selltiz, Jahoda, Deutseh and Cook state "a research design is an arrangement of the essential conditions for collection and analysis of data in a form that aims to combine relevance to research purpose with economy in the procedure." A research design should be based more or less on methodology. It should be made once, the topic and problem for research have been selected and formulated, objectives have been properly outlined , concepts have been properly defined and the hypotheses have been properly framed. The presentation of the guidelines for the design, some of the practical difficulties, deficiences and shortcomings in the planning and execution of research projects in the light of the experiences of some researchers, are highlighted. The intension is to help the future researchers to learn from the lessons and formulate systematic research design.

Characteristics of a good research design

A good research design should possess the following

four characteristic features, viz. objectivity, reliability, validity and generality.

Objectivity

The objectivity of the findings pertains to the methods of collection of data and securing the responses. Any research design should permit the use of measuring instruments which are fairly objective in which every observer or judge seeing a performance arrives at precisely. This ensures the objectivity of the collected data which will be , used for the analysis, inferences and generalizations.

Reliability

Reliability refers to 'consistency throughout a series of measurements. That is to say, if a respondent gives a response to particular item, he is expected to give the same response to that item whenever he is asked subsequently. The investigator should frame this item in such a way that the respondent cannot but give only one genuine responses. There are different methods in determining the reliability of the responses given out by a respondent. Some of these methods are using 'check item' administering the same test repeatedly using a series of 'parallel' forms, etc.

Validity

Any measuring instrument is said to be valid when it measures what it purports to measure. For example, an intelligence test constructed for measuring intelligence should measure only intelligence and nothing else.

Generality

The next important thing is that a well planned research design has to answer the 'generalization' of the findings of the study. That is how best the data collected from a sample can be utilised for drawing certain generalizations, applicable to a larger group from which the sample is drawn. Thus, a good research design should ensure that:

— the measuring instruments can yield objective, reliance and valid data;

— the population is defined in unequivocal terms

— the requisite size or the sample is collected by using the most appropriate techniques of sample selection,

— the appropriate statistical analysis has been employed; and

— the findings of the study can be generalized without being contaminated by the errors of measurement or sampling errors or any other interfering factors.

Components of a research design

A good research design consists of the following components. They are:

Title of the study: The title of any research project

— should be as brief as possible

— should be as precise as possible

— should project the scope of the problem in generalized terms.

2. *Statement of the problem:* The researcher should state his research problem in unambiguous and more precise terms. While stating the research problem the usage should be clear, simple and concise which are of most preferable. A problem well put is in half-selved.

3. *Review of literature:* A brief survey of studies under taken earlier has to be given. This is meant to fill up the gaps in the contribution of knowledge. Such survey would entail a study of a relevant literature.

The review has to be done in such a manner that when the proposed study is completed, it would add its own contribution to the quantum of knowledge in the subject concerned. Earlier studies are not only reviewed but also critically appraised, then only it is more meaningful, useful and a correct approach in any field of investigation, In other words, this type of review would pinpoint the stage from where further research is called for.

4. Area *and scope of the study:* Scientific projects differ widely in their geographical, temporal and functional dimensions. However, it will be better and purposeful if individual researchers do micro studies that may spotlight the dark and obscure lacunae in the data. As far as the time dimension is concerned benchmark surveys related to a particular data is undertaken. Generally, surveys cover a period of time, with the object of studying the trend of some variable or other. For example, a study meant to assess the impact or credit on socio-economic improvement of farmers in Rayalaseema region in Andhra Pradesh Could period of ten years.

The functional dimension refers to a research project concerning with a particular industry or section of the population covering certain functional variables. Besides the above, the scope of the investigation is depended on several aspects such as money available to the researcher and availability of sample, etc.

5. *Objectives of the study:* The main purpose of the research study is to lay down the objectives precisely. It may be mentioned in the form of questions to be answered, or it may be in the form of an explanation to a particular issue or phenomenon. In other words, the objectives should be worded in a lucid and precise form. For example, if the investigation is on

interlocking of leadership in a village organizations, the objectives may be:

— Assessing the extent of interlocking leadership

— Identifying the socio-economic characteristics of such interlocking leaders

— Evaluating the effects of such interlocking leadership on the growth of institutions involved

6. *Formulation of hypothesis:* Hypothesis is a tentative solution of the problem facing the scientist. It is usually framed depending on one or more of the following sources:

— The facts established by previous investigations in the related areas

— The history or science

— The analogies

— The findings of other studies

— The body of theory

In framing the hypothesis, the investigator has to resort to null hypothesis which means possible reasoning rejection of the variables under the study. A hypothesis should be empirical, conceptually clear, specific, close to things observable and related to the body of theory.

7. *Definition of concepts:* The researcher needs to know clearly the meaning and contends of every term that he -uses. It clarifies the issue as well as explains the investigators, respondents and other readers of the research report specifically and pointedly. The term concept must be defined both (a) in abstract term giving general meaning it is intended to convey. This, may be called the 'formal definition'. Formal definition is necessary in order to link the study with

the body of knowledge using similar concept, (b) in operational term by which it will be represented in a particular study. This type of concept is known as 'operational-definition' (some times, the workable definition). The operational definition helps in collection of data and in carrying out all research.

Care must be taken in defining concepts. Every definition is the product of the purpose for which and the environment in which the enquiry launched. This is generally accepted in all types of research projects. To illustrate the operational definition of the concept, size of the land holding operationally defined as that the land owned by a cultivator minus the land area leased out plus the land area leased in. All important terms and concepts, like the above, in a study should be operationally defined. New definitions and new concepts are put in all enquiries, precedents and past practices which deserve respect.

8. *Methodology:* The decision pertaining to method of investigation is to be done in this section. The worker has to decide whether the research project is going to be empirical in the sense of being based on primary data collected from the field, or analytical in the sense of being based on secondary data collected from published reports. In both cases research analysis will be crucial. Further, the researcher has to decide the method, either census method or sampling method to be adopted in the study with justification and the reasons for the same

Census method involves comprehensive or complete enumeration. If a survey covers all the units of the universe, under investigation, it is called census. Example of census survey is livestock. This method is time consuming and expensive process. The method of sampling has gained increased popularity in recent times.

The study of a few representative individuals or units is called a sample study. In social science research technique both the census and the sample survey methods have their relative merits, and the researchers can adopt the suitable one, according to nature and purpose of the given research project besides time and money factors.

9. *Sampling design:* Complete coverage of a population on a scientific enquiry is never possible nor advisable, even if it is possible. It may be possible when the population is very small. What is to be done is to take a sample from the population which is numerically adequate and culturally representative. While selecting sample units, the worker should be taken utmost care in adopting a particular criteria for stratification. The researcher should keep in mind the following facts while selecting sampling method:

— The definition of the universe or Population

— The size of the sample

— The representativeness of the sample

10. *Constructing of schedule or questionnaire:* A questionnaire or schedule refers to the tool or instrument of data collection. The data collected thus, become the empirical material for, testing the hypothesis/hypotheses of the study on hand.

The terms questionnaire and scheduled are treated as synonyms in social science research. Technically, a difference between them existed not in the format or contents but in the way of response obtained from the respondents with the help of them. In other words, questionnaire or schedule consists of a number of questions printed or typed in a order on a form. In case of questionnaire the responses to the questions are to be filled up by the interviewee himself. In case of schedule the responses to the questions are to be noted down by the interviewer. The questionnaire is usually associated with mail and therefore it is called mailed questionnaire. This method is used if the respondents are educated.

The form or questions may be either close or open. Open-ended questions are designed to permit a free response from the subject while the closed questions have the advantages of being standardizable or categorical. In other words, the closed questions many require the respondents himself to make a judgment about his attitude rather than leaving this to the interviewer. The questions to be asked should be direct bearing on the problem, avoiding the personal questions. The wording of questions is to be simple and should exact information that is needed avoiding multiple meaning and emotional connotations.

11. *Collection of data:* The choice of method for collecting data is administered by the subject matter, the unit of enquiry and the scope of the study. A study of behaviour of a group would call for observational technique. For a simple enquiry among the class people a questionnaire is adequate. A survey of general population entailing many complicated questions would call for personal interviewing.

12. *Analysis of data:* After collecting data, the classification and analysis are to be taken up. Depending on the nature of the data, and information required to fulfil the objective or hypothesis the researcher should analyse the data subject to the appropriate statistical analysis besides tabulation.

13. *Interpretation of results:* After organising the data into a meaningful form the researcher should draw inferences. Drawing inferences or interpreting data

will call for statistical inference based on usual test significance.

1. To the previous findings of the study
2. To a wider field of generalizations
3. To scientific objectivity
4. To uncover any additional factors which would not be visualised by the investigator earlier

14. *Reporting the findings: No* research is an end in itself. The investigator must report of what he discovered or innovated based on the data collected to fulfil the need for which the study taken tip and to ensure proper directions to other investigators in carrying out of similar researchers.

Time and financial budgeting: In carrying out the research, the time factor is very important, otherwise the work carried by the investigator and the findings of the study become a mere waste. That means research is meant to solve the problems of the society in the sense the researcher has to, respond quickly and in time.

Advantages of research design

1. The research design may result in the desired method of study with useful conclusions
2. It may lead to more accurate results or help to reduce inaccuracy
3. It may give optimum efficiency and reliability
4. It may minimise the wastage of time as well as money
5. It may be helpful for the collection of material and testing hypothesis/ hypotheses
6. It is a guide-post for carrying research in the right direction

5

Interactive Capacity

Still another form of this obstacle arises in obtaining data on the *combined* behaviour of various people. Even if I know how many pages of a magazine we read, we do not know how many other people have read how many pages of the same copy, even if it is my family copy. One way to overcome this obstacle is to add up the pages looked at by all people (actually, a sample of all people) and divide by the number of copies. A more amusing technique was tried about thirty years ago.

A researcher counted the number of fingerprints on magazine copies whose pages had been dusted with special fingerprint powder. (This is another example of the intellectual kinship between detective work and empirical scientific research.) Businessmen's lack of knowledge of their own behaviour is an interesting example. Two economists asked businessmen how they set prices, and many replied that they added fixed markups to their costs. But other analyses that assume prices are set according to what the market will bear explain actual prices better than do the businessmen. Apparently the businessmen fail to recognize when they make adjustments to meet competition and otherwise maximize their profits.

One can, however, ask different kinds of questions of the businessmen. A used-car dealer may be able to tell you very intelligently and accurately why he set a price of $825 on a particular two-year-old Valiant even if he cannot tell you how he sets prices in general. Still another way is to infer his procedure from his answers to various relevant facts. I asked newspaper executives what they thought their sales to two classes of customers would have been if their prices had been 10 per cent lower or 10 per cent higher. Their answers explained satisfactorily why one class of customers was charged more than the other.

Though we cannot ask a native about abstract, general rules, we can always enquire how a given case would be treated. Thus for instance, in asking how they would treat crime, or punish it, it would be vain to put to a native a sweeping question such as, "How do you treat and punish a criminal?" for even words could not be found to express it in native, or in pidgin. But an imaginary case, or still better, a real occurrence, will stimulate a native to express his opinion and to supply plentiful information. Sometimes one group of respondents can answer with more knowledge and accuracy than another group. To rely more heavily upon the answers of combat veterans seems sensible because their knowledge is greater.

The fallibility of memory

One of the ways that we can learn about human behaviour is to ask people how they have acted or what has happened in the past. But it is not news that people sometimes forget things. If you intend to use the products of people's memories as data, you must guard against the inaccuracy of their memories. A. Kinsey recognized that his subjects might have forgotten what they had done in the past, at what age they had first done it, and how often. To estimate the importance of memory loss lie checked up on subsamples of interviewees' memories by various devices. One of these important devices lie called "take and retake." Subjects in the take-retake group were asked for their sexual history and then were interviewed again many months later.

The two interviews were then compound to see how well the subject later statements checked against their earlier statements. Kinsey was able also to check the quality of subjects' memories by asking questions about their physical development (such as the age of growth of pubic hair) and then comparing those answers against objective physical data. Physical checks of memory were obviously impossible for most parts of the Kinsey study, however. Kinsey's checks revealed that forgetting differed among, types of questions. Forgetting had little effect on the reported *types* of behaviour people had engaged in. It had more effect on the reports of *frequency* of behaviour. And there was most memory loss about the *age* at which subjects first engaged in various types of behaviour. Several devices offer some protection if you think memory loss may be large.

One method of reducing memory loss is to have subjects keep *diaries* of their behaviour, so that no remembering is necessary—a common practice in television-viewing research and in market research. No consumer would be likely to remember after a week just what products she had bought the week before and how much of each. But if you get her to write down her purchases *immediately after* she makes them, memory loss can be negligible. Mechanical counting devices are sometimes useful. For example, if you want to know how often a man on a special diet thinks of food, you can ask him to click a pocket counter. Or, P. F. Lazarsfeld and F. Stanton developed a "program analyser" with which a person registered his like, and dislikes of various parts of radio programs by pressing buttons. (Stanton is now president of CBS, and we wish be would put a program analyser in my house.) In some cases you can circumvent people's bad memories by referring to existing records. For example, you can ask to see their bank books and other financial records instead of asking people how much they have saved.

In other cases, you must substitute observation techniques for question techniques. The Nielsen Audiometer is a mechanical device that automatically records when a television set is on and when it is off. And another device actually *photographs* people watching the television screen to measure who is actually watching, as well as -whether or not the set is on. The type of forgetting euphemistically called "confusion" is a bugaboo of readership research. Show a person a magazine and ask him whether or not lie has read it. He may say "yes" even though he has not read it.

Actually, memory (or other faculties) plays tricks on people, and they confuse what you show them with something else that they have seen. To overcome this confusion, one group of people is shown a dummy magazine that has never been printed. The proportion that says "yes" to this "placebo" is subtracted from the proportion that says " yes " to the real magazine.

Percentage who say they read actual magazine	42%
Percentage who say they read dummy magazine	12%
Percentage estimated to have read actual magazine	30%

Here is a general precept for dealing with memory loss: It is always (rood practice to reduce the time period between the event to be remembered and the interview to the shortest possible interval.

Cover-up

There are some factors that people do not want to reveal to strangers (even to intimate friends, or especially to intimate friends) because of embarrassment, guilt, shame, or other social motives. The subject, may therefore deny exaggerate, minimize or otherwise knowingly operate upon the truth to shape it into a form that lie feels is more acceptable. Barry Goldwater believed that this obstacle was operating strongly in pre-election polls in 1964;

> Senator Goldwater's own polls show that President Johnson has a large lead over him. Sources close to Mr. Goldwater said last week lie believes that if his position in the polls does not improve lie will be politically dead.
>
> But the Senator is also said to believe that "subtle impulse," many of which the voters will not discuss candidly with pollsters or with any other questioners, are at work among voters this year and could bring him victory Nov. 3.

Observation call sometimes operate as a check and prevent misinformation, as, for example, when the subject claims a level of income quite inconsistent with his home or Job. Or the researcher can build into the interview internal checks that get at the truth in several different ways and therefore show up inconsistent answers.

The take-retake technique can also be used to check on how much cover-up is operating; as cross-examining lawyers know, falsehood can be revealed by discrepant answers to repeated questions when the subject forgets his original lie. The intuition of a highly trained interviewer call often distinguish truth from falsity. Kinsey's interviewers, for example, were trained to recognize and use the vocabulary of prostitutes in order to elicit responses that would help them to judge whether or not a woman was really a prostitute. Kinsey relied heavily upon this sort of ability in his interviews. But each of the Kinsey interviewers had a full year's training, in these skills. There are few interviewing, staffs that can be so well trained and upon whose intuitive capacity it world be enable to depend to any great extent.

Trying to please the observer

People like to please other people, and subjects in research studies are no exceptions. Interviewees often answer questions the way that they think the interviewer would like them to answer. And subjects ill experiments often act the way they think the observer wants them to act. This is very nice of them, but such genial behaviour has a ruinous result unless the researcher does something about it. Psychologists have given much thought to protecting themselves from subjects who alter their normal behaviour during experiments.

Psychologists often camouflage the experiment and its purpose so that the subject cannot know what the experimenter wants or expects. For example, Clark L. Hull wanted to find out how people learn a concept or make a generalization when they are not trying to find a generalization. But human beings are always trying to "solve the problem, especially in psychology laboratories. Hull therefore convinced the subjects that they were participating in a *memory* experiment, and the task was to learn the names of various Chinese characters, whereas in reality the subjects were gradually learning general rules about the names of types of characters. If Hull had not camouflage the experiment, the subjects would have shown *sudden* learning, rather than gradual learning- of the concept.

Animals need no such camouflage because (I think) they do not have a whole set of rules of thumb to help them solve problems. In questionnaire surveys asking the questions in all impartial way so that the interviewer's own prejudices are hidden call help to overcome the obstacle of subjects' trying to please the interviewer.

Rationalization and repression

We discussed conscious distortion of the truth. Freud convinced us, however, that much lies in the human mind that either comes into consciousness as a subconscious distortion of reality or else does not come into consciousness at all because it is repressed.

> When a group of men who had said that they wanted to avoid serving in the Infantry were asked why, only 8 per cent said that this was because the Infantry "sees too much combat" or because "Its casualty rate is too high." The great majority indicated such reasons as "I don't think I'm physically qualified for it ... .. It would not give me a chance to do the kind of work I can do best," and "It would not give me training for a better job after the war." The analysts felt that, in a number of cases at least, such responses were rationalizations of the "true" motive—desire to avoid danger. In an effort to determine the extent of such rationalizations, they studied the relationship between reluctance to serve in the Infantry or in overseas combat, units and reported worries about battle injuries. They discovered that there was marked relationship: the great majority of those who said that they worried often about battle injury—79 per cent to he exact—wanted to avoid both the Infantry and overseas combat service. This is in contrast to 37 per cent of those saving, that they never worried. Frequently a set of interlocking, questions of this type permits an intrinsic, check on evasions, and their analysis many of more convincing results.

Digging out the real beliefs and reasons for behaviour may involve the use of one or more or the variegated ingenious processes that psychologists have developed.

6

The Observer

Observer variability occurs even when it would seem easy to be objective. For example, in library-science research it is sometimes necessary to decide whether two similar works by an author are two different works or two editions of the same work. Even ail experienced observer will decide differently about the same pair of books from one day to the next. In other words, there will be variability (dispersion) in the observer's judgment from time to time. Variability of traffic policemen in giving tickets for speeding is part of our folklore.

The state of the officer's digestion and the degree of amicability between him and his wife, as well as the sex of the driver, are believed to influence the outcome. In the physical sciences too-especially in the early stages of it physical discipline-observer variability is ail important obstacle. For example, a human laboratory assistant does not read a thermometer perfectly. One important reason is that on repeated trials the observer looks at the thermometer from slightly different angles, giving slightly different readings.

The difficulty is compounded if the observer cannot get close to the thermomeer, as, for example, when he reads it from inside a window. Many other minor influences also cause variability and prevent precision. As the natural sciences progressed and as more accurate instrument readings were needed, ingenious researchers developed such ways of surmounting, variability in instrument reading as the following:

1. Repeat the observation, and take an average of the observed values. If the observer-variability errors are unrelated to (independent of) one another, the average of the observations is likely to be closer to the actual value than is a single observation.

2. Reduce the variation in the viewing angle with a mechanical device that holds the chin of the observer in a fixed place and thus fixes the location of his eye. Placing a mirror behind the needle is another common device to increase precision in reading instruments.

3. Read and record electronically, and print the reading automatically. But electronics has not completely licked this obstacle. Variability in observing stars is a major difficulty in astronomy, for example.

Observations are repeated and averaged whenever possible, to cancel out random variation. And analogous to the use of the in reading thermometers, the social scientist often *reduces the scope* of the observations. If a field worker is to gather data on family income, he call be instructed to determine only how *many* cars are owned, how *many* rooms the house contains, and the occupation of the breadwinner. This list leaves less scope for judgment than would a general instruction to estimate the income level. Reducing scope is a device to restrict the observer to gathering knowledge that he call obtain reliably. Earlier we said that it is easier to state accurately what magazine you yourself read yesterday than to find out what a stranger read or what the average person read. This decreasing accuracy parallels the continuum of confidence you call place in an observer.

You rely heavily on his statement of how he himself will vote. You may place considerable credence in his statement of how his wife will vote. You do not have much confidence in his casual statement about how his neighbours will vote. And you are politely skeptical about his prediction of how his state will go in the next election. Here are two general principles about observer accuracy and the scope of observation: First, the sharper and more measurable the Categories, the more accurate the judgments.

All observer who estimates the year of a respondent's car will be more accurate about its *age* than if he judges it to be simply "old" or "new." And a judgment of old or "new" will be more accurate if he specifies a cut-off point, say three years old. On the other hand, it is a waste to ask for more categories of accuracy than he needs. Second, the less the observer must summarize, the more accurate he will be. He will be more accurate in judging the intelligence of a single person than in judging the average intelligence of a whole group of people. Learning from experience usually reduces observer variability.

Professors often take advantage of this process when they grade exams by reading several exam books and giving only tentative grades before beginning to grade in earnest—and then regarding the exams that were read first. A. Kinsey required a full year of practice from his interviewers before he would accept their data. The Kinsey interviewers, however, needed such an extraordinarily long training period because they had to exercise a great deal of judgment. Mechanical and electronic devices can occasionally be employed in the social sciences to reduce observer variability. For example, College Board Examinations are graded and totaled mostly by machines. Of course, instruments cannot make observations and measurements that require judgment. In educational examinations, this limitation sometimes means ignoring some kinds of complexities in responses and not measuring some kinds of abilities.

Tape recorders and cameras are frequently used in anthropology to produce a permanent record that can be reviewed repeatedly, either by the observer himself or by other people, in order to check on and reduce the extent of variability. And the experimental psychologist uses many gadgets to reduce observer variability-running wheels to measure animal activity, water and food meters to measure intake, and timers of all kinds to ensure exact timing of stimuli.

Observer bias

The tall fellow records a lower temperature than the short fellow because the tall fellow looks down at the thermometer. This innocent propensity to take a lower reading that inheres in the tall fellow we shall call by the ugly name "bias." In scientific usage, bias is merely a tendency to observe the phenomenon in a manner that differs from the "true " observation in some *consistent* fashion. But usually there is no way to determine the "true" value, especially before the study is complete.

Therefore, we assume that every observer is biased in one direction or the other. Our job is to determine each observer's bias and to allow for it. Most biases in the social sciences are social. Social-scientific topics and situations stir up and involve the observer's beliefs, emotions, and other mental baggage. For example, sportswriters lament the fate of the noble boxer Battling Siki, who underestimated the problem of observer bias; he fought Mike McTigue for the light-heavyweight championship in Dublin on St. Patrick's Day 1923 and lost by a decision. In a survey of anti-Catholicism and anti-Semitism, a Catholic interviewer perceives responses somewhat differently than does a Jewish interviewer.

And whether an interviewer's own values are puritan or libertine may affect a sex survey. Anthropology has suffered worst and longest from observer bias. Modern anthropologists regard most early anthropological accounts by sea captains missionaries as almost useless simply because the authors' perceptions were so warped by their own cultural background. Their bias was often that all non-Europeans were heathen, savage, primitive, and without law or social organization. Overcoming the obstacle of observer bias in physical problems like thermometer reading is reasonably easy.

The simplest tactic is to obtain reading as from several observers and to calculate their mean value, on the assumption that their biases will cancel out. The tactics used to reduce variability *within* observers also reduce variability from bias among observers. In the thermometer case, such tactics, might include careful instructions, devices that put the tall and short men's chins on the same bar, and automatic reading with instruments.

Most observer bias in the social sciences is not dealt with so easily, however. Here are some tactics that prove helpful. First, train observers very carefully. In a famous study of racial bias, G.W. Allport found that many whites who were shown a picture of a white man and a Negro later said that the Negro was holding, a razor, even through it was the white man who really held the razor in the picture. The better trained the observer, the less likely he is to make such biased observation. Careful training is the keystone of modern anthropological method.

Second, specify the observer's task as closely as possible, to reduce the area of discretion within which bias may operate. As with observer variability an observer's bias in estimating family income can be controlled by having him count the age and number of cars owned or the number of rooms in the house. Third, require observers to refer frequently to detailed instructions. This requirement is a sort or training, for it forces the observer to retrain himself by constantly rereading his instructions. It also reduces his area of diseretion by reducing the, chance that he will drift away from his instructions. Fourth, require immediate and detailed reporting whenever possible.

Anthropologists try to record their field notes every day, to minimize the chance that their memories will play biasing tricks upon them. Police officers are also trained to take on-the-spot notes, to prevent bias and inaccurancy from creeping in, and court give special attention to such notes. Fifth, mechanical devices like the camera and the tape recorder can sometimes reduce the discretion of the field observer.

The permanent record can be checked later against the observer's observations, to evaluate bias. This technique has been used extensively in anthropology, market research, and social psychology. The coming of recording devices drastically altered the working habits of anthropologists. Sixth, have several observers observe the same phenomena, and compare their observations. Note that often all observers must observe at the same time, because, for example, all interviewee may answer differently or not at all in a second interview.

Complete duplication is usually too expensive, especially in interview studies in fact, the cost of interviewing is the basic limitation on the size of the study. Comparing the data from several observers to establish their individual biases is usually feasible only on a small part of the study; those biases can then be taken into account when the rest of their data are analysed. Such a comparison can also test whether or not the observers have been trained well enough to squeeze their biases out of them. An example is a study in which two well-trained psycholinguists counted the number of pauses of various kinds in a recorded speech. Both of them practiced and compared their counts until these practice counts agreed with each other. Then each could observe individually without fear of undue bias creeping in. It is often wise to select observers who differ on relevant dimensions, for example, foreign-born and native-born, old and young, white and Negro, and so on.

This technique of comparing ratings among observers, and of averaging the ratings among observers if the ratings differ, can be especially powerful when the observers themselves are part of the situation and therefore have strong emotional reactions that affect their judgments. For example, the average judgment among a sample of several enlisted men is likely to provide a less biased rating of an officer than will that of just one enlisted man; averaging samples of students and patients is likely to provide "better" judgements of teachers and doctors, respectively, than are judgments by just one student and one patient. The previous examples show how observers can inject bias into what they hear and see and also into their judgments of what they hear and see. But bias can also come from the way that the researcher himself affects the human subjects, as we shall see shortly.

Cheating by interviewers

Some of these deviations are not larcenous; for example, the interviewer may merely skip ail interview because the house does not look pleasant from outside. But some of the deviations are pure theft; the interviewer may fill out the questionnaire schedules in his armchair at home, and, worst of all, he may do it with such skill that the answers are hard to distinguish from the real thing without some independent check.

Prevention and detection of interviewer cheating require detective's imagination and resourcefulness, Here are some frequently used techniques. First, the study supervisor may, check to see whether or not the interviewer really carried out the interview by contacting some or all of the subjects by telephone or postcard. This tactic is not feasible if the respondents are guaranteed anonymity.

One hopes that such ethical breaches do not have serious consequences. Second, someone once told me of a mechanical device that rolls the questionnaire past a writing window, one question at a time and irreversibly. It prevents the interviewer from skipping some of the questions and later filling them out at home. Finally, some researchers claim to have developed special cheatcatcher questions, but they are kept as trade secrets.

If you detect cheating, find out how much cheating there is, and report it in Your write-up, even though unsophisticated readers of your study or critics with vested interests may seize upon this report as a means of damning the study. Commercial motivation researchers raised a howl because this finding threatened their livelihoods, and one of the motivation researchers, seized upon evans' report that one of his interviewers had cheated—which Evans had allowed for by discarding those data—to discredit the study. But sophisticated readers gained confidence from his report because they were reassured that there was no unreported but worrisome cheating.

Variability among observers

Variability among observers is not a special type of difficulty. Rather, it is a combination of variability within individual observers and systematic bias differences among observers. Avoiding these two sources of error separately automatically solves the problem of variability among observers.

Observer-caused effects

The observer is inevitably a part of the same environment as is the phenomenon he is studying. Therefore, the observer, like all other aspects of the environment, must influence the phenomenon. Sometimes the effect is so slight that it may be ignored, as is usually the case in the physical sciences. For example, the act of measuring the time it takes a ball bearing to roll down an incline affects the ball in some infinitesimal way; there is gravitational attraction between the observer's eyeballs as they roll in his head and the ball bearing as it rolls down the incline, but the attraction is too small to measure.

On the other hand, a chemist's breath may well affect a reaction he is running. The observer effect in medical examinations straddles the physical and social sciences. When a doctor (or especially a young nurse, in the, case of male patients) takes a patient's blood pressure, fear or excitement often forces the blood pressure far above the normal level. A danger of observer-caused effects is that the researcher may not realize that they are operating and affecting the results.

The consequent interaction between subject and observer must have consequences. We humans spend large parts of our lives learning to pick up and act upon subtle cues given us by people with whom we are in contact. Therefore, even very subtle behaviour of the observer can affect the study results. For example, the inflection and tone of voice in which an interviewer asks a question can produce one response or another. But Kinsey's crosschecking techniques Satisfied the official reviewers that error from this source was not great. One might argue that in history, economics, or political science there are no observer-caused effects because the research' generally takes place after the events are complete. Brutus killed Caesar no matter what the historian says about it now. And ill economics the course of economic events is clearly affected by the kind of records that are kept, which are the raw material for the economist later.

7

Sampling Designs

Several criteria must be taken into consideration when selecting a sampling plan or design. These are divided into four categories.

A statement of objectives: GIGO (garbage in, garbage Out), the acronym that used to adorn the walls of computing centers, is particularly applicable to sampling. If the researcher is Unclear as to the objectives of the study, the data will be useless, no matter how many are collected. In deciding upon the appropriate sampling design, it is essential to know what data need to be collected and why. Having some idea of what statistics the sample is expected to generate is also essential. Is the objective to generate point estimates such as a mean or a total for a particular variable, or are the data to be used to test a multivariate relationship? It is important to know, because a design that could probably generate precise and economical results for a point estimate will not necessarily do so if several variables are of equal interest. Specifying the objectives of the study also refers to specifying the unit of analysis for the objective at hand. For example, is the focus on individuals, households, enumeration areas, or what? Clusters require one form of strategy, element samples another.

Measurability: Measurability is what distinguishes probability samples from all others. The researcher must know the probability of selection of every element of' the population from which the sample is to be drawn. In the absence of, this information, drawing inferences within estimable credibility limits is not possible. Measurability then, requires a complete and accurate sampling frame.

Practicality: The sample design must be doable. From the outset, it can be determined that some plans cannot be executed. Questions that require overly precise answers ("I want to know what percentage of the population has hangnails within one tenth of 1 percent, 99 times out of 100.") are not practical. When considering whether the design can be executed, it is essential to specify the resources that are available, the period in which the Study needs to be conducted, and whether the phenomenon under consideration can be measured by means of the proposed techniques.

A key issue of practicality is whether the research ought to be done at all. If a lot is known about a topic, yet another survey might add nothing further to our understanding. Often the most that can be expected from such enterprises is a congressional "golden fleece" award. All research activity carries with it an opportunity cost. This opportunity cost may be as funds that could be diverted into a more worthwhile project or as time wasted by the researcher.

Economy: Cost is a major factor in any Survey. Cost may be measured in many ways, such as money, time, or other nonmonetary resources (e.g., available personnel). A primary objective of a sampler is to achieve the highest precision possible per unit cost. Two elements of exactitude may be differentiated: precision and accuracy. Precision refers to the inherent variability of the phenomenon in the population while accuracy takes into consideration the inherent variability plus any included bias.

Formally, precision and accuracy may be defined as follows:

$$\text{precision} = \frac{1}{\text{var}(\bar{y})}$$

and

$$\text{accuracy} = \frac{1}{MSE(\bar{y})} = \frac{1}{variance + biases}$$

Practically, this means that the researcher either (a) fixes the desired precision and then determines the sampling design that would yield it for the minimum cost, or (b) fixes the cost and attempts to achieve the maximum precision within that cost constraint.

Some of these issues can be addressed by the researcher, spending some time at a desk and thinking through the process step by step. Yet other issues are best dealt with through a pilot study. A trial run on 30 to 50 cases can usually pinpoint the major weaknesses of a study. Except for extremely rare populations of interest that may not be captured in a small sample, pilot studies identify failings in the measurement instrument and provide valuable feedback on the data collection mechanism.

Furthermore, it pilot study can often provide a rough estimate of the sampling variance, which can be used to fine-tune it sample size estimate. Conducting a pilot study is no guarantee of success; however, not doing one is it harbinger of failure.

Selection procedures

As Kish tells us, "Simple random sampling (srs) is the basic selection process, and all other procedures can be viewed as modifications of it, introduced to provide more practical, economical, or precise designs." The basic elements of, srs sampling were addressed. What is important to note about all probability samples, however, is that whatever the approach taken, at the ultimate stage the elements must be selected randomly.

Sampling with or without replacement

Sampling with replacement assures that the probability of selection stays constant. Sampling without replacement results in higher selection probabilities for items chosen later in the sampling procedure. On the other hand, sampling without replacement can often produce more efficient estimates, especially when sampling with replacement results in many duplicate selections.

The issue of which approach to take (where a choice is available) is moot if the sampling frame (the eligible Population) is sufficiently large, since the fpc becomes so small that the results are indistinguishable front one another. Clearly, sampling with replacement has some advantages in that it simplifies the statistical calculation of the standard error; however, this strategy is not always available to us, especially when the sampled element is somehow modified through the measurement process. For small samples without replacement, the sampling distribution best approximates a hypergeometric distribution.

EPSEM (Equal Probability of Selection Method) vs. Unequal Probabilities Methods

In equal probability of selection method samples, the population elements have equal probabilities of inclusion into the sample. EPSEM samples are essentially self-weighting, thus allowing for the simple and direct estimation of parameters such as the mean. EPSEM samples may also be achieved through compensating unequal probabilities at several stages. The opposite to EPSEM samples are Unequal probability samples, usually corrected by using inverse weights. Unequal probability samples are often used when the selection frame is not complete or has problems, or when it is necessary to oversample some class of elements. Oversampling is often useful when a given class of interest is a rare event. In these situations, an srs would generally not produce enough cases to yield reliable estimates.

Random vs. systematic selection of elements

Random sampling involves the independent random selection of elements within a stratum. A common variant for selecting elements from a population or a particular stratum is what is known as systematic selection. This approach is worthy of some consideration because it appears quite often in practice and, under most circumstances, produces results that would occur if the sample had been drawn as srs. Systematic selection first involves a determination of the sampling fraction, *n/N*. For the sake of example, let us assume that this is 1/100. As a second step, a uniform random number between 1 and 100 is generated.

This random number (say.39) *Is* used to select the first element from the sample frame-in this case, the 39th element. After the first element has been selected, each successive I 00th element is chosen for sample inclusion (i.e., 139, 239, 339, . . .) until the total sample has been chosen. Systematic selection is extremely practical when the sample frame does not include a discrete listing of all elements in the population. Aerial Sampling that uses map grids as frames is a good example of such it case.

Another application the author came across some years ago involved the auditing of a selection of professional case files. No complete listing of the case files existed; however, the files were arrayed on a series of shelves and the total number of files was known. In this circumstance, a random start number was generated and every f th file corresponding to the sampling fraction was selected for examination. Since several thousand files were involved, this procedure saved considerable time and expense over having to create an initial listing or frame from the population of case files. Clearly, systematic selection has its uses. In some situations, however, bias can be introduced. One danger is that *periodicities* may exist in the implicit frame, with the result that the selection of every f th element produces a very nonrandom sample.

The traditional example used to illustrate periodicity is that of houses on uniform blocks. Through bad luck, the researcher may generate a start number that results in almost every selected house being a corner house. Periodicities also are highly probable when elements must be selected within a time frame. Using systematic selection to examine retail sales patterns over time may result in the selection of sales on a specific day of the week or, if the units are months, on a seasonal basis, Such as months in which there are holidays. Another problem that might arise is that of linear trends. Here, the values associated with the population elements increase or decrease across time or distance.

From a statistical perspective, this situation results in serial correlation among the selected elements. Overall, however, periodicities and linear trends are rare in most social science sampling applications. Where they might exist, the researcher can still use systematic sampling, although with some modifications. For example, it may he possible to "shuffle" the frame if it is known to be sorted in some specific, periodic order. It may also be possible to stratify the frame and to generate a new start number from each stratum. Where linear trends exist but little can be done to alter the sampling plan, the best solution may be to acknowledge the situation and correct for the serial correlation during the statistical analysis.

Stratified vs. unstratified sampling

Unstratified selection implies that the sample is drawn front the entire population in one Stage (or a single stratum). Stratified samples require the population to be segmented into homogeneous subpopulations, with random samples drawn independently from each segment. At worst, ineffective stratification generates results similar to those for an srs. The most general form of stratified sampling is what is known as *disproportionate stratified sampling.*

Two subtypes are often discussed in the literature, and these are *proportionate stratified sampling* and *optimum sampling.* In disproportionate stratified sampling, the sampling fraction is allowed to differ across strata. Thus, in stratum 1, the sampling fraction might be 1/100 and in stratum 2 it might be 1/25. Disproportionate sampling fractions are generally used when the strata differ substantially in size or the costs of measurement are different across strata. When conducting a labour force participation study, for example, it might be worthwhile to stratify by sex and by class of worker.

Since salaried work is the norm for both men and women, it would likely be more efficient to stratify by class of worker—for example, salaried, self-employed, unemployed, and not in the labour force—and to use a lower sampling fraction for the salaried workers than for the remaining groups. Disproportionate stratification poses little difficulty for analysis if the analyst remembers to weight the data by the sampling fraction for each stratum. Thus, if $f_h = n_h/n$, then the appropriate weight for all elements in stratum h would be f_h. To obtain an estimate of the sample total, one would obtain the product $n\bar{y}_{st}$, When it is necessary to estimate a population total, the strata elements should be weighted by the corresponding population values.

Therefore, the corresponding fraction would be $W_h = N_h/N$, and the total would be estimated by $N\bar{y}_{st}$. Proportionate stratified sampling is the special situation of all f_h being equal and, as such, requires no further comment. Optimum allocation, however, is a procedure used to allocate more of the total sample to those strata with the largest variances. That is, as s^2_h increases so does n^2_h Optimum allocation is achieved when $\Sigma^H_{h=1} (s^2_h / n_h)$ is minimized.

An estimated optimal sample size for the hth stratum may thus be determined by

$$n_h = n \frac{N_h S_h}{\Sigma^H_{h=1} N_h S_h}$$

Optimum allocation requires reliable existing information on the strata variances. Consequently it is a procedure that is normally applied when the same survey is to be conducted repeatedly. For example, monthly labour force surveys, repetitive political attitude surveys across several regions, and periodic market trend Surveys are prime candidates for optimum allocation as a rule, "one-shot" Surveys are not.

A further difficulty with optimum allocation is that what might be optimal for one variable is not likely optimal for another. Thus, multipurpose Surveys rarely incorporate optimum allocation. Where the researcher obtains a copy of a survey based on optimal allocation, the analysis is conducted in the same manner as a survey based on disproportionate stratified sampling.

Single-phase vs. multiphase samples

Single-phase sampling refers to a process whereby the entire sample is drawn in it single operation. Multiphase sampling, however, involves drawing the sample in two or more stages. The second phase of a multiphase sample involves selecting a subsample from a larger preselected sample. The advantage of multiphase samples is that the first phase can often provide detailed information for improving upon the final selection. The general procedure in multiphase samples is to conduct a less costly general or screening interview for the first phase and then revisit a selected subsample for more detailed interviewing in the second phase.

This type of strategy might be employed in a fertility survey. Here, a general interview schedule could be presented to all women included in the sample. As a second phase, one might wish to conduct more detailed interviews with women who have had miscarriages or who, based on the initial results, may appear to be infertile. Often multiphase samples are multimodal. That is, it less expensive telephone interview procedure might be used at the first phase, while more expensive in-person interviews might be reserved for the second phase. Effectively designed sampling strategies may employ different combinations of the foregoing dimensions. As a practical endeavour, sampling involves a trade-off between costs, "doability," and statistical considerations.

Sampling proportionate to size

It often happens in practice that the psus vary considerably in size but the researcher wishes to select a sample of a fixed overall size, *n*, and of similar sizes within each of the primary units. For example, a criminologist may wish to estimate how much violence takes place in schools. It is decided that the overall sample size should consist of 1100 students out of the total regional population of 220,000. Furthermore, to maintain consistency in the size of the variance of the estimates, the criminologist decides that approximately 50 students be selected from each school. This suggests that 22 initial psus (schools) are to be selected. If the schools are of approximately equal size, it would be a simple matter to randomly select 22 schools from the study region and then further select a random sample of 50 students within each school. In practice, the schools in a given region vary considerably in size from, say, 600 students to 2000 students.

Thus, an srs of schools would be biased against students in the larger schools. That is, the probabilities of selection for students in the larger schools would be less than for the smaller schools. To address this problem, it is common practice to select the psu with probabilities proportionate to their size. Thus each student in the region has a constant overall probability of selection. The situation can be illustrated by examining the selection probabilities separately at the two stages. Again, f is the overall sampling fraction n/N. Let N_α, be the number of students in cluster α; let b represent the number of students to be selected within each cluster, and consider F as $1/f$. In essence, F *is* N/n.

Since the sample to be selected within each cluster is fixed at b, the probability of selection for the second stage is b/N_α. Now we need to determine the probabilities of selection for primary sampling units. Since the overall sampling fraction is fixed at f the solution may be achieved by substituting the appropriate Values in the equation

$$\frac{N_\alpha}{Fb}\frac{b}{N_\alpha} = \frac{1}{F} = f$$

Thus, the appropriate probabilities of selection for the clusters at stage one are N_α/Fb. Since the denominator, Fb, *is* a constant, the selection probabilities are proportionate to the cluster's sizes, N_α.

Occasionally, the exact cluster sizes are not known. In these situations substituting a measure that proxies N_α is often possible. For example, if in a study of manufacturers employees, reliable data on the number of employees per firm were not available, it might be possible to substitute a reasonable proxy such as annual total sales, or amounts paid by the firms in benefits. This proxy for the number of employees per firm is known as a *measure of size* and is usually designated as Mos_α. By substituting Mos_α for N_α we obtain the equation for the two-stage selection probabilities as

$$\frac{Mos_\alpha}{Fb}\frac{b}{Mos_\alpha} = \frac{b}{Fb} = f$$

Again, the probability of selecting the α th psu should be equal to Mos_α/Fb. Some consideration might prompt us to ask how the population total, *N*, can be determined if the exact sizes of the individual psus are not known. Occasionally, this information is available from selected industry or census documents. All is not lost, however, if the information is not available. If it can be assumed that *Fb is* again fixed, with a psus, then we can substitute

$$Fb = \frac{\sum_{\alpha=1}^{A} Mos_\alpha}{a}$$

What is important here, however, is that if Mos_α is used for the calculation of the selection probabilities for the primary units, it must also be used for the calculation of the selection probabilities for the secondary units. That is, Mos_α, cannot be used for one and N_α for the other.

A Caution

Why should we bother selecting clusters proportionate to size when the frame could just as easily be stratified according to size and psus chosen on that basis? The answer is that these are two very different processes, and while both are statistically "legitimate" things to do, the, procedures address two very different problems. In sampling proportionate to size, we assume that the units of interest are the elements within the Clusters, In the preceding example,•that would be the students within the schools.

Stratifying the psus by size and then conducting an srs selection within the strata implies that the unit of interest is the cluster itself. Thus, the focus would be on the characteristics of the school as a unit, not the individual students, or on the firm as opposed to the individual employees. The distinction is one of units of analysis. Hence, it is again essential that the person designing the sample be fully aware of the objectives it is supposed to serve.

Poststratification

Occasionally, a researcher has prior knowledge of a distribution of a population on some criteria in conjunction with the survey. These data may be obtained from analyses of census files or from larger, multipurpose samples. Where minor differences exist between the distribution of characteristics in one's sample and the known distribution of the characteristics in the population, it may be appropriate to reweight the sample. When used judiciously, this reweighting, known as *poststratification,* can lead to improved estimates in samples that have succumbed to the vicissitudes of chance. Some researchers use poststratification as a procedure for correcting for nonresponse in the Survey. This is a much more tenuous enterprise and one that should not be engaged in lightly.

The use of weighting to correct for nonresponding or missing cases may be a viable approach to the problem. However, weighting is but one possible way of addressing the issue. The researcher should be aware that there are many approaches to the missing data problem, and the advantages and disadvantages of each.

Design effects

The issue of estimating an appropriate sample size for testing hypotheses. Here we examined the simple relationship between the size of a sample, the variance of the estimate, and the impact of DEFF and roh for Cluster Samples.

Random sample

The relationship between n and the standard error can be illustrated as follows. First, recall that the variance of an estimate such as a proportion is

$$\text{var}(p) = (1-f)\frac{s^2}{n} = \frac{s^2}{n^*}$$

It is possible to solve for n*:

$$n^* = \frac{s^2}{\text{var}(p)}$$

and for n:

$$n = \frac{n^*}{1+f} = \frac{n^*}{1+n^*/N}$$

Example: estimating sample size for an srs

From a previous survey s^2 is estimated to be .2491 and the population, N, *is* known to be 10,000. The researcher wants a standard error of no more than 1%. By substitution,

$$n^* = \frac{.2491}{(.01)^2} = 2491 \text{ and } n = \frac{2491}{1+2491/10{,}000} = 1994$$

There are two significant points of note here. First, n^* is very sensitive to the size of var(p). and as var (p) becomes smaller, n^* increases geometrically. Second, except where f is very large, the fpc has only a small impact on the required sample. These two points are well illustrated in Table 1, where the researcher considered how sample size varied with differing values of the standard error of p. To illustrate the impact of the population total on n, two cities have been assumed: one with a population of 10,000 and the other with a population of 100,000. Where f is small, n remains similar whether the population from which the sample is to be drawn is 10,000 or 100,000.

This pattern, illustrated by the estimates reported in Table 1, appears counter-intuitive to many people, who assume that if a sample is to stay "representative," sample size must increase as the population increases. In fact, for a given sample size with negligible fpc, the precision of a sample is essentially the same whether the sample is drawn from a population of several thousands or several millions.

Table 1

Relationship between SE(p) and n for selected SE(p)

			n	
Standard error	*var(p)*	*n**	N= *10,000*	N= *100,000*
0.01	0.0001	2491	1994	2430
0.015	0.000225	110	997	1095
0.02	0.0004	623	586	619
0.025	0.000625	399	383	397
0.03	0.0009	277	269	276

Sample size where s^2 is known

It is assumed that a researcher is interested in obtaining a point estimate rather than testing a hypothesis. Consequently, the issue of statistical power can be ignored. Following the logic of the preceding section, estimating the required sample size for an srs is relatively straightforward. Prior to being able to estimate an acceptable sample size, however, the researcher needs to know three things. First, some estimate is required of the variance of the variable or phenomenon under investigation. Second, an acceptable level of error needs to be specified. That is, for some parameter, θ, to be estimated, it must be decided how large an error limit, L, is acceptable, where $|\theta - \hat{\theta}| < L$. Third, the probability 1—α needs to be stated to specify the expected proportion of the times the estimate must be less than L. Typically, if α = .05 were acceptable, L Would be 1.96 SE(*).

Under these circumstances, we know that

$$L = z\frac{s}{\sqrt{n_0}}, \text{ thus } L^2 = z^2\frac{s^2}{n_0}$$

Solving for n_0,

$$n_0 = z^2\frac{s^2}{L^2}$$

Sampling for votes

The basic principles are easiest to illustrate where the statistic of interest, θ is a proportion. Suppose that in the last elections held in a particular jurisdiction, 35% of the voters cast their ballots for the Democratic candidate. Before deciding to run again, the candidate wishes to estimate the likely proportion of votes she would receive, *plus* or minus 2.5%, with a 95% level of confidence that the estimate falls within that range. From the previous election, the variance (s^2) is estimated as pq or (.35)(.65) .2275. The candidate wishes to estimate $P \pm z$ SE(p), where z. SE(p) = .025. To simplify notation, let L represent the acceptable limit of $z_{\alpha/2}$ SE(p). Furthermore, it can be assumed that the candidate is running in a jurisdiction with a large population (say several million), so the fpc factor is moot. By Substitution, we have

$$n_0 = (1.96)^2 \frac{.2275}{(.025)^2}$$

$$= 1398$$

A sample of 1398 voters is required to estimate the proportion of votes the candidate might receive within ±2.5% 19 times out of 20.

Where the population from which the sample is to be drawn is finite, the preceding formulas can be used it they are adjusted for the fpc. It the jurisdiction in which the candidate is running is a town of 5000, the following adjustments can be made:

$$L = z\frac{s}{\sqrt{n}}\sqrt{1-\frac{n}{N}}, \text{ thus } L^2 = z^2\frac{s^2}{n}\left(1-\frac{n}{N}\right)$$

Solving for n, we obtain

$$n = \frac{\frac{z^2 s^2}{L^2}}{1+\frac{1}{N}\left(\frac{z^2 s^2}{L^2}-1\right)}$$

This formula is somewhat unwieldy. However, it will be noticed that the term $z^2 s^2/L^2$ which appears in both the numerator and the denominator, is the estimator for n_0. By Substituting n_0, n can be expressed more manageably, as follows:

$$n = \frac{n_0}{1+\frac{1}{N}(n_0 - 1)}$$

Sampling for votes

Again, substituting the appropriate values, n determined as follows

$$n = \frac{1398}{1 + \frac{1}{5000}(1398 - 1)}$$

$$= 1093$$

Since the population is now considered finite, the fpc results in a reduction of the necessary sample size by 22%.

Sample size where s^2 is unknown

In some situations, s^2 either is not known or is of questionable reliability. Under these circumstances, one must generate an estimate of s^2 . There are three ways in which this is typically done. First, the researcher can search the available literature for similar studies conducted elsewhere. As indicated previously, the estimate of s^2 need not always be very precise, especially when one is dealing with proportions. In other Situations, it is possible to conduct it sensitivity analysis by using the best estimate of s^2 and then generating several estimated *ns* by varying the value of s^2.

For example the desired formula for n can be entered into a spreadsheet. A first expected n can be generated by means of the best estimate of s^2, and subsequent values for n can be obtained by increasing s^2 by 25 %, 50%, . . . , 100%, and so on. A second approach to obtaining an estimate of s^2 is to conduct a pilot study. Where possible, pilot studies are highly recommended for many reasons. Not only is it possible to obtain an estimate of s^2, but the measurement instrument can be assessed, and any research assistants or interviewers involved in the study can get firsthand experience with both the instruments and the design procedure. Unfortunately, quality pilot studies can be difficult to execute. When the design costs of doing the research are very high compared with the cost of collecting the data (e.g., conducting face-to-face interviews in the Himalayas), doing a pilot may not be economical. A third approach that can be used is generally attributed to Cox and Stein. The Cox-Stein procedure involves estimating the final sample size "on the fly." This approach has the advantage of combining the pilot and the actual study into a single process. Its primary disadvantage is that the final sample size is not known until after the study has started; hence, the final cost is not known at the start. This contrasts with the pilot approach, where the cost usually can be fixed and the results from that study allow a fixed cost estimate to be produced for the final Study.

The Cox-Stein approach includes the following steps

1. Select an initial subsample of size n_1, and estimate s^2_1.
2. Calculate n_2 as follows:

$$n_2 = \frac{s_1^2}{V}\left(1 + \frac{2}{n_1}\right)$$

   where V is the level of precision required.

3. Calculate n as follows:

$$n = \max\left[n_1, \left(n_2 \frac{1}{(\frac{n^2}{N}) + 1}\right) + 1\right]$$

4. Take $n - n_1$ additional observations.

Cluster size and sampling error

The preceding chapter introduced the concepts of DEFF and roh with respect to clustering, the point being that the expected homogeneity of clusters reduces their effective standard error in comparison to an srs based on the same number of elements. The loss in precision can also be seen to depend on the size of the clusters.

For the random roadside survey, roh was estimated to be .03 1. By assuming that rob is reasonably constant in such surveys, the relationship between Cluster Size and DEFF can be illustrated. In Table 2, DEFF has been calculated for rob of .03 1 and cluster sizes from 10 to 100 (assuming either a constant b per cluster or a stable $\bar{n}_\alpha$. Clearly, as the Cluster size increases, DEFF increases and the effective sample size relative to an srs decreases correspondingly. If achieving the smallest sampling error

Table 2

DEFF and effective sample sizes for different sized clusters

Cluster size	DEFF	Effective Sample where srs = 1783
1	1	1783
5	1.124	1586
10	1.279	1394
20	1.589	1122
30	1.899	939
40	2.209	807
75	3.294	541
100	4.069	438

for a given *n* were the only consideration, the smallest cluster size possible should clearly be selected. Unfortunately, other factors come into play, complicating one's task in establishing an optimal cluster size.

For example, in the roadside surveys, the proportion

of drivers with BAC levels over the legal limit was estimated to be about 5%. Thus driving in a state of statutory intoxication is a relatively rare event; and with small clusters, it is likely that few (if any) drivers over the limit would be captured at any given site. With an average cluster size of 20, we could expect only one driver to be over the limit.

Clearly, reasonable sized clusters are required in this instance to capture the point estimate, p. Even with $\bar{n}_\alpha$ = 42 (as here), only two drivers on average can be expected to be over the legal limit. Cost is another significant factor that must be considered with cluster samples. Often, it costs 20 to 50 times as much to identify and reach the cluster as it does to measure the elements in the cluster. Surveying students in classrooms across a state or province illustrates this problem.

The costs of travel and of the interviewer's time to appear on location are substantial. At each site, however, the cost of surveying a classroom of 20 to 30 students is negligible. Since cost is a major factor in determining how much data can be collected, it is worth turning our attention to this issue.

Survey costs

The costs may be measured directly in monetary terms, as is done when a for-profit agency is hired to conduct a survey, or they may be indirect, as they are when doctoral students invest time in collecting their own data. In the latter case, the data are not "free." There is an opportunity cost involved, since time the doctoral candidate puts into data collection could be used for other activities—writing the thesis, spending time with one's family, or working full time. Determining the cost of data collection is an iterative process. Initially, sample size requirements are based on how precise one would like the estimate to be. This may be based on a practical motive, such as a political candidate's wanting to be able to estimate with a reasonable degree of certainty how many voters are likely to be captured, or it may be based on theoretical criteria, Such as the desire to be able to estimate DEFF or another important parameter.

These demands for accuracy, however, are tempered by the resources available. If the cost of collecting the desired sample is prohibitive, then the sample size may be scaled back (consequently decreasing the precision of the estimate), or the enterprise may be abandoned. Usually when we collect data, we wish to know how much the exercise will cost, but we also work within the confines of a predetermined budget. Thus, sampling is the art of compromise, and the key question is, Can we satisfy our desire to generate an estimate having an acceptable level of precision for an acceptable cost).

The issue of precision, which varies with the sampling- error, has been examined in some detail. The next step is to examine the factors that enter the cost equation. The total cost of data collection can be broken into two components: filed costs and variable costs. The fixed costs are those associated with aspects of data collection that are somewhat independent of the size of the sample. For example, in executing a survey, the cost associated with developing the questionnaire is the same whether the instrument is presented to 10 people or 10,000 people.

The variable cost components are the items driven by the number of elements. In a telephone survey, this would include items such as the per-interview cost for the interviewer. Some items may cross categories depending upon the situation. For example, the cost of phone calls in telephone surveys may be fixed if the surveyor is making local calls on a flat-rate billing system, but it may be variable if per-call or long-distance charges apply.

Kish presents a four-component cost model that works well in the main. Specifically, Kish's model for total costs, C_t, is defined as follows:

$$C_t = C_k + C_{kv} + nc + nc_v$$

C_k represents fixed costs that apply despite the size of the survey or the specific design chosen. These include such elements as the process of deciding upon the survey design, the per-diem expenses of a consulting statistician, the development of the measurement instrument, the performance of the data analysis, and the cost of publishing and distributing the final report.

C_{kv} are design-dependent cost factors that do not vary with the sample size. Hence, they are independent of n but they do depend on the strategy selected. These factors may include differential costs of training and Supervising interviewers to collect data in a cluster as opposed to an srs survey. The third component, nc, consists of variable costs related to the sample size but independent of the design . Typically these costs are the per-unit cost of collecting data (interviewing or another form of measurement), the incremental costs of supervising the data collection, and some elements of overhead (e.g., cost of renting more office space or a fixed office space for a longer time).

One issue that may be overlooked is the tendency of large samples to take longer to collect than smaller samples, thereby imposing an opportunity cost by delaying the analysis and publication of the results. The fourth component, nc_v consists of items that vary with both the number of elements sampled and the design of the sample. Thus, a cluster sample sometimes requires regional offices to reduce the cost of travelling to the sites, and the cost of supporting those regional offices is proportional to the number of clusters and the number of elements sampled. Because of the fixed costs, larger surveys tend to cost less per element than small surveys. On the other hand, increases in precision often have a steeper incremental cost function (because of the geometric requirement for data) than the per-unit savings function associated with a larger sample size. As with most human activities, the cost-precision relationship is one of marginal incremental returns to scale. Initially, significant increases in precision are obtained as more resources are put into increasing the sample size. After a point, however, the costs per unit increase in precision become prohibitive.

Optimal strata sizes

It has been suggested that the optimal strategy for allocating elements over a stratified sample is to allocate disproportionately to strata that have either the largest variance or the largest N_h. If the total cost is fixed, this approach can be modified so that the strata with the largest variances get the largest proportion of elements and those with the highest associated costs receive a smaller proportion of the overall sample. Different models can be used to estimate the total cost of carrying out different sampling designs.

Some of these can be defined analytically, while others are based solely upon field experience. The simplest model, however, is a linear cost model that assumes constant incremental unit costs as the sample size increases or decreases. Thus, the assumption is made that the total cost, C_t, is composed of a fixed cost component, C_k, and a variable stratum-dependent component, C_h, associated with H each element in the hth stratum. That is, $C_t = C_{k+}\Sigma^{H}_{h-1} C_h n_h$. Cochran shows that under these criteria, the lowest variance is obtained when the stratum sizes are proportionate to $N_h\ S_h / \sqrt{Ch}$. Thus, for a fixed overall cost for the sample, the best estimate for the total sample size is given by

$$n = \frac{(C_t - C_k)(N_h S_h / \sqrt{C_h})}{\sum_{h=1}^{H} N_h S_h \sqrt{C_h}}$$

Once the total sample size has been estimated, the stratum allocations, n_h/n, may be estimated by

$$\frac{n_h}{n} = \frac{W_h S_h / \sqrt{C_h}}{\sum_{h=1}^{H} (W_h S_h / \sqrt{C_h})} = \frac{N_h S_h / \sqrt{C_h}}{\sum_{h=1}^{H} (N_h S_h / \sqrt{C_h})}$$

It has been assumed that the cost is fixed. Cochran also provides a discussion on estimating n_h, based on the requirement that var($\bar{y}$st) be fixed and the total cost be allowed to vary instead. When the size of a cluster increases (all other things being equal), the DEFF increases and the effective sample size decreases. Consequently, the following question is often posed: What is the optimal cluster size?

The answer to this problem is best addressed in two steps. The first step is to decide the optimal sample size for an srs of an acceptable precision. Once determined, n is multiplied by the design effect to compensate for the fact that the effective sample size is less than the normal sample size. Needless to say, the difficulty here lies in obtaining reasonable estimates of both s^2 and DEFF. Based on this exercise, however, the researcher call often determine roughly whether the available budget call support the research. For a cluster sample, the basic cost model may be defined as follows:

$$C_1 = ac_1 + nc_2 = ac_1 + \bar{n}_\alpha ac_2$$

where again, C_1 is the total cost, a is the number of clusters, c_1 is the cost associated with the cluster, and c_2 is the unit cost associated with the elements. By knowing, roh, it is possible to estimate the optimal cluster size, $\bar{n}_{opt}$

as

$$\bar{n}_{opt} = \sqrt{\frac{c_1}{c_2}\left(\frac{1-\rho}{\rho}\right)}$$

After $\bar{n}_{opt}$ has been determined, the number of required clusters becomes $a = n\sqrt{n}_{opt}$. A side benefit of this formulation is that the actual values of c_1 and c_2 need not be known to calculate $\bar{n}_{opt}$. It is sufficient to know the approximate ratio between these two elements to estimate the optimal cluster size.

Where the total cost, C_t is fixed, however, a may be estimated within that constraint as follows:

$$\frac{C_t}{c_1 + \bar{n}_{opt} c_2}$$

societies to maintain their professional status) but incomplete for accountants (for whom membership may be voluntary). Upon completion of the analysis, however, the researcher must be careful not to generalize the findings beyond the redefined target population.

Response rates and survey tactics

Decreasing response rates are becoming an increasingly important problem in the social sciences, particularly in survey research. Professional survey firms are finding it more and more difficult to maintain the response rates of previous years, despite constant improvements in survey technology. In a review of more than 500 face-to-face interviews, telephone surveys, and mail surveys, Goyder reports mean response rates of 67, 60, and 58%, respectively, Groves and Lyberg show a long-term decline in response to telephone surveys. In their review of surveys conducted primarily by academics as opposed to private research firms, Hox and DeLeeuw (1994) suggest that over the period 1947-92, responses to telephone and face-to-face surveys have converged with those of mail surveys. Variations in response rates and how they might be dealt with depend upon the survey procedures employed.

Some people are difficult to locate (thus necessitating callbacks or setting of appointments), and some are reluctant to participate in surveys of any kind. Telephone surveys were very successful tools before direct-dial marketers latched onto the procedure and succeeded in souring the level of consumer cooperativeness. Ever more people are now perceiving any form of telephone soliciting as harassment and an infringement on their privacy. Because response rates are declining universally, it is even more important that researchers use whatever procedures are available to maintain the overall response rate. Fortunately, there are some tried and true techniques at our disposal if we are, willing to make the effort to use them.

In-person interviews

In-person surveys generally involve house-to-house interviews with area residents. This has been the traditional procedure used to collect information for censuses and large-scale surveys. Recently, however, in-person interviews for large-scale projects have fallen out of favour. They are exceedingly costly, and there is some evidence that both response rates and data quality can be improved through other procedures, particularly telephone surveys. Still, in-person interviews do offer some advantages over other techniques. They allow for ancillary information to be gathered through on-site inspection.

Thus, for example, the interviewer can later provide qualitative assessments of the condition of the respondent's residence or the physical condition of the interviewee. The, interviewer can also perform quick validity checks on such items as the apparent age of the interviewee or the apparent standard of living maintained in the household. Furthermore, it is possible to cross-check some aspects of' the sample frame through direct observation. This may be particularly useful in canvasses of dwelling units that have been subdivided and not reported to municipal authorities (as happens with illegal suites). The negative aspects of in-person interviewing generally relate to cost.

This type of research is very expensive in terms of personnel, time, and travel. Not only are interviewer costs high, but the costs of training interviewers are high as well. Other difficulties relating to in-person interviews involve quality control. Unlike mail or telephone interviewing, supervisors generally do not have firsthand contact with interviewers in the field. It must be assumed, therefore, that these employees are conducting the interviews as expected and that the sessions are essentially consistent across interviewers. Procedures for increasing response rates for in- person interviews revolve around the traditional callback.

Unfortunately, a dozen or more tries may be necessary to achieve an interview with one person. Indeed, many interviewees feel little obligation to honor their commitment to keep appointments arranged over the telephone. Given the travel costs associated with in-person interviews, this unreliability can force the researcher to select a lower overall sample size than might be warranted. Occasionally, an interviewer who has been stood up by the person who made the appointment can interview another household member who may have similar characteristics or may be knowledgeable about the objectives of the survey. Also, some pertinent data may be collected through direct observation that might either suffice per se or supply data for an analysis of missing cases. The use of interviewers with characteristics similar to those of the interviewees (e.g., ethnic affiliation, gender) may also increase response rates, although dissimilarity in such respects does not appear to be a major problem.

Telephone interviews

The primary advantages of the former are reduced cost and the timeliness of data collection. In some automated teledialing centers, the data are entered directly into microcomputers, thereby allowing for both internal consistency checks on answers and virtually instantaneous analysis. Advances in random digit dialing also allow for simple random samples as opposed to the heavy reliance oil stratified samples for in-person interviews.

Because of travel costs, in-person interviews often made heavy use of clustering, and stratifying which, in turn, complicated the simple design (DEFF). Other advantages of telephone interviews generally relate to the degree to which supervisors have control over the interviewers. It is possible to monitor interviewers to make sure that standards are adhered to at least at minimum levels and that each expected interview is both conducted and conducted as it ought to be. Telephone interviews are not without costs, however. While almost universal coverage exists in many parts of the world, not everyone has a telephone. In fact, for some surveys, the target population might be the one whose members are least likely to have private telephone service.

Validity checks are much more difficult to make, and the relative anonymity of the telephone (which may be an advantage for some things) makes it difficult to uncover lies or misleading answers from respondents. Furthermore, some individuals in the sampling unit may be less accessible by telephone than through in-person interviews. Overall, however, the telephone interview is becoming the technique of choice for more and more surveyors. Calls around supper time are most likely to find people home, but are also likely to find people most upset about intrusions. Precalling to set up interviews (especially with professionals, etc.) is one way to schedule a more convenient time for the interviewee.

Mail surveys

The mail survey is fraught with problems, however. It generally has the lowest response rate of all survey techniques; there is no control over the sequencing of questions; there is no opportunity for internal consistency checks, and no control over the return time for the survey. The telephone interview is also much more timely. Another disadvantage of the mail survey is that the interviewee has no opportunity to ask for an explanation of difficult-to-understand questions. Ultimately, of course, mail surveys require respondents to be functionally literate. Unsolicited commercial mail surveys are often considered successful if the response rate is beyond 20%.

Since the response rate for this procedure has generally been among the lowest, more techniques have been devised to increase response here than with any other procedure. As Hox and DeLeeuw suggest, those improvements in mail survey methods have led to general increases in response rates over the last few years. Much of this is undoubtedly due to Dillman's for-step "total design method." This process, which has engendered variants in recent times, essentially encompasses the following.

First, an initial mailing is sent out with a questionnaire, covering letter, and postage-paid return envelope. Second, a postcard reminder is sent out a week or two later. Third, after another couple of weeks, a second mailing similar to the initial mailing is sent out. Finally, a special mailing is sent out.

Among the other useful techniques for increasing mail response are:

- precalls by phone to provide notice of incoming surveys
- offers of small gifts in the survey (e.g., pens to complete it or nominal amounts of cash)
- offers to donate small tokens to charity if the survey is returned completed
- pointing out the procedure's lack of intrusion in comparison with other survey techniques (in-person or telephone)

Nonscientific Samples

Probability samples are only a small segment. In many Situations, nonprobability procedures may be more than acceptable, particularly if a wealth of supporting evidence exists. Convenience samples of the type found in shopping malls and supermarkets are a good example of nonscientific sampling strategies that often "work." These procedures typically target the user population of a particular good and provide adequate indicators for marketing purposes. As an indicator of population preferences, however, they can be suspect.

A classical example here is the flawed procedure Ford Motor Company executives used to assess demand for the Edsel, which was introduced in the mid-1950s. Snowball sampling is another procedure that has its uses. Snowball samples are particularly good at identifying sample frames. Working on the basis of "birds of a feather flocking together," this procedure requires the location of an individual of a given characteristic; then that person is asked to provide names of other suitable subjects. Initial research into AIDS was based on snowball sampling procedures. This approach is very useful when (a) there is no preexisting sampling frame, or no obvious alternative to one, and (b) the issue in question is a rare probability event that tends not to be (near) randomly dispersed throughout the population.

Snowball samples may appear to be cluster samples, but they are not. Unlike Cluster samples snowball samples are not probability samples. Another commonly used nonscientific sampling procedure is the quota sample. Quota samples as originally conducted, appeared to parallel stratified samples. Again, unlike true stratified samples, quota samples are not probability samples. Original quota samples were essentially convenience samples directed at subpopulations. A more recent use of the term is what Sudman calls "probability sampling with quotas."

Some particularly interesting populations often constitute rare events or hard-to-locate individuals. For example, the proportion of drunk drivers on the roads, those infected with AIDS, Americans of Danish ancestry, and persons with incomes over$ 1 million would likely be missed in a typical general-purpose survey. The cost of identifying and surveying hard-to-find elements through normal sampling techniques can be prohibitive. Consequently, we turn to alternate strategies. Before examining those strategies in detail, we focus briefly on the issue of why the elements of interest might be difficult to find.

Spreen distinguishes between what he terms "rare" and "hidden" Populations. Essentially, difficult-to-locate populations may possess the trait either because they are small of, as Spreen terms them, "insufficient" proportions of the population, or because they wish to remain hidden. Diagrammatically, the situation may be depicted as follows:

	Easy to reach	*Hard to reach*
Sufficient proportion	Sufficient subpopulations	Large hidden population
Insufficient proportion	Rare population	Small hidden population

Sufficient subpopulations comprise the group most often captured in standard survey sampling. Rare populations are easy to reach (i.e, once identified, they pose no greater problem than sufficient populations) but pose a problem of high unit cost because of the many ineligibles that need to be screened to identify a single element of interest. Hard-to-reach populations, however, may or may not be rare events. They are difficult to locate because the trait being investigated is socially sensitive. Studies that focus on drug use, tax evasion, or pedophilia and other nonmainstream sexual practices will find the target population difficult to find.

Generally, members of "hidden populations" are reluctant to cooperate and, when they do agree to participate, often provide unreliable responses. At one level, the techniques we employ to capture these difficult-to-locate samples differ. Easy-to-reach but rare populations require techniques that either reduce the perunit screening cost for large populations or increase the likelihood of selection for the rare elements relative to the sufficient ones.

Hard-to-reach or "hidden" populations require an approach that will induce the respondent to cooperate. As Spreen notes, "it will take a lot of time to gain the confidence of the respondents for getting reliable answers and low nonresponses. Clearly, this will be a very time consuming and expensive way of sampling." At another level, the same techniques used to identify rare elements can often be used to gain an entree into a hidden population. Link-tracing designs, for example, use informants to direct the researcher to other members of the target population.

Frame location

Finding specialized lists that can act as sampling frames for normally hard-to-locate populations is possible. This is particularly the case with easy-to-reach but rare populations. Surveys of professionals fall into this category. A general survey would likely capture few if any physicians, accountants, or lawyers. On the other hand, persons in those occupational groupings tend to belong to their respective professional associations, and those membership lists are potential frames.

The same can be said for other rare groups, such as Volunteers, persons with unique hobbies, or individuals with rare diseases of certain types. Depending upon the circumstances surrounding the study, these specialized frames may be made freely available to the researcher by the agency or organization holding the list, or the list may be purchased. Before relying on a special list, however, the researcher should explore the likelihood of duplicate entries and rates of inclusion and exclusion.

A list of physicians provided by the American Medical Association is likely it good census of all licensed physicians. A list of members of a local philatelic society Would likely underestimate the total number of stamp collectors in that community; it is also possible that some persons on the list are no longer collectors. The issue of dulicate listings can be alleviated sometimes by using computerized sort and search programs, although the outcome might be frustrating to someone who has purchased the list on a cost-per-entry basis. How much inclusion or exclusion exists can often be "guesstimated" based on one's knowledge of the organization owning the list. As always, the crucial dictum is Know thy field-statistical acumen is no substitute for substantive knowledge of one's area of Study.

Multipurpose surveys

Many government and private organizations conduct large-scale surveys regularly. The National Opinion Research Center's General Social Survey (GSS) or the monthly labour force surveys, contain data on thousands of respondents. Often a sufficient sample can be drawn from one or more existing general-purpose surveys. This is particularly the case with large surveys conducted frequently with nonoverlapping samples. In other situations it is possible to use large multipurpose Surveys as screening mechanisms for locating rare populations. The sponsoring agency may collect a small charge per question for each element; however, that cost is likely to be only a small fraction of the cost of constructing one's own screening survey. Once the rare elements have been located, they may be asked a series of questions added to the multipurpose survey, or they may be followed up on a subsequent occasion.

Correlated factors

Occasionally, it is possible to find rare elements by knowing that they are correlated with some readily identifiable indicator. Heavy drinkers, for example, are more likely to be captured by conducting "exit interviews" at a randomly selected sample of liquor outlets than by means of a random digit dialing telephone survey. Again the crucial element is researcher familiarity with the behaviour under Study.

The more knowledge one has of the correlates of the trait of interest, the more likely it is that one will be able to specify a correlate that can be used to identify the target population.

Large clusters

We have already noted the relative cost advantage of

many cluster samples. For reasonably common events, cluster samples impose a high cost because of the adverse impact they have on the variance. For rare events, however, even extremely large clusters may not invalidate a sample, since only a few elements will be found per cluster. The problem of locating drinking drivers is a good example of the value of large clusters. Some studies that have focused on the prevalence of rare genetic disorders have found clusters as large as a village to be cost-effective. The key here, of course, is the relative cost of travelling to the cluster site and setting up the screening mechanism compared with the cost of surveying the elements within the cluster. Where the fixed costs are high, but the variable cost of surveying individual elements is low, samples with large clusters hold a particular advantage.

Disproportionate stratified sampling

The key to disproportionate stratified sampling is to find small strata with a large proportion of rare elements. Usually, we look for special lists that identify the trait in question or have a highly correlated variable. Occasionally, specialized frames such as aerial census data will serve to identify areas with a high proportion of a target population.

Link-list procedures

The procedures discussed above work well with rare but easy-to-reach populations. For hard-to-reach or hidden populations, it is often necessary to use something other than general screening procedures.

One technique that has received considerable attention lately is the use of link-lists. This technique is an umbrella term for several related procedures variously known as snowball samples and adaptive sampling techniques; other specialized approaches are included, as well. Once an individual of interest has been found, he or she is asked to identify others with the same trait of interest. As Spreen defines the term, link-tracing is "a sample design in which the respondent is asked to mention other persons, according to some inclusion criterion defined by the researchers." Link-list procedures have proven effective in putting together sampling frames of rare and hidden populations.

Once the frame has been constructed, all the individuals in the frame, or a selected sample of the frame, may be included in the study. Unfortunately, link-list frames are not without their share of problems. One set of problems is strictly methodological and relates to the issue of inclusion and exclusion. Specifically, "popular" elements are more likely to be included on the list than "loners." That is, link-list procedures generate better frames among groups that are highly social and interactive. Furthermore, link-tracing procedures are based on the assumption that there is a clear structure in the target population.

Thus, if the individuals within the target population are largely unknown to each other, frame construction will not be very successful. For example, link-list procedures are not very good for identifying pedophiles, who tend to be loners. A second set of problems surrounding link-tracing procedures involves statistical inference. Most standard statistical applications using data collected through link tracing are biased. The seriousness of this problem depends on several factors. Techniques have been developed to generate reasonably unbiased estimates when the initial respondents are selected at random. Clearly, this is a less worrisome problem when one is trying to identify simply rare as opposed to hidden Populations. Most ethnographic approaches that identify the initial respondents based oil their quality as "informants" produce biased results, since the informants are generally more widely known individuals. How much bias is involved is unknown. Given the extensive base of "qualitative" and ethnographic research in the social sciences, it is perhaps surprising that more attention has not been focused oil this issue. For those interested in using snowball or link-tracing methods to estimate population parameters, it should be noted that these procedures are similar to what are known as adaptive sampling designs.

These designs have been studied extensively and under many conditions are known to give unbiased (albeit sometimes inefficient) estimators. One advantage of the estimators discussed by Thompson is that they are often design based, opposed to model based. That is, one need not make any assumptions about the distribution of the estimable parameters.

Problems with panel surveys

Increasingly, social researchers are turning to panel surveys to monitor social trends cross-sectional surveys, panels provide for and to test theoretical propositions. Unlike the collation of data across a series of slices in time. From a theoretical perspective, panel data provide more opportunity to address issues of causality than do static, cross-sectional surveys. While allowing the researcher to address a wider range of questions than their point-in-time cousins, panel Surveys pose a few unique problems, not the least of which is tracing respondents across panels. Most survey respondents, however, can be traced using at least one of three basic techniques, namely, and reverse tracing.

Retrospective tracing simply involves trying to find a respondent for a follow-up by revisiting the interviewee's previous address. It the respondent is found at that address, the interview is conducted as planned. If the respondent has moved, attempts are made to trace him or her. Typically, the interviewer would contact the current resident or immediate neighbours to start the tracing procedure.

The important point relating to retrospective tracing is that it is reactive as opposed to proactive. That is, the surveyor is only concerned about the possibility of having to trace a respondent once the person has moved. If the population of interest is not very mobile, retrospective tracing may be less expensive and less time-consuming than other tracing procedures. The obvious disadvantage is that for highly mobile Populations, this approach can be extremely expensive and cumbersome.

Panel conditioning

Survey researchers have noticed that responses tend to change across panels. Specifically, response change according to the length respondents stay in the panel. For example, it is common for respondents to victimization surveys to indicate fewer victimizations per unit time the longer they remain in the panel. Labour force surveys often generate higher monthly rates of unemployment, the greater the number of follow-up waves. Those changes may result in greater accuracy or more error, depending upon the substantive focus of the research.

Several candidates have been put forward as the specific Cause of those changes; however, all are encompassed under the term panel *conditioning.* The phenomenon of panel conditioning raises two *immediate* issues. The first relates to our ability to decide which panel estimates are the most accurate. Should we accept the results from the first interview or are the results of the later panels more accurate? Few studies have been conducted that included cross-validation of survey responses with other data sources. So far, the results appear inconclusive. The second issue relates to our ability to identify the specific factors that produce the conditioning in the first instance.

The potential candidates often parallel those raised in application of test-retest methodologies for estimating test reliablity. Briefly, we may classify those conditioners into two general categories: intrinsic factors and extrinsic factors. Intrinsic factors consist of items related to the interview itself. For example, some researchers have suggested that panel conditioning is a consequence of learning and memory effects-the respondents' acumen increases as they become more familiar with the test instrument and the interviewing process.

Other factors intrinsic to the interview process include all increasing loss of interest or commitment to the task, an increased comfort level with the test situation (thus resulting in more responses to less socially desirable questions and fewer "don't knows"), and a lack of memory aids, such as bounding, oil the first interview. Extrinsic factors relate to components outside the specific instrument. Attrition, for example, might lead to increased respondent bias as the remaining respondents in the panel become ever more selected. Where the unit of analysis is the household, the respondent may change.

Other factors are attributable to the implementation of the research. That is, the researcher may use different modes on follow-up interviews. In the Canadian Labour Force Survey, for example, it is common for the first interview to be a face-to-face meeting, to allow the respondent to become "familiar" with the interview and the interviewer. Subsequent interviews, however, are usually conducted over the telephone. The researcher may also use slightly different versions of the questionnaire over time, with subtle changes in the wording of key questions. Often, the interviewer will change, resulting- in the confounding of the interview results with interviewer bias. These and likely many other factors not yet identified call contribute to varying degrees of bias, and error in survey results. How great a problem panel conditioning poses is an empirical question. If panel conditioning were constant or additive, the difficulties could be mitigated by means of' appropriate statistical controls.

Unfortunately, if the biases that form panel conditioning do not follow these conditions (and it is likely they do not), their identification and melioration become much more difficult. Where those biases affect the estimated mount of change across surveys, they undermine the reliability and validity of any inferences we might draw.

Attrition and nonresponse

The discussion of problems associated with panel surveys started with the inherent problem of following up respondents. Where that follow-up fails, the researcher is left with missing data. Attrition has already been mentioned as a possible source of difficulty in panel conditioning.

The overall difficulties posed by attrition are generally more extensive, however. Most panel surveys, even the best designed and executed, experience some attrition. Over a series of five interviews, a panel that experiences a 10% dropout rate after each interview will end with a retention rate of only 66% at the end of the fifth period. Matters are made worse when attrition is lumped with ordinary nonresponses to create a generic "nonresponse" or "missing" observation.

Of course, actual panels vary in their attrition experiences. Kalton, Kasprzyk, and McMillen review several panel surveys generally respected for their "quality" and find considerable variability in rates of attrition. For ex, the 'U.S. National Medical Care Utilization and Expenditure Survey generated a nonresponse rate of 9.9% on the initial wave that increased to 22.1% on the fifth wave. The waves were spaced at 3-month intervals. The U.S. Panel Study of Income Dynamics reportedly generated a cumulative nonresponse rate of 50% after 17 years, and the British National Child Development Study, which followed a cohort of young people from age 7 to age 23, produced a 76% response rate at age 23 (after exclusion of respondents who had died or emigrated).

While it might be argued that the retention of 76% of respondents over 16 years is commendable, the missing data still pose a substantial problem. As we will see later, it both the cases lost to attrition and those lost to traditional nonresponses were random, the problem could be solved relatively easily.

However, addressing the problem when the data are not missing at random is much more difficult. Where attrition or nonresponse is systematically related to the outcome variable, the missing data can cause substantial bias in the results. The difficulties inherent with systematic attrition are well documented by Singer's discussion of how the relative effectiveness of drug treatment programs might be evaluated. Wainer also provides an example of the difficulties involved in the temporal assessment and interpretation of SAT scores.

Statistical analysis and panel data

The statistical analysis of panel data presents a series of problems not found in with cross-sectional Surveys. Obviously, database management problems connection matching cases across waves. The sheer volume of data, and the are associated with decision about whether the cross-sectional aspects as opposed to the longitudinal aspects ought to be one's primary focus, also contribute to the complexity. Those issues might be considered to be exogenous, however, in that they do not necessarily influence, either the content of the questionnaire or interview, or the manner in which the data are collected.

More germane to the scope of methods, is the impact of measurement error oil our ability to estimate unbiased and efficient parameters. Two central concerns in the analysis of any temporal data are the impacts of measurement error associated with the independent variables (often referred to in econometrics as "errors in measurement") and the impact of model misspecification. Misspecification in this context refers to the exclusion of key "causal" and control variables from the model, and the inclusion of extraneous indicators. Classical regression approaches to the analysis of panel data can easily generate inaccurate estimates when either the model is misspecified or the independent variables are susceptible to measurement error.

The error need not be systematic: even random measurement error can have a deleterious impact upon our results. The problem can be addressed partially by respecifying the model in terms of the dependent variable. Analyzing difference scores across waves (i.e $\Delta Y - Y_{1+1} - Y_1$) as opposed to raw scores helps to mitigate the problem of overall model misspecification.

On the other hand, in the absence of misspecification, estimates based on raw or cross-sectional data are often far more accurate than those based on differences. For applied researchers, classical regression poses a Hobson's choice, with neither solution being completely palatable. A better but technically more complicated solution to the problem is to analyse the data within a structural equation model framework. In this approach, both the structural model of interest and the measurement model are addressed explicitly. To address the measurement model, however, multiple indicators or measures of the concepts are required.

Thus, for example, a single question asking whether a respondent supports "abortion on demand" cannot be used to estimate the impact of measurement error on the structural parameters. At least two, and occasionally several more, indicators are required to allow for an analysis of the measurement model. We address measurement error in greater detail in the chapters relating to measurement. At this point it is important to note that before a given study is conducted, the researcher should have some inclination about how the data might be analysed. If it is expected that the analysis will be limited to classical regression approaches, then single indicators will suffice.

On the other hand, the expectation that the data will he analysed within a structural equation framework requires a questionnaire structured to include multiple indicators. Prudence would also suggest that those indicators be subjected to rigorous pretesting to assess their overall reliability before the actual survey is begun.

Estimating mobile populations

Most sampling procedures devised for human populations assume that the population is relatively immobile. That is, dwelling units are fixed locations and people have an attachment to those units, at least for the duration of the survey. For certain subpopulations, these assumptions are simply untenable. The homeless in big cities and nomads in parts of Africa and other areas of the world are highly mobile. Thus, for example, standard enumeration and sampling techniques for estimating the number of prostitutes, drug addicts, or "street people" tend not to work very well. Many procedures have been devised to address this problem, but one technique that appears to be gaining in popularity is the *capture-recapture* approach. Capture-recapture methods grew out of biologists' attempts to estimate the size and distribution of animal populations. If the underlying assumptions are met, the estimation algorithms are simple.

Assume, for example, that Y_c roaches are captured, marked with a dot of red paint, and released. Subsequently, y roaches are recaptured and y_c are discovered with a red dot. If both the Y_c and y roaches were captured at random and without replacement, then the total population of roaches can be estimated by

$$Y = Y_c \frac{y}{y_c}$$

The corresponding estimate of the variance of Y, S2, is given as follows:

$$S_Y^2 = \frac{y^2}{y-1} \frac{Y_c}{y_c} \left(\frac{Y_c}{y_c} - 1 \right) \left(\frac{y}{y_c} - 1 \right)$$

Elaborations on these formulas have been developed, but these two equations stand at the heart of those developments. While conceptually very simple, the capture-recapture technique stands or falls on how well its underlying assumptions are met. The essential assumptions may be defined as follows:

- The population is closed so that N is constant
- All individuals have the same probability of being selected in both surveys.
- Measuring (observing, interviewing) the individuals in the first survey does not affect the likelihood of inclusion in the second survey of this set of individuals.

- We can identify which individuals are included in both surveys, and all individuals canvassed in the first survey are indicated as such in the second survey.

Unfortunately, it is extremely difficult to ensure that these assumptions are met in actual field conditions. Consider the first assumption. The homeless population of most major cities is constantly in flux, with people moving both into and out of the big urban areas. The difficulty of framing a population suitable for analysis by means of capture-recapture techniques call be mitigated to some degree by reducing the duration between surveys. While those ~~point~~ estimates might be relatively accurate at the time of the study, estimates for narrowly defined areas with high rates of migration will soon be outdated. The second assumption is likely the most difficult to meet in practice.

Many studies of drug addicts, for example, rely for their basic estimates on appearances and reappearances at street clinics. This approach is highly unreliable, since both initial and Subsequent appearances at a clinic are not at all likely to be random events. Taking an aerial approach and randomly selecting certain street segments or dwelling units in areas generally known to have high concentrations of the target population would theoretically produce better results. Without some form of "impersonal" selection procedure, near equal likelihood of selection is almost impossible with human populations because of the high variation in behavioural patterns related to selection. Although of less importance than the second assumption, the third assumption also raises major concerns. It is possible that those who are successfully observed or interviewed in the first survey are also more likely than their compatriots to be selected in the second Survey. This may be a consequence of a personal relationship built up in the first interview; alternatively, fear that the observer poses a personal threat may have been lessened. Unwarranted reliance oil the third assumption is most likely to pose a problem when the individuals in the surveys are merely observed rather than interviewed.

However, many mobile populations, such as indigents, are elusive and reluctant to be identified. Thus, determining whether someone in the "recapture" survey was observed in the initial survey may be easier said than done. The analogous conditions for animal surveys are also rarely met. Thus, when complementary estimates arc available against which to compare survey results, the population total is almost invariably found to be underestimated.

Statistics concerning the relative distribution of the target population on the other hand seem to fare better. Despite the difficulties in ensuring that the appropriate assumptions are met, variations on the capture-recapture theme have been carried out in several areas, including the estimation of drug addicts and homeless mentally in people. Theoretical progress is also being made on circumstances under which some basic assumptions, such as that of population homogeneity, do not hold.

Counting the homeless

The variation in the number of observers captured by the enumerators was astounding. The percentage of observers interviewed by the enumerators ranged from a high of 67% in New Orleans to a low of 7% in Chicago. Some observers were not interviewed but were either clearly or probably Counted. That proportion ranged from a high of about 29% in New York to a low of 6% in Los Angeles. The percentage of observers who did not see an enumerator or were not counted ranged from 15.% in New Orleans to 75% in Chicago. Overall, the variability was such that in one city, approximately 85% of the observers were apparently captured by the enumerators while at the opposite end of the spectrum, only about 25% were captured. The ex post facto construction of an explanation for why so many observers were not counted reads like a litany of what can go wrong in applied sampling. Among the more important factors identified were the following:

- Some enumerators arrived at their sites early or left late. Observers' field notes showed that "enumerators typically stayed at each site only 15 minutes, on average".
- Some enumerators apparently chose to drive by the sites in their cars rather than inspect them oil foot as they bad been instructed. In drive-by situations, it is possible that the observer might have missed the enumerator, or vice versa.
- Despite substantial work pill into identifying sites beforehand many instructions regarding site locations were vague or ambiguous. More than 90% of the enumerators reported difficulties in finding their sites. At some sites, enumerators reported conflicts between street numbers and building names oil the official lists and in the actual neighborhoods.
- Many sties posed intrinsic difficulties. They either were dark or hard "visual barriers" that made observation difficult.
- While the obvious falsification of data ("curbstoning") was ruled out as a significant factor, it did appear that some enumerators simply chose not to spend much energy in locating and counting the people at their assigned sites.

Like litany of the enumerators, some observers apparently had difficulties finding sites. Some observers also chose not to spend the entire duration at the site.

Furthermore, the observers were tired when asked to fill out questionnaires at the end of their shift, and some appeared to be functionally illiterate or not fluent in English. Consequently, many follow-up questionnaires were of questionable value. It is commendable that the Bureau of the Census has been so open and has allowed for so litany detailed descriptions of the S-Night experiment to be published.

The practical difficulties faced in the S-Night survey are clearly an eye-opener, and given the professionalism and expertise of bureau personnel, one inevitably is much more inclined to suspect surveys conducted by less experienced researchers. Undoubtedly, some major lessons have been learned from the S-Night experience. Clearly, many problems with S-Night related to the difficult conditions surrounding this type of survey-at night, often in less desirable parts of town, and with a highly transient population.

8

Statistical Methods in Economics

Simple methods of data presentation like the Bar Chart, the Pie diagram, and the frequency curve are so well known that they need no elaborate introduction at this level. What one should know about them at this level, is how not to misinterpret them or not to get misled by them, due to ignorance oft he actual implications of such representation.

(a) *Scale distortion in dimension:* Linear vs Area vs Volume. What is a circle 'double' the size of second circle? Double the diameter? Double the area? Example: A dosa of 1 foot diameter is not equal to 2 dosas of ½ foot but is equal to '4 dosas' of ½ foot diameter.

However, in a piechart, percentage is proportional to the angle at the centre and hence is a correct representation. In graphical display, distortion of scale along the two different axes can mislead on to think that one variable shows a large variation over a small range of variation of another related variable.

(b) *Percentages:* Often one may speak of percentage when it is not at all meaningful or vice versa. Example: "There is a 100% pass result in an institution, but the number of candidates from that institution is only 1." Similarly among all the candidates who appeared for an examinations there is only one failure (what is not told is that the number of candidates who appeared is also one).

Choice of a measure to describe a situation or compare different situations is not a trivial matter. The right choice depends on the purpose to which the answer is utilised.

(c) *Location & spread:* Measures of location (Typical values or Averages) can be very misleading when not accompanied by a measure of spread (range, Standard deviation, etc.). The story of the expert, of height 5′6″ entering a river, to cross the same, because the average depth of the river is only 3 feet-but not coming out on the other side, is well known. In taking decision under uncertainty —Risky decision—it is required to be known, for a right choice among more than one, risky alternatives. The Game theoretic modelling of Socio-Economic political activities is well known.

Consider the following two cases: Prices of a commodity in 5 locations in a district are Rs. 15, 30, 20, 35, 40 per Kg while for the same commodity in 5 locations in another district are Rs 27, 30, 24, 29, 30. Going by the averages, one can claim that price is (on the whole) the same in both the districts. Is it appropriate to draw this conclusion? or should one think that, In the second district, this conclusion that the price is Rs. 28/- per Kg. is meaningful while the fact, of the average price being Rs. 28/-, in the first district is actually more of a fiction and that the average price does not reflect the price situation in the district properly. Another important measure for reporting both the measure of location (usually the mean μ) and of spread (usually the standard deviation σ) is that it enables one to obtain a clearer picture of the 'distribution of the variable concerned'.

A very general theorem in probability theory states that, "the interval $\mu \pm k\sigma$ contains at least $(1-\frac{1}{k}2)$ of all the values of the variable." Thus if it is known that the average is 28 and standard deviation is say 2.5, one can be sure that more than 75% (or using a more refined inequality, more than 90%) of values of x will be between 28 ± 2(2.5), i.e., between 23 and 33. Rarely will the values be beyond these limits. If instead, with the same mean, the S.D. is known to be 20, one has to conclude that to cover 75% of cases, one is to have the limits 20 ± 2(20), i.e., –20 to + 60. [of course, if the variate of interest is price, in 'absolute terms' a negative value may not be meaningful. A word of caution is, perhaps, in order.

A relatively large S.D. or an unreasonably large 'Range' may be due to 'outliers' one or two values which are far from the rest of the values. Thus, in examining average and standard deviation, one should make sure that the data are not vitiated by such outliers. Depending on the purpose to which the summary statistics are to be put, one may have to exclude the outliers (but noting their presence) and recomputed the mean and standard deviation if the purpose is to get a meaningful picture (17 the situation. As an obviously artificial illustration, consider a locality where one Millionaire (with income of Rs.10 lakhs per month) and 49 other families each with an income of Rs.4,000/- per month live.

What is the average income and the corresponding standard deviation? Do you think that this average is representative of the group? If instead, it is the case of size of land holdings, one family owning 1000 hectares and the other families owning 20 hectares each of arable land, what, is needed is the total land available for agriculture, would you exclude the big 'land-lord' from consideration?

(d) *Distribution*: Often, data are collected from which a frequency distribution or a histogram is drawn in order to get an overall picture of the situation. Very often histograms are constructed using the frequencies in various class intervals, which are of equal width If the distribution is asymmetric (as is often the case with income distribution), equal width intervals give a patchy picture of the situation, with many class intervals having practically 'no frequency at all.' An appropriate remedy is to have class widths which are small in the region of high frequency while keeping larger class widths in the regions of low frequency. Quite often, another approach is also used, a new variable got by suitable 'transformation' of the original variable is introduced; by a frequency distribution of this variate-even with equal intervals, one can get a meaningful picture of what one wanted to study in the first instance.

A classic example is the lognormal distribution for studying the income distribution. When the income value changes from 100 to 10,000 (= 100^2) the log value changes from 2 to 4 only, i.e., doubling the log value changes the original x to x^2. The frequency distribution of log (income) is often found to be well-enough represented by a normal distribution. It may not be easy to test for equality of other relationships between two income distributions directly, but the same can be tested using the distribution of the logarithm of actual incomes, using all the properties of tests based on the normal distribution.

(e) *Regression:* One is often required to study the relationship between two quantities, e.g., land under cultivation and final yield of a crop in a season, or the amount of 'finished product' from a knowledge of the amount of the raw material used or the yield of, say, cane juice by a knowledge of length and thickness of sugar cane from a field. In particular, one may want to make an intelligent guess of the values of y based on the value of x connected with it. This is the general regression problem. To predict on variable as a function of other variables x_1, x_2, ... x_k whose values are known.

A natural procedure to answer this question starts with collection of relevant 'past data.' The value of x_1,s and corresponding *y* are recorded on various occasions. This serves as a data bank from which one 'builds up a regression model' to guess the value of *y* when values of the relevant x's are given. Starting with simple regression—with only one *x*, the data consist of *n* pairs of values (x_1, y_1), i = 1 .... *n*.

These points are plotted (the scatter diagram) and a visual picture of the possible interrelationship is obtained. If the points are randomly scattered with no visible pattern, perhaps no worthwhile relationship exist and any attempt at predicting y by knowing x is futile. If a pattern emerges, one can use this picture to guess the y value when *x* value is given. The pattern is often describable approximately by a mathematically definable simple curve—a straight line, a parabola, a power curve, etc. Then, one can obtain this curve which fairly represents the data and enables one to guess the y for a given *x* by substitution of *x* in this function.

Of course, the predicted value will not exactly coincide with the actual value that may be subsequently obtained but, if the 'regression is good', the actual value will be fairly close to the proscribed one. What is more, one can even set up a 'confidence interval' within which the actual '*y*' value with a high degree of reliability. Of course, if this confidence interval is small, the prediction is more precise while if it is rather larger, the prediction may be not useful and no better than a random guess. The problem of regression can be loosely stated as follows: Given a set of points (x_1, y_1), i = 1, 2 ... *n*, find a curve of given type $y = f(x, \theta)$ (e.g., $y = \theta_0 + \theta_1 x$ gives a straight line, $y = \theta_0 + \theta_1 x + \theta_2 x^2$ gives a parabola, $y = \theta_0 e^{\theta_1 x}$ gives an exponential and $y = \theta_0 x^{\theta_1}$ gives a power function.) which represents the value of y as closely as possible when the corresponding x value is substituted in it.

Consider the following example:

x	1	2	3	4	5	6	7
y	10	13	17	19	23	25	50

Fitting a linear regression line to predict y means, obtaining the value of θ_0, θ_1, in $y = \theta_0 + \theta_1 x$ such that, when substituted, the predicted value, of y will be as much in agreement with the observed value as possible.

Let us try out some θ_0 and θ_1 and see how good a prediction is got in each case.

x	1	2	3	4	5	6	7
y	10	13	17	19	23	25	30
8 + 12x	10	12	14	16	18	20	22
8 + 3x	11	14	17	20	23	26	29
7 + 4x	11	15	19	23	27	31	35
10 + 2x	10	12	14	16	18	20	22
10 + 3x	10	13	16	19	22	25	28

Which of these, if any, can be accepted as good enough for our purpose? Can we get some other (θ_0, θ_1) pair which is even better than all these, in fact, the 'best' (θ_0, θ_1)? The answer depends on the criterion one adopts for comparing the different 'fits.' One common criterion, as a measure of disagreement, is the 'sum of squares of deviations' (of y's form the corresponding 'predicted y's).

Thus for θ = (8, 3), i.e., for the model $y = 8 + 3x$, the deviations are 10-11, 13-14, 17-17, 19-20, 23-23, 25-26, 30-29, i, e., –1, –1, 0, –1, 0, –1, 1 and the sum of their squares is 5. For θ = (10, 3), i.e., for the model $y = 10 + 3$, the deviations are 0, 0, 1, 0, 1, 0, 2 with sum of squares of deviations (ssd for short) = 6. For θ = (7, 4) they are – 1, –2, –2, –4, –4, –6, –5 with ssd = 102. Obviously (7, 4) gives a bad fit while (10, 3) as well as (8, 3) give relatively much better bit. Using differential calculus one can get theoretically the best (θ_o, θ_1) in the sense that the ssd is the smallest among all possible choices of (θ_o, θ_1).

$$SSD = \Sigma (y_1 - \theta_o - \theta_1 x_1)^2; \quad \frac{\partial SSD}{\partial \theta_o} = 2\,\Sigma(y_1 - \theta_o - \theta_1 x)(-1) = 0$$

$$\frac{\partial SSD}{\partial \theta_1} = 2\,\Sigma(y_1 - \theta_o - \theta_1 x_1)(-x_1) = 0$$

i.e. (θ_o, θ_1). should be such that

$$n\theta_o + (\Sigma x_1)\,\theta_1 = \Sigma y_1$$

$$(\Sigma x_1)\,\theta_o + (\Sigma x^2)\theta_1 = \Sigma x_1 y_1$$

For our case n = 7 and we have $\Sigma x_1 = 28$, $\Sigma y_1 = 137$,

$$\Sigma x_1^2 = 105, \ \Sigma y_1^2 = 2973, \ \Sigma x_1 y_1 = 638.$$

Hence we have $7\theta_o + 28\theta_1 = 137$

$$28\,\theta_o + 105\,\theta_1 = 638$$

with the solution $\theta_o = \frac{47}{7} = 6.71$ and $\theta_2 = \frac{90}{28} = 3.21$

The best fitting line is therefore $y(x) = 6.71 + 3.21x$ which will give a sum of squares of deviations as 2.4286 only. In a way, the average of squared deviations (error), the MSE is $= \frac{2.4286}{7-2=5}$ 5 0.485. The division of SSD by 5 instead of 7 is because what we have obtained are 'estimates' of the true relationship between y and x incidentally an asymmetric relation, in that $y(x) =\{y_{\text{theoretical}}(x) = (\theta_o + \theta_1 x)\} + e$, where e is a 'random' error, which, on the average is zero but in particular cases (here, in the 7 cases of observed (x_1, y_1) will take-values randomly and hence, what we observed as deviations are not the exact deviations (which we cannot actually observe), but only the deviations as determined by 'guessed prediction.' In this guessed prediction formula, θ_o, θ_1 are estimated by solving two equations—putting two restraints on θ_o, θ_1 while we have 7 observations. We say that 2 degrees of freedom (d.f.) are lost and (for this purpose), the SSD is based effectively (essentially) on 7 – 2 = 5 observations only.

Incidentally, it is not necessary to compute the individual predicted values in order to get this SSD for the best fit; one can get the SSy (predicted as equal to (θ_o) (RHS of first equation) + (θ_1)(RHS of second equation) = 2968.61 in our case. This is necessarily less than SSY $_{\text{observed}}$ (in our case, 2973) and the difference is (= 4.31 in our case). To repeat, for convenience, in the present case the two 'normal' equations are: $7\theta_o + 28\theta_1 = 137$,

$$28\theta_o + 105\theta_1 = 638,$$

The solution obtained is $\theta_1 \frac{90}{28}, \theta_o = \frac{47}{7}$

Hence the $SSy_{th} = 137 \left(\frac{47}{7}\right) + 638\left(\frac{90}{28}\right) = 2970.5714$

Hence, SS Error = 2973 – 2970.5714 = 2.4286.

Similarly, for a given type of curve (even other than

straight, line) one can theoretically get the best fitting curve and compute the SSD, but the Normal equations—the equations got by setting the derivatives to zero-one gets in nonlinear cases, is not easy to solve. Hence, and also for some other reasons to be noted later, one transforms *y* or *x* or both to get a new pair of variables where the new y may have a linear relationship with the new *x* variables.

C-D function: For instance, one can consider the Cobb-Douglas production function where yield is expected to have a relation of type $y = \theta_o\ x_1{}^{\theta 1} x_2{}^{\theta 2} \ldots x_k{}^{\theta k}$ with the different factors of production x_1. Then if y = log y and x_1 =log x_1, the equivalent 'ideal' relationship will be $y = \log(\theta_o) + \theta_1 x_1 + \theta_2 x_k + \ldots \theta_k x_k$ which, with error added gives $y_{obs} = \log(\theta)_o + \theta_1 x_1 + \theta_2 x_k + \ldots {}_k x_k +, \varepsilon$, the error term ε being random with 0 mean. One can now carry out linear regression with these variables and get a predictive relation of Y on the X_1's. However, when one gets back to 'actual' variables y, x_1, x_2 ,.... x_k, one ends up with $y = (\theta_o\ x_1{}^{\theta 1}\ x_2{}^{\theta 1} \ldots x_k{}^{\theta k})e^{\theta}$, the error term being now not additive but multiplicative. Correspondingly, the SSD with these (y; x's) will not necessarily be a minimum among all possible (θ_o, θ_1,... θ_k) that one can try out.

However, linearised regression on transformed variables is often preferred to direct regression since often errors are riot additive, but may be multiplicative and estimated values of θ's which are often the main motive for analysis, obtained by this transformed method will serge the purpose; also, as already noted, the determination of best θ_k's directly is too cumbersome and does not give any compensatory advantage over those obtained by the linear analysis of transformed data.

Step-wise regression: A natural corollary of the problem of Regression considered above is: Just because data are available on many variables, is it necessary to use all of them in predicting y or can one possibly drop out any of the predictors as either not relevant or redundant when already other variables are included in the model.

This leads to the problem of Stepwise Regression. Broadly speaking the logic used is as follows:

Let a predictor us a set of variables say x_1, x_2 and x_3, i.e., we have $y = g(x_1, x_2, x_3; \theta) + \theta$ as the model and let it be giving a good prediction: what happens if we drop out, say, x_3, and got a predictor with only x_1, x_2 included? Obviously, the fit (in terms of SSD, say) cannot be better now than earlier. But the deterioration may be meager the MSD increasing only slightly. In this case, it is obvious that degree of predicting of y using only x_1, x_2 is effectively as good as when using all the three variables.

Hence, one may drop out x_3 from further consideration if anyway x_1 and x_2 are included in the predictor equation. If instead, a dropping of x_3 leads to considerable drop in predictability (i.e., MSD now becomes substantially larger), obviously the role of x_3 in predicting y is substantial even when x_1 and x_2 are also used in the model; one should retain x_3 in the predictor. Using this argument appropriately, one can often substantially reduce the number of variables to be used for getting a good prediction of y.

However, one should not conclude that because a variable, say x_3, is dropped from the set of predictors, it has no influence on the value that y takes; all that it says is that in the presence of the other variables which are retained, use of these variable is redundant; not that it is irrelevant in the context of prediction. If it is actually relevant, that fact will be revealed by the analysis which established that the variable can be dropped out from every set of variable for prediction and it is simply, of no use as a predictor.

A word of caution: A good predictor equation $y = g(x_1,...x_k; \theta)$ close not simply a causal relationship between the x's and y. The problem of investigating, among many variables, as to which of them may be causes and which may be effects—if at all—is quite a challenging one. Unless a time element is involved and one goes .into more complicated models (and the problem of identification etc.) this question cannot be answered. (e.g.: Identification and casual ordering: etc. in 'Models of Man: by Herbart A. Siman and few monographs of Cowels commission).

Logic of statistical inference: The general logic of statistical inference could be summarised as follows: If according to our assumption, some observations are not likely to occur (i.e., rare enough) we would rather discard or change our hypotheses than stay put, consoling ourselves that what has occurred is rare and we are unfortunate in having this occur to us. Let us take a crude example: When a coin is tossed, we expect that head and tall will fall with equal chance; hence that when the results of tossing of a coin 100 times are reported, we expect around 50 heads and around 50 tails to be reported.

We do not expect that only 4 or 5 heads fall up with 96 or 95 times tails turning up. Suppose somebody reports that when he tossed a coin 100 times, he found that all of them fall heads up only. What would be one's reaction? Since each toss can turn up either as a head or tail, it is quite possible that a head turns up a first time, a second time... the hundredth time, i.e., it is not impossible to get all the tossed giving heads only. But we do not expect it to happen; it is a very rare event (if the coin is a fair coin). Hence, we feel that if the coin gave such unusually large number of heads in a set of tosses, there must be something uncanny about the coin; it is not likely to be a fair coin at all. May be it is a coin with both sides marked head only!

Null hypothesis: To formalise the logic: We start with a hypothesis—the null hypothesis H_0. The outcome, of course, is not always expected to *be* the same even when the hypothesis is true. At best, all that we can say is, if H_0 is true and we notice the outcome, which is a 'random variable', i.e., the outcome can be any one of the many possibilities but we can attach a probability to each of these outcomes.

Some outcomes are much more probable than others and we can divide the set of all possible outcomes into two-the set of events which it is reasonable to expect to happen and the complementary set of events (outcomes) which it is felt to be unreasonable to expect to happen (the so-called critical region): This requires a knowledge of the probability distribution of x, the outcome variable. In the case of our example above, x the number of heads in n (=100) trials follows binomial distribution, with probability mass function $p(x) = \binom{n}{x} p^x q^{n-x}$ where p is the chance of head and q =1 −p is the chance of tail. For a fair coin p = q = ½.

The 'expected value' of x (i.e., the theoretical average of number of heads) = np (100x ½ = 50 in our case) and variance = n p q (25 in our ease). Though x is discrete, taking values 0, 1, 2.... 100 only, one can treat it as if it is a continuous variable and that (it can be shown that to a good approximation) it follows a Normal distribution with mean = 50 and variance = 25 (SD = α = 5). Since the normal distribution has the mode (most likely values) at the mean itself and is bell shaped, one naturally assumes that x = 50 is the most reasonable value and values nearer to 50 are more reasonable to expect than values away from 50. Taking the 2α or 3α rule, one should expect the x should take values in the interval 50 ± 2(5) 40 – 60 with a high chance. (For normal, it is 95%) and in 50 ± 3 (5) ≡ 35 - 65 with even a higher chance (97.73%) for normal case). Further the Mode being in these intervals, one should expect x to fall in "35 – 65" with as high a chance as 99.73% and it is unreasonable, (as unreasonable as - being expected to occur only about 3 times out of 1000 times) to find x outside that region.

Hence when a coin, supposedly fair, is tossed a hundred times and is found to fall heads 95 or 96 times, such an event is unreasonable, rare. In the face of this evidence, we revise our hypothesis and conclude that perhaps the coin is not fair.

Type I & II errors: Thus, if the coin is really a fair coin but we follow the above rule for accepting and rejecting the hypothesis, there is a chance of about 3 in 1000 that we wrongly reject the correct hypothesis. This is called the Type I error—of not accepting the hypothesis when really it is true—(because, by chance, a rare event can turn up). The chance of this type of error being committed—(here about 3 in 1000) is called the significance level. There is also mother side to this type of inference. We can commit an error of type II, the error of accepting H_0 when something else (say, H1: e.g., chance of head is 80%) is true. It is quite possible that a based coin (with p = 0.8 say) is what we are unknowingly using and it gives x as 42.

Since x = 42 falls in the reasonable region according to the rule, we shall be accepting the claim (hypothesis) that the coin is fair and thus committing another type of error. The actual probability of this type of error is usually denoted by β, and can be computed for any specific H_1. Whenever one can state a hypothesis and work out the probabilities of different observable events when the hypothesis is true, one can define (a) a level of significance (i.e., the probability of error of first kind, that may be acceptable, denoted by 'α') and (b) partition the set of all possible observable outcomes into 'reasonable or acceptable set of outcomes' and 'the set of outcomes considered as rare and unreasonable (the 'critical' region)' at that significance level.

It is now straight forward task: Observe the event that happens and depending on whether it falls in the acceptable or in the critical region, accept or do not accept the (null) hypothesis. The statistic—the calculated value whose distribution in general is used to decide as to what is reasonable outcome—is said to be not significant (ly different from what one expects if H_0 is true) or significant (ly different for what one expects if H_0 is true), at the given level of significance a, as the case may be. Consider the situation when it is claimed that the average income of households in a locality is Rs. 4000/- per month.

How to go about, to answer this question? Suppose it is further known that for the incomes x, the standard deviation is 500/-. Then, if a sample of 16 householders is randomly selected and their incomes $x_1, x_2, \ldots x_{10}$ are obtained, we can show that their x (which of course is a statistic, changing randomly depending on which particular families are picked up by the sampling process) has a distribution which is approximately normal with mean = mean of individuals x's = 4000 (under the null hypothesis) and with variance $\dfrac{\text{variance of x}}{\text{sample size}}$ Hence in the above case the standard deviation of sample mean

$$= \sqrt{\frac{\text{variance of x}}{\text{sample size}}} = \frac{\text{SD of x}}{\sqrt{n}} = \frac{500}{\sqrt{16}} = 125$$

Thus using 5% level of significance (equivalently, 95% as the probability of reasonableness required for acceptness), we set up the limits 4000 ± 2(125), i.e., 3750 – 4250 for $\overline{x}$. If the observed $\overline{x}$ lies in this interval, we say that $\overline{x}$ is not significant (i.e., not significantly different from what we expect if the true value of the average is 4000); if the observed $\overline{x}$ is outside this range, we say that it is significant (i.e., significantly different from what we expect if H_0 is true) and hence consider that H_0 is not true. All the relatively more sophisticated tests, also are basically resting on this type of logic.

A similar logic can be used also to test, for regression. If there is no regression, i.e., if y is not predictable on the basis of x, it is equivalent to saying that $y = \theta_0 + 0\,x = \theta_0$. Similarly; if θ_0 and θ_1 are fixed as known, one can suitably reframe the question and test for the difference between the observed the observed θ_1 (estimated θ_1) and hypothesised θ_1 to be taken as zero.

Estimation: Another question of interest is that of estimation. Often we observe data and make assumptions about their probabilistic structure—often, their distribution or some parameters connected with the same. For instance, one may wish to estimate the proportion of people below the poverty line in the country. One relatively simple method of estimation is introduced below: For any distribution usually one can compute the movements, i.e., averages of powers of x, the variate of interest.

These movements theoretically obtained by using the well-known mathematical techniques are naturally dependent on the value of the 'parameters' of the distribution. When a sample is taken, one can always calculate the movements (as observed—calculated on the basis of the data). Hence, one way of estimating the parameters is to equate the movements which are known functions of the parameters with the corresponding observed' movements and solving for the parameters. Thus, for instance, let p be the proportion of householders which are 'well to do' (according to well defined criterion) in a locality. Let a sample of, say 100 households be selected at random and let the total income of household be the variable of interest. Let the income of these households be $x_1, x_2 \dots x_{100}$. It is often considered reasonable enough to assume that the average in any sample is distributed approximately normal (even when the individual values are 'not normal'), the theoretical mean of $\bar{x}$ will be the same as theoretical mean of x, while the theoretical variance of $\bar{x}$ will be $\frac{1}{n}$ th of the variance of x.

Hence, if $\bar{x} = \frac{1}{100}\Sigma x_1$ is computed, the result (changing from sample to sample randomly) will he a variable which is effectively normal, with $E(\bar{x}) = \mu$, the Theoretical Average income of the household in the locality. In other words, if we want to estimate μ, we can take $\bar{x}$, the sample mean and equate it with the theoretical mean. Thus $\bar{x}$ is an estimate of the population mean (i.e., mean income in this locality).

A natural question is: how 'reliable' or 'precise' is this estimate? This can be answered if one can calculate the variance (or the standard deviation) of this estimator. As already hinted, the variance of $\bar{x}$ is $\frac{1}{n}$ th of the variance of x. Hence, if V(x) is known, one can get, the $V(\bar{x}) = \frac{V(x)}{n}$ 'How to get V(x)?' is the next question. Most often, one has, in turn only to estimate V(x) from x_1,

$x_2 \ldots x_n$ and one proceeds by computing sample variance

$$s^2 = \frac{1}{n} \Sigma (x_1 - \overline{x})^2 = \frac{1}{n}\left(\Sigma x_1^2 - \frac{(\Sigma x_1)^2}{n}\right)$$

$$= \frac{1}{n} \text{ (corrected sum of squares)}$$

However, it is theoretically shown that E (corrected sum of squares) = $(n - 1)\sigma^2$, and not $n\sigma^2$. Hence, a more appropriate thing to do is to divide the slim of squares by n – 1, in place of n to get a good ('unbiased') estimate of σ^2. Of course, when n is large enough, this nicity may not be observed. Then, $V(\overline{x})$ is estimated as s^2/n. Hence, one can say that the estimated "Standard Error" (the name used for the standard deviation of any statistic) of $\overline{x}$ is $s/\sqrt{n}$. As is already noted, smaller the standard deviation, better is the reliability of the estimate, the estimate will be quite close to the true value with a high chance.

Hence, by increasing n, the sample size, one can get as good an estimator as one wants (in that, estimate so derived can be made to come as close to the true value as one wants, with a quantifiably high chance). Suppose one wants to have 95% confidence—meaning thereby one wants to have an interval within which the trite value lies with a 95%, chance. We know that if a variable U is normal, the interval $\mu_u \pm 2\alpha_u$ covers 95% of the cases. Hence, treating $\overline{x}$ as the statistic U, we have

$$P\{\mu_{\overline{X}} - 2\sigma_{\overline{X}} - \leq x \leq \mu_{\overline{X}} + 2\alpha_{\overline{X}} -\} \cong 0.95$$

The same event as given in the brackets can be described as $P\{\overline{x} - 2\sigma\overline{x} \leq \mu \leq \overline{x} + 2\sigma\overline{x}\} \cong 0.95$ That is, using $\overline{x}$ and $\alpha\overline{x} = \alpha_x/\sqrt{n}$, we have got a random interval which has a chance of including the value of μ within it equal to 95% and we say that a 95% confidence interval for μ is $\overline{x} \pm 2(\alpha_x/\sqrt{n})$.

One small note: the above is correct if α_x is known prior; otherwise, when it is itself estimated, the distribution of $\bar{x}$, though has $E(\bar{x}) = \mu$, cannot be specified fully, since $\alpha_{\bar{x}}$ is not known.

However, if a new variable t $\frac{(\bar{x} - \mu)}{s/\sqrt{n}}$ = is defined, it follows a distribution almost normal if *n* is large enough but has a normal like distribution which also depends on n, but not on μ or α. This is the *t*-distribution with *n* –1 degrees of freedom. From tables one can choose for a given level (like 95%) the interval of the *t*, say ($-t^* \leq t \leq t^*$) which includes *t* with that probability. For the normal distribution it would be a ± 1.96 and for the actual t it will be a little larger usually. From this '*t*' value corresponding to required confidence level, one can compute the confidence interval for μ. One can have many 'tests' like the *F* test etc. to test different types of hypotheses by defining suitable 'statistic' whose distribution—under the null hypothesis to be tested—is known or can be determined.

Time series analysis: We may conclude this brief presentation with a discussion on time series analysis. A common enough problem is to project the value of a variable at some point in future, on the basis of the past data. At a first glance, one is tempted to treat it as a regression problem with *y* (the variable to be predicted) at t-the time in future, that is one thinks of *y*(*t*), the value of *y* at time '*t*' as a function of '*t*', instead of some other specific variable. One can fit a curve of regression of *y* on *t*, for example, of population *y* while at times *t* = 1, 2, 3,... and if found 'good', use it for projection of population into the future.

Similarly, if one has monthly sales figures of say, woollen clothing or seasonal goods, one can try to do the same taking t as month number. However, it is obvious that this would not do; in a year, during different months the sales figures will not show a regular behaviour as one may expect when considering yearly sales figure—they will be cyclic within each year though their average may go up from year to year. In such cases one is tempted to make a two-way analysis: by using y_j to indicate sales in month *j* in year *i*.

One can take out the overall monthly average and the deviations can now be analysed for seasonal effects and for annual growth separately in a sense. One can then try forecasting the monthly average for a given year in the near future by the trend analysis as indicated earlier, and then, for given month make adjustments. However, success of this approach though often good enough, does not give any insight into the phenomena under study. Essentially, it assumes that as time passes, the same trend and same seasonal ups and downs are to be expected in future also.

Autoregression: A more meaningful approach is that of autoregression etc., in which models it is not time alone, but the past history also decides the future, i.e., instead of using t to predict $y(t)$, one predicts $y(t)$ on the basis of $y(t-1)$, $y(t-2)$.... Analysis of this model is relatively more sophisticated though the concept is easy to understand and many dynamic economic models are based on such auto and serial regression of one series on other series and on the past values of the series of the interest.

9

Statistical Analysis

The first component is the selection process that tells us how individual observations or elements are to be selected. The second component tells us how to make inferences from the characteristics of the chosen elements to the larger population from which they are selected. The two processes are not independent, since different selection procedures imply modifications to the inferential process, and concerns with inference instruct our selection procedures. In this chapter the focus is on some basic statistical concepts as they apply to commonly encountered sampling strategies. We introduce a standard notation, as well as a number of elementary statistical approaches that allow for inferential conclusions.

Statistical basics

The first question one might ask is: Why should we sample? Frequently, sampling is a less desirable procedure for data collection, second to measuring the entire population. Conducting a census is either impossible or impractical for many reasons, however. Among those commonly cited are the cost involved in measuring an entire population (monetary and temporal), the logistics, the intrusiveness of the measurement procedure, and possible damage to the measured units. Ultimately, we accept sampling as a necessary compromise that may allow us to make an inferential statement about the population from which the sample was drawn. Since sampling is a compromise based on expediency, we must first decide how good the sample needs to be.

Sampling plans vary as to accuracy and generally speaking, the more accurate it sample is, the more expensive it will be. In some applications such as the Canadian Labour Force Surveys, a high degree of accuracy is required to estimate worker participation and unemployment rates within a tenth of a percentage point. On the other hand, exploratory surveys and some general-purpose surveys are "good enough" if they are accurate within ±20%, 85 or 90 times out of 100. Obviously, as researchers, we want results that are accurate enough to be worthwhile, but we do not want to waste resources in attempting to obtain more accuracy than a project requires. It must also be kept in mind that measurement is generally an intrusive enterprise and people have a right to their privacy.

Surveys that are needlessly at the extremes of the accuracy continuum present unwarranted intrusions in people's lives and as such, ought to pose an ethical problem for the researcher. If a high level of accuracy is required but the resources are not available, the researcher should either consider an alternate strategy (such as downscaling the project) or put of the project until a later date. As Sudman states: "Almost all researchers will agree that a small study well-designed and executed is superior to a large study that has been botched." Sudman also rather poignantly continues, "Frequently, research is labelled as 'exploratory' merely to protect it from criticism directed against a poorly designed or executed sample."

Before starting any survey then, the researcher should seriously consider the ethical issues surrounding his or her proposed intrusion. This consideration can be helped a great deal if the researcher provides a clear statement of the objectives and implications of the study, identifies the required level of accuracy, and clearly lists the resources that are available for getting the job done. If, having considered this information, the researcher still agrees that the project is warranted, this information will greatly help in developing the most appropriate sampling strategy.

Inference

The sampling procedure we use is judgmental, based on convenience, fortuitousness, or selectivity. We might, for example, choose based on the assumption that it is likely the least the smallest grape on the bunch developed and consequently, the least sweet. Or, we might pick a grape in the middle of the bunch on the assumption that it is "most typical" of the remaining grapes. Outside the grocery store we might be accosted by a "market researcher" soliciting opinions on sour grapes.

The surveyor's selection of respondents is based on a convenience sample—whoever is willing to respond is included in the sample. Unknown to us, the solicitor may have been asked to select a quota sample, in which a fixed number of men or women or people of another identifiable characteristic were to be chosen for the survey. While this approach *may* produce usable results for the surveyor, such judgmental sampling procedures are not open to quantitative assessment. That is, there is no way to assess the validity of the inferences drawn from such samples, nor is it possible to estimate their precision. It is only by conducting a scientific sample that we can have any measurable confidence in the estimates and conclusions we draw from the sample. For a sampling procedure to be minimally scientific, it must be based on a random sampling procedure that is independent of the volition or wishes of the sampler or the respondents. Furthermore, the likelihood of selection for each element in the population must be known (or at least knowable) and nonzero. These conditions lead to the selection of what is termed a probability sample. When all the elements and all combinations of elements in the population of interest have an equal probability of inclusion in the sample, the sample is known as a simple random sample; or srs. Normally, such a sample is selected by using a random number generator. Many sample Surveys that come to our attention are not probability samples.

For example, readership surveys by magazines that ask readers to respond with a mail-in form are not probability samples. It is not possible to know what the probabilities of selection are among those who choose both to read a particular magazine and to respond to its queries. Thus, certain readers' attitudes toward their spouses, their sex lives, space aliens, or the president of the United States give us little insight about how the general population views these phenomena. Within a true srs, each element has an equal probability of selection. This, however, is not a prerequisite for a probability sample.

Elements may have unequal probabilities of selection if the selection probabilities are known. For example, for a consumer survey of cosmetics, one might wish to oversample women in comparison to men. If the women in the sampling frame are twice as likely to be selected as men, then for the tabulation of the results, the sampled womens' responses should be weighted by one half. When responses are weighted by the inverse of the selection probabilities, the sample results can be corrected to the respondent's actual distribution within the population. Samples in which the sampled elements are likely to be selected in the same proportion as they appear in the population are known as self-weighting samples. Samples with differential likelihoods of selection for the elements are known as weighted samples. The use of a probability sample allows us to estimate the precision of whatever statistic we wish to estimate—such as a mean, proportion, or total.

The bases of the determination of the precision of an estimate are the law of large numbers and the central limit theorem. Thus for any nontrivial sample (nonsmall *ns*), the central limit theorem (CLT) allows us to form a confidence interval around a sample estimate that will likely include the population parameter with a specifiable or known chance of error. Convenience sampling and other judgmental approaches cannot appeal to the CLT and, consequently, the precision of any statistic that might be generated from the results cannot be estimated. The selection of a scientific sample does not necessarily mean that the results we obtain will be useful—the resulting estimates may simply be too imprecise for our purposes. For example, a survey that estimates the proportion of women in the United States as 51 % plus or minus 10% is of little practical use. However, the selection of a probability sample enables us to make that determination. Nonscientific samples are not open to such an assessment. Researchers who rely on nonscientific samples are like the proverbial ostrich who puts faith in the adage that ignorance is bliss.

Basic notions

As with any scientific endeavour, it is essential to start by defining the basic terms. Sampling is best understood as relationships between sets. In set theory, the primary unit of analysis is the "element." An element is the simplest, most basic observational unit. Elements Could represent anything from human beings to grapes to grains of sand on the beach.

It is useful, however, to consider different aggregations of elements (sets) and to look at the relationship among those aggregations. In sampling, we often refer to three hierarchical and subsuming sets: universes (or superpopulations), populations, and samples.

— *Universe or superpopulation:* a theoretical infinity of all elements that might exist throughout all time—space coordinates; "all humanity."

— *Population:* the set of all elements bounded by a particular set of time-space coordinates; for example, all people living within the geographical boundaries of Uganda on July 1, 1991. The observation and measurement of an entire population is called a census.

— *Sample:* a subset of a population chosen according to some procedure that allows for the observation and measurement of elements fewer than the population.

For all practical purposes, there should be a close correspondence between the universe and the population. The two concepts should not be taken as identical, however, since the universe defines a theoretical concept while the Population defines an operational entity. An understanding of the distinction between the universe and the population does allow for greater understanding of the problem some researchers face when deciding how statistics based on populations should be treated. Some researchers argue that statistical analysis performed on population data should be limited to descriptive statistics alone.

The essence of the argument is that if the data are truly population data, then any characteristics calculated from the population data constitute "real" relationships (point estimates, differences, correlations, etc.) and are not Subject to sampling variation. Often this argument is invoked when official statistics that purport to measure the entirety of events are analysed, or when the population under analysis is small. By appealing to the concept of the universe or superpopulation, it is possible to recognize that what we believe to be a population is but one possible manifestation of a broader possible set of theoretical outcomes —that is, outcomes that might be observed on different occasions (other than on census clay, or at the end of the fiscal year) or in different places. From this perspective, it makes sense to conduct statistical tests on data that may be defined as constituting a population.

A more compelling reason for not doing statistical analysis on population data sterns, not from the idea that any data set designated as a Population provides a "true" parameter measure, but from the practical problem inherent in large numbers. It an empirically defined population is large (such as the population of the United States on Census day), then any estimate of the standard error will lead to values that are so trivial as to be of no practical value. The normal formula for the standard error of the mean is $s/\sqrt{n}$. Consider how small this value would be *n* were the size of a city (possible of a million inhabitants) or a country (of 50-200 million inhabitants). Clearly, conducting inferential statistics on population data makes practical sense only if the population is relatively small.

Other important concepts that are central to the understanding of basic sampling include the following:

— *Sample frame:* a complete listing of the population from which the sample of interest is to be drawn. If there is no preexisting frame, it is impossible to determine the probability of selection for any given element; hence, the precision of our statistics cannot be estimated.

— *Sampling units:* the basic observational units on which upon which the measurements are taken. Sampling units contain elements and are used for selecting elements into the sample. If there is one element per unit, we use the term "element sampling." Where natural groupings of elements occur, such as in a household or in a-school classroom, the sampling units are called "clusters."

Drawing a sample

To reiterate, two sets of rules are needed when we conduct research with samples: one for drawing a sample and another for making inferences back to the parent population. For "scientific" samples, the first set of rules generally implies that the primary sampling units are drawn on some probabilistic basis using impartial rules. That is, they are drawn independent of the researcher's volition by some "impartial," mechanical procedure following some predetermined probability distribution. Where every element in a population has an equal probability of selection, and every combination of elements has an equal likelihood of selection, a special form of sample known as a simple random sample (srs) is produced.

The second set of rules corresponds to the rules of statistical inference, which should be familiar to readers through their exposure to statistical techniques.

The basic principles behind drawing an srs apply whatever actual procedure is used to collect the data (e.g., telephone- surveys, face-to-face interviews, mail). Essentially, in drawing an srs there are four steps to follow:

— List all of the elements in the population from 1 to N.

— Decide on the required sample size

— Using either a table of random numbers or a random number generator, select n uniform random numbers between 1 and N.

— Select the elements indicated by the n random numbers and conduct the survey.

Simple random samples come in two variants: sampling with replacement and sampling without replacement. In sampling with replacement, any selected elements are returned or replaced in the original frame for further possible selection. This may lead to selected elements being chosen subsequently, in which instance the duplicated case is simply counted or weighted by the number of times it is chosen.

The advantage of sampling with replacement is that the probabilities of' selection remain constant over all selections. In sampling without replacement, the probabilities of selection for later selected elements increase. For example, consider a population with five elements. On the first selection each element has a .20 probability of selection. If the first element is not replaced, the second selection is based on the remaining elements, each having a .25 probability of selection, and so on. For extremely large populations from which a modest sample is to be selected (such as a market survey of a sample of 1000 from a population of 100,000), the issue of sampling with or without replacement becomes moot; however, for small populations, it may be crucial. Occasionally, sampling with replacement is impossible, even from small populations. Consider our problem of testing the sweetness of grapes on a bunch.

The measurement process leads to the destruction of the sampled elements. In these instances, the analysis may be carried out; however, we must correct the primary variance term, which is s^2/n for an srs. The correction term is known as the *finite population correction factor* (fpc) and is $1—f = 1—n/N$, where n is the number of elements in the sample and N is the number of population elements. Essentially, the common variance estimate is weighted by $1—f$. The impact of the fpc can easily be seen if a couple of hypothetical examples are considered. First, assume that a sample of 250 is drawn from a population of 1000. In this, instance, the fpc = 1—n/N = 1—250/1000 = 75. If the same sample of 250 is drawn from a population of 10,000, however, the sampling fraction becomes, 1— 250/10, 000 = .975. In the first example, the variance estimate s^2/n, will be reduced by .25; in the second example, it is reduced by .025—a relatively trivial amount.

Drawing a random sample

Those Students might be considered a population, and the complete listing of the students Would constitute a sample frame. After the fourth week of the semester, the instructor distributes a questionnaire to all the students. Among the questions asked are "How many hours did you spend studying last week?" and "Do you work part time?" The first 70 students (as indicated by the boldface numbers) are males and the remaining 130 students are females. The second column represents the students' answers to the question of how many hours they worked in the preceding week; column 3 tells whether they work part time (1 = yes, 2 = no). The instructor decides to select a 20% random sample for detailed analysis.

Normally, if the instructor were interested only in a sample of students, information would not be available on all the remaining elements (students) in the population. For pedagogical purposes, however, it suits us to have information on the entire population. There are several ways in which the sample could be chosen.

Thus to select this 20% sample, the instructor might generate a list of 200 uniform random numbers between 0 and 1 corresponding to the 200 elements in the population. If the random number had a value of less than .2, the corresponding population element would be included in the sample. Here, 41 of the random numbers have a value of less than .2; therefore, the sample size is higher than the exact value of 20% by one.

Since each element within the population can be chosen only once, this procedure is a variant on sampling without replacement. As suggested, this procedure can result in more or fewer than an exact number of expected elements. If generating an exact number for some reason is necessary, the procedure can be modified to do this. Alternate ways of selecting the sample do exist. A common procedure is to generate a list of 40 random numbers between 1 and 200.

One possible outcome of this approach is the same number being generated more than once, forcing us to address the issue of sampling with or without replacement. If we are willing to accept duplicate entries (sampling with replacement), then the 40 random numbers will be sufficient. If we wish to have a sample of 40 unique individuals from the population, then we probably will have to generate more than 40 random numbers, since it will be necessary to skip numbers that have already occurred.

Sampling notation

One of the biggest problems faced by students entering the sampling literature is the apparent lack of consensus in the held over notation. In this text, we will parallel that used by Kish. Complementing this material, we may usefully review some basic statistical concepts and notational conventions that impinge directly on our future discussion of sampling.

As indicated, $\overline{Y}=Y/N = (1/N)\ \Sigma Y_i$ is the "true" or population value. Sometimes this is represented in the literature as m. Since this parameter is generally unknown, the sample mean, $\overline{y}=y/n=(1/n)\Sigma y_i$ is used to estimate the population parameter. Because the sample mean is a random variable, it will have it sampling distribution that is the theoretical distribution of all possible values of an estimate (statistic), each with its own probability of occurrence. The standard deviation of the sample means about the population mean is known as the standard error of the estimate. Unfortunately, the standard error (SE) is known only theoretically, since we usually only have a single point (sample). It can be shown (by the CLT), however, that for an srs with replacement, the standard error is $\sigma_y/\sqrt{n}$ Since σ^2 cannot be estimated from the sample, we use s^2 as an estimate. Therefore, the standard error of the mean (say) can be given as:

$$\text{SE}(\overline{y})=\frac{s}{\sqrt{n}}.$$

At this point, it makes sense to provide a more precise theorem.

> If all possible random sample of size *n* are drawn from a population with a mean μ and a variance of σ^2, then as *n* increases, the sample means will be approximately normally distributed, with mean μ and variance σ^2/n.

Notice that this theorem does not make any assumptions about the shape of' the from which the samples are drawn. The original data may be normally or population uniformly distributed, or even distributed as a cross section of the Rocky Mountains. The key notion is that despite the distribution of the original data, the distribution of a statistic such as $(\overline{y})$ will be normal. It is this very powerful and critical assumption that allows its to make inferences about sample statistics. It should also be noted that the accuracy of the approximation increases with *n*.

Sampling errors

Assume for a moment that an extremely large number of nontrivial samples are drawn at random front a population. The CLT assures us that the estimated means of each of those samples will form a distribution about the true population mean $(\bar{y})$ and eventually. There are, however, other sources of error that creep into our design. These are called nonsampling errors. Some of these errors are random and cancel themselves out; others are systematic and result in systematic- bias. Nonsampling errors are typically a consequence of some systematic bias in the collection of the data. In this situation, it is the case that $\bar{Y} \# \bar{Y}_{true}$.

For example, the tendency of some questionnaires to generate response sets produces a systematic directional bias in the results. Other sources of nonsampling error include selectivity bias that results when some classes of elements are not included in the sample frame, unwillingness among certain groups to participate in the survey, interviewer biases, or systematic mistakes at data entry. This combination of sampling and nonsampling error is known as the total error of a sample. Since all sources of error contribute to variations over samples, decomposing this variation into its constituent components is possible. Thus, the mean squared error of the sampling distribution is related to the variance in the $(\bar{y})$ values. That is:

$$MSE\ (\bar{y}) = \text{var}\ (\bar{y}) + [E(\bar{y}) - \bar{Y}]^2$$

When the latter term, $[E(\bar{y}) - \bar{Y}]^2$ is not zero, the estimate is biased. In well-designed samples, however, the bias is generally very close to zero.

Estimates from simple random samples

The standard formulas for point estimates such as sample means and standard errors presented in introductory statistics generally assume that data are collected through all srs with replacement. Thus, the standard formulas for estimating the sample mean ($\bar{y} = \Sigma\, y_i/n$) and the standard error of' the mean ($SE[\bar{y}] = s/\sqrt{n}$) readily apply. The situation is somewhat different, however, when the selected sample is srs but without replacement. The traditional formula for the mean, ($\bar{y} = \Sigma\, y_i/n$) remains appropriate. The standard error for $\bar{y}$, however, requires modification, especially when the sample is drawn from a relatively small population. In this situation, the standard error of $\bar{y}$ is defined as:

$$\mathrm{SE}(\bar{y}) = \sqrt{(1-f)\frac{\sum_{i=1}^{n}(y_i - \bar{y})^2}{n(n-1)}}$$

or

$$SE(\bar{y}) = \sqrt{(1-f)\frac{s^2}{n}}$$

For proportions, the corresponding formula for the standard error is:

$$SE(p) = \sqrt{(1-f)\frac{pq}{n(n-1)}}$$

with $q = 1 - p$. When the standard error of a population total must he estimated, the formula SE (Y) = N SE($\bar{y}$) or N SE(p) can be used. Although we have used the finite population correction factor (1—f) in these formulas, it should be again noted that its impact becomes negligible when the sample size is small compared with the overall population. For example, if a sample of 500 is to be drawn from a population of 100,000, the fpc essentially becomes 1. In this instance, whether one uses the fpc formula for estimating SE($\bar{y}$) noted above, or the more familiar $s/\sqrt{n}$ is irrelevant.

Stratified samples

Simple random sampling (srs) schemes lead to very large estimates of the standard error of the estimate. Sometimes, exceedingly large SEs can result in estimates of little practical value. Fortunately, it is often possible to reduce the SE of an estimate at minimal or no cost to the sampler. One procedure that is frequently employed is stratification. Typically, stratification increases the efficiency of the sample. Efficiency, it will be recalled, is the relative size of the sampling error of a sample to other samples of the same sample size and the same cost of execution. By "homogeneous" it is meant that on average, any two items chosen at random within a stratum or segment are more a like than any two elements chosen at random from the total parent population. Essentially, stratification increases efficiency through the loss of between-strata variance.

The key to success in stratification is to find variable that is strongly related to the estimate or outcome variable. Thus, for example, if income is strongly related to geographical region, then region could serve as a stratification variable. To obtain unbiased results in stratified samples, the elements "within each stratum must be selected as an srs. That is, we select the stratum elements independently from each other and from the elements in the other strata and at random. How this increase in efficiency is gained can be shown through a trivial example. Assume for a moment that a hamlet consists of two blocks. Ail srs of four houses is selected from *within* each block, and the number of occupants or household members is recorded.

Stratum	*Household members*	*Stratum means*
Block 1	1224	$\bar{y}_1 = 2.25$
Block 2	66 87	$\bar{y}_2 = 6.75$

The overall mean, $\bar{y}$ is 4.5. The total sums of squares, $\Sigma(y-\bar{y})^2$ is 48: thus, the estimated variance across all the households (which is what we would estimate for in srs) is $s^2 = 48/7 = 6.857$. The corresponding sums of squares and sample variances for stratum 1 are 4.75 and 1.583, and lot stratum 2 are 2.75 and 0.913, respectively. Since the elements within each stratum were selected independently of one another and of the elements in each other stratum, the overall variance, s^2_{st} is simply the sum of the variances within each Stratum.

Thus, $s^2_{st} = s^2_1 + s^2_2 = 1.583 + 0.917 = 2.50$. By stratifying the hamlet by block, we have reduced the estimated sampling variance by [(6.857 - 2.500)/6.8571100, or 64%. This procedure is analogous to performing a one-way ANOVA. Within the ANOVA framework, the total sum of squares is equal to the within-group sums of squares (which is an element of the error variance) plus the between- group sums of squares. If there is no group effect (in this case, stratification effect), then the total sum of squares is equal to the sum of the within-group sums of squares.

On the other hand, if the grouping (stratifying) variable is related to the outcome variable, the within-group sum of squares is reduced by the size of the sum of squares attributable to the grouping variable. In stratified sampling-then, the worst that can happen is that the stratifying variable has no effect and the estimate of s^2_{st} becomes no worse than s^2_{srs}. On the other hand, finding an effective stratifying variable can reduce the estimate of the error variance considerably.

Estimating the standard error

Let us assume that a sample is divided into H strata, with each stratum having N_h elements in it out of a total, N. The relative sizes of the strata will be W_h, where $W_h = N_h/N$ and $\Sigma W_h = 1$. The population mean becomes a weighted mean calculated across all H strata. Consequently, $\bar{y}_{st}$ is defined as:

$$\bar{y}_{st} = \sum W_h Y_h = \frac{\sum N_h \bar{Y}_h}{N}, \quad h = 1, \ldots, H$$

This can be estimated from the sample data by using the analogous formula:

$$\bar{y}_{st} = \frac{\sum n_h \bar{y}_h}{n} \qquad h = 1, \ldots, H$$

Estimating the sampling error of $\bar{Y}_{st}$ is more complex than for the mean of an srs. The complexity, however, is more an issue of bookkeeping rather than any major conceptual distinction. First, apply the formula for sample variance within each stratum.

$$s_h^2 = \frac{\sum (y_{ih} - \bar{y}_h)^2}{n_h - 1}$$

Once the individual stratum estimates have been obtained, the overall variance of the estimate of $\bar{Y}_{st}$ becomes:

$$V(\bar{y}_{st}) = \sum W_h^2 \frac{s_h^2}{n_h} (1 - f_h)$$

$$= \sum \frac{N_h}{N} \frac{s_h^2}{n_h} \left(\frac{N_h - n_h}{N} \right)$$

$$= \frac{1}{N^2} \sum N_h (N_h - n_h) \frac{s_h^2}{n_h}$$

where again, the fpc becomes negligible for large samples. An estimate of the standard error is thus

$$SE[V(\overline{Y}_{st}] = \sqrt{V(\overline{Y}_{st})}$$

Standard errors of population totals

An estimate of the population total, Y, is given by $N\overline{Y}_{st}$. (i.e.,$\Sigma^{H}_{h-1} N_h \overline{Y}_h$) The estimated variance of $N\overline{Y}_{st}$, becomes $N^2 V(\overline{Y}_{st})$ or:

$$N\overline{y}_{st} = \sum N_h^2 \left(\frac{N_h - n_h}{N_h}\right)\left(\frac{s_h^2}{n_h}\right)$$

An estimate of the standard error is thus

$$SE[V(\overline{Y}_{st}] = \sqrt{V(N\overline{Y}_{st})}$$

Example: stratifying students by gender

An example of the impact of stratification on an estimate can be obtained by considering our earlier project involving study time spent by students. In the original sample of 200, it was known that the first 70 students were males and the remaining 130 students were females. Thus, the sample frame contains two strata defined by sex.

Intuition tells us that the male students are less conscientious and spend less time, on average, studying. This suspicion is borne out when we calculate the mean number of hours spent studying by the two strata. For the first stratum, $\overline{Y}_{\text{females}}$ is 8.47 and for the second stratum, $\overline{Y}_{\text{females}}$ is 14.04. The weighted mean for the whole sample is calculated as follows:

$$\overline{y}_{st} = \Sigma^{H}_{h=1} w_h.\overline{y}_h$$

$$= \left(\frac{70}{200}\right) 8.60 + \left(\frac{130}{200}\right) 14.04$$

$$= 12.14$$

Our primary interest, however, resides in the estimation of $\bar{y}_{st}$ and SE $\bar{y}_{st}$ from the random sample of 41 students. The weighted sample mean for the stratified sample becomes:

$$\bar{y}_{st} = \sum_{h=1}^{H} w_h \bar{y}_h$$

$$= \left(\frac{26}{41}\right) 14.04 + \left(\frac{15}{41}\right) 8.47$$

$$12.0$$

Again, the sample was drawn without replacement; consequently, the standard error, SE($\bar{y}_{st}$) is estimated as follows:

$$SE(\bar{y}_{st}) = \sqrt{\sum_{h=1}^{H} \frac{w_h^2 (1 - f_h) s_h^2}{n_h}}$$

$$= \sqrt{(.65)2 \left(\frac{\left(1 - \left(\frac{26}{130}\right)\right)(3.36)}{26} + \frac{(.35)^2 \left(1 - \frac{15}{17}\right)(3.84)}{15} \right)}$$

$$= \sqrt{.04 + .02}$$

$$= .26$$

If the samples within each stratum had been drawn with replacement, the fpc (1-n/N) would be dropped from the formula. Regardless, a 95% confidence interval may be estimated as $\bar{y} \pm 1.96$ (.26). It is readily apparent that this estimate of the standard error is almost half the corresponding srs standard error of .46. Thus, it seems that our original objective of increasing the efficiency of the estimate has been successful.

Corresponding estimates may be made for proportions. If we consider the proportion of students with part time jobs, *P* may be estimated as follows:

$$P_{st} = \Sigma_{h=1}^{H} W_h p_h$$

$$= \left(\frac{70}{200}\right).23 + \left(\frac{130}{200}\right).09$$

$$= .22$$

For the sample of 41 students, the sample proportion, p, and SE(p_{st}) have estimates equivalent to those for continuous data. Thus,

$$p_{st} = \Sigma_{h=1}^{H} W_h p_h$$

$$= \left(\frac{15}{41}\right).40 + \left(\frac{26}{41}\right).12$$

$$= .22$$

and for the standard error,

$$SE\ (p_{st}) = \sqrt{\sum_{h=1}^{H} \frac{w_h^2\,(1-f_h)\ p_h q_h}{n_h - 1}}$$

$$= \sqrt{\frac{(.65)^2\left(1-\frac{26}{130}\right)(.40)(.60)}{14}} + \sqrt{\frac{(.35)^2\left(1-\frac{15}{17}\right)(.12)(.89)}{25}}$$

$$= \sqrt{.0014 + .0016}$$

$$= .06$$

In this instance, nothing is gained through stratification, since the srs estimate, of the standard error is also approximately .06.

A Caveat

When well executed, a stratified sampling design can be highly effective. Unfortunately, it is not the panacea that some would believe. Stratifying works best with simple Surveys designed to measure only a few variables. Basically, what may be a good stratifying variable for one measure may not be so for another. Thus, in complex, multipurpose surveys, identifying strata that work with more than a few variables is very difficult.

Cluster sampling

It has been assumed that the primary sampling units (psus) consist of the individual elements as listed in the frame. In many situations, the psus are not individuals but some other element containing a bunch or cluster of individuals, such as a household or a school. In this situation, the sample frame consists of a listing of clusters (e.g., households), not individual elements. Common psus that make up clusters are road locations for random roadside checks for drinking and driving ("spot checks"); work groups; city blocks; industrial organizations, and classrooms. More so than with other sample designs, the notation for cluster samples can become complicated. Any cluster samples.

Within the population, it is as given cluster will be indicated by the subscript α where α =1...A. Inside a given cluster, it will be assumed that there are B elements, subscripted by β where $\beta = 1, \ldots, B$. From the population of A clusters, a sample of size a may be selected. Similarly, within a particular sampled cluster a subset of b elements may be chosen from the total, B. If it is considered desirable to stratify the clusters, then the strata would be indicated by the previous notation where h signified the hth stratum and h = 1, . . . , H.

Equal sized clusters

It is rare for clusters to be of equal size; however, the basic concepts of cluster sampling are best identified by using that configuration as a starting point. Let $Y_{\alpha\beta}$ represent the Yth variable associated with the βth individual in the βth cluster. In total, there are A clusters with B individuals in, each, therefore, $N = A \times B$. For each cluster, we may calculate a cluster mean as follows:

$$\bar{y}_\alpha = \frac{1}{B}\sum_{\beta=1}^{B} y_{\alpha\beta}$$

For a clusters out of A, the overall cluster mean (i.e., the mean of the cluster) is:

$$\bar{y}_{cl} = \frac{1}{a}\sum_{\alpha=1}^{a} \bar{y}_\alpha$$

and the equivalent formula for the variance among the clusters is:

$$\text{var}\,(\bar{y}_{cl}) = (1-f)\frac{s_a^2}{a}$$

where

$$s_a^2 = \frac{1}{a-1}\sum_{\alpha=1}^{a}(\bar{y}_\alpha - \bar{y}_{cl})^2$$

Do note, however, that for var($\bar{y}_{cl}$) the variance is among the clusters and not the individuals.

Unequal sized clusters

In most practical situations dealing with "natural" clusters, the number of elements varies from cluster to cluster. Furthermore, whenever we deal with a probability sample of clusters that are unequal in size, the ultimate sample size that results is itself a random variable. From a statistical point of view, this is an anomaly, since we generally treat the sample size as fixed. Thus, in traditional samples where we are trying to estimate the proportion of some phenomenon, the numerator is a random variable, but the denominator is fixed. Where the Sample size is itself unknown, the proportion is estimated by the ratio of two random variables. This complicates the math somewhat, and exact estimates become difficult to generate. Assume, for a moment, the outcome variable, Y, is coded 0, 1. Where both numerator and denominator are random variables, the estimated proportion is termed a *ratio mean* (R), which may be defined as follows:

$$R = \frac{Y}{X} = \frac{\sum_{\alpha=1}^{A} \sum_{\beta=1}^{B} Y_{\alpha\beta}}{\sum_{\alpha=1}^{A} X_{\alpha}}$$

In other words, the ratio mean is the ratio of cluster totals to the total sample size.

For a random subset of clusters then, the sample ratio mean, r, is:

$$r = \frac{y}{x} = \frac{\sum_{\alpha=1}^{a} \sum_{\beta=1}^{b} y_{\alpha\beta}}{\sum_{\alpha=1}^{a} X_{\alpha}}$$

Because the sample mean is a ratio, it is subject to some bias [i.e., $E(r) \neq R$]. In large surveys, this bias is usually quite small, being in the order of $1/x^2$.

While estimating the ratio mean is reasonable straightforward, estimating the variance of the ratio mean is more complex. Specifically,

$$\text{var}(r) = \frac{1-f}{x^2}\ a\ (s_y^2 + r^2 s_x^2 - 2 r s_{xy})$$

where f is the sampling fraction, a is the number of clusters, and r is the ratio mean (not to be confused with Pearson's). If f is reasonable small (as often happens in large-scale surveys), then the first component may be reduced to $1/x^2$. The individual variances and covariances for the numerator and denominator are:

$$s_y^2 = \frac{\sum_{\alpha=1}^{a}(y_\alpha - \bar{y}_{cl})^2}{a-1}$$

$$s_x^2 = \frac{\sum_{\alpha=1}^{a}(x_\alpha - \bar{x}_{cl})^2}{a-1}$$

and

$$s_{xy}^2 = \frac{\sum_{\alpha=1}^{a}(y_\alpha - \bar{y}_{cl})(x_\alpha - \bar{x}_{cl})}{a-1}$$

Cluster sampling is often used when it is impossible to put together a frame of all individual elements or when the random selection of individual elements is extremely expensive or ineffective. The roadside survey example suggests a prime situation in which element sampling procedures are simply unworkable. It is impossible to list all drivers on the road at a particular time and to draw it random sample; drawing a random sample of road locations is, however, possible. While cluster sample designs are often much more practical and cost-effective than element samples they are not without their associated costs. Usually, the standard errors of cluster samples are much larger than element samples of the same size (n). Sometimes this problem can be mitigated by stratifying the clusters. For example, if it is known that urban drivers are more likely to be driving intoxicated than rural drivers, the roadside clusters could be stratified along a rural/urban dimension.

Example: Estimating the proportion of drives over the legal Blood Alcohol Concentration (BAC) limit in a cluster sample

In one typical application of cluster sampling, random roadside surveys are conducted to estimate the proportion of drivers who have a blood alcohol level above the legal limit. This example entails a number of sites chosen from the 1986 random roadside survey conducted in Ontario, Canada. The original survey consisted of 298 sites selected at random throughout the province. The actual sampling design consisted of it two-step affair. The province's census tracts and enumeration areas were stratified by population, and site selection was conducted proportionate to population size.

The underlying assumption here was that vehicle registration and more importantly, traffic volume, would be proportionate to the population of the census area. Census tracts and enumeration areas were randomly selected within each stratum. Once that selection had been made, grids were laid over the census area and sections were drawn at random until a suitable survey location had been selected. Site suitability was judged on the basis of whether there would be sufficient traffic flow, whether there was a location at which the survey could be conducted, and other logistical issues, such as whether the safety of the survey crew could be assured. For the current example, 42 sites have been selected from the original 298.

Two variables have been included: the total number of vehicles stopped at each site and the number of vehicle drivers who had blood alcohol concentrations (BAC) over the local limit of 90 mg %. To simplify matters, the weights and sampling fractions have been omitted. From the sample data, the mean number of over the limit drivers, $\overline{y}_{cl}$ is estimated to be 2.143 and the mean number of drivers stopped, $\overline{x}_{cl}$ is 40.310. The corresponding totals are y_{el} = 90 and x_{cl} = 1693, and sample variances are s_y^2 = 3.686. s_x^2 = 280.902, and s_{xy}^2 = -2.143 Thus, the estimate of the proportion of drivers over the legal BAC limit of 80 mg % is the ratio mean:

$$r = \frac{y}{x} = \frac{90}{1693}$$

$$=.053$$

The variance of *r* (omitting, the fpc) is estimated as:

$$\text{var }(r) = \frac{1}{x^2} a\,(s_y^2 + r^2 s_x^2 - 2rs_{xy})$$

$$= \frac{1}{(1693)^2}\ 42[3.686 + (.053)^2\ 280.902\text{-}2(.053)\ (\text{-}2.143)]$$

$$=.69 \times 10^{-4}$$

Consequently, the standard error of *r* is the square root of the variance, √[var(*r*)] .0083.

Based on these results, it is possible to form a 95% confidence interval around *r*(.053) as *r* ± 1.96(.0083), or

$$.036 \leq r \leq .069$$

Design effects

The differences in the variances produced by different sampling schema for a sample of a given size are termed design effects. Formally, the design effect (DEFF) is the ratio of the variance of a particular sample to the variance of a simple random sample of the same size. That is:

$$DEFF = \frac{\text{var}(\bar{y})}{(1-f)s^2 / n}$$

Harkening back to the student example, it will be recalled that the standard error for the stratified design was .26, while that for the srs design was .46. In this instance, the design effect is:

$$DEFF = \frac{(.26)^2}{(.46)^2}$$

$$= .32$$

Design effects of less than 1 suggest improvements in efficiency of a particular design over its srs counterpart and are consequently considered more cost-effective. DEFF values greater than 1, suggest a relative loss of efficiency compared with an srs of' it similar sized sample and are considered less cost-effective than a simple random sample. Design effects for cluster samples are almost always larger than 1, even with the judicious use of' stratification. Typical design effects of three for cluster samples are not uncommon. This implies that a given cluster sample is about 1/3 as efficient as an srs of the same sized sample, or conversely, an srs would require only 1/3 the sample of the cluster sample to achieve a similar efficiency.

In the roadside example illustrated above, the variance of the ratio mean is estimated as $.69 \times 10^{-4}$. The estimated variance for an srs with the same number of sample elements would be pq/n = [(.053)(.947)1/1693 = $.30 \times 10^{-4}$. Thus, the approximate design effect is DEFF = $(.69 \times 10^{-4})/(.30 \times 10^{-4}) = 2.3$. Cluster samples generally produce DEFF values greater than because the intracluster homogeneity is greater than the intercluster homogeneity. Consider the example of measuring religious affiliation within households. Generally, all members of a household have similar religious affiliations. Thus, knowing the affiliation of one person in a household suggests the affiliation of all the other household members.

Because DEFF is based on a ratio of variances instead of standard errors, Kish suggests that it is sometimes convenient to use DEFT, where DEFT= √DEFF. Since homogeneity is such an integral concept of DEFF, it makes sense to present a statistics that represents this phenomenon directly. Hansen, Hurwitz, and Madow were the first to explore this issue of homogeneity within clusters in detail. They offer a statistic designated as ρ that Kish prefers to call roh, or the rate homogeneity. Rob is derived from DEFF as follows:

$$\text{DEFF} = \frac{s_{cl}^2}{s_{srs}^2} = 1 + \rho\,(\bar{n}_\alpha - 1)$$

By isolation,

$$\rho = \frac{s_{cl}^2 - s_{srs}^2}{(\bar{n}_\alpha - 1)\,s_{srs}^2} = \frac{DEFF - 1)}{\bar{n}_\alpha - 1}$$

In the formula above, $\bar{n}_\alpha$ represents the mean cluster size. The formula is not exact, but it is reasonably accurate if there is not too much variation in $\bar{n}_\alpha$. With equal size clusters, this value would be replaced by *b*. For the sample of 42 roadside clusters, the mean cluster size is 1783/42 = 42.5. Thus, roh is estimated as

$$\rho = \frac{DEFF - 1}{\bar{n}_\alpha - 1} = \frac{2.3 - 1}{42.5 - 1} = .031$$

Theoretically, roh has a range of —1 to + 1; however, roh is usually greater than zero. Negative values of roh occur only when the elements within the clusters are more heterogeneous than the randomly selected elements across clusters.

When we address the issues of cost and optimal cluster size. One of the major limitations of using DEFF and roh to depict the relative impact of one design over another is that both measures often vary according to the variable upon which the estimate is based. In multipurpose surveys, DEFF can vary radically depending upon which variable is considered.

In these situations, it is usual practice to base DEFF on the primary variables identified when the objectives of the study are initially established. Where DEFF is relatively consistent across a number of indicators, the mean DEFF is sometimes used both for planning purposes and for generating approximate standard errors for complex statistical analysis, where corrections for the design cannot be directly incorporated into the calculations.

Statistical software

Although the need to correct for design effects and to introduce the fpc into the analysis of samples drawn from small populations without replacement has been known for most of this century, few software packages incorporate these dimensions into their standard routines. Most of the major statistical analysis programs assume that the data are gathered as an srs and generate results on that basis. In fact, many packages do not even allow for the use of fractional weights in the analysis and require the researcher to recode the weights into integers. Weighting is then done by the "case duplication" method, where a given case is generated *I* times. Depending upon the magnitude of the integer weights, this can be a very cumbersome and time-consuming process, even on modern computers.

In this chapter, we discuss the basic concepts underlying statistical inference and examine what is now known as the "classical" approach—the Pearson—

Neyman or, PN model of hypothesis testing. Statistical inference deals with chance events and stochastic processes as opposed to deterministic ones. It is for this reason that many statisticians consider statistics the practice of decision making in the face of uncertainty. Within a deterministic framework, where A *always* leads to B, modern statistics has no value beyond describing the observed data.

On the other hand, statistics can help us assess the relative veracity of statements concerning relationships based on chance. That is, statistics helps us assess the empirical veracity of statements of the form: "There is a high probability that A will result in B" or "The likelihood of A leading to B is 75%." We can start by asking what distinguishes a stochastic event or process from a deterministic one. Simply stated, *stochastic events* are those whose outcome on any given trial or manifestation is not strictly predictable or predetermined. Thus, for example, no one can say for certain on the flipping of a fair coin whether any specific outcome will be heads or tails.

Let us consider what we mean when we say that there has been an outcome of a stochastic process. By definition, if an outcome is stochastic, its exact nature or characteristic cannot be predicted. The event space or the range of total outcomes of that process can be defined, however. Thus, for example, with a coin it is heads or tails. Within a survey of left-handed people, the event space is a proportion within the range 0 to 1 inclusive of left-handed as opposed to right-handed people that will be captured in a randomly selected sample.

What is important here is that the outcome has a range of possible values, which will form a distribution around the "true" value. In other words, while the "true" proportion of left-handed people is 10%, that exact value is unlikely to occur on any one given survey. Now, speaking about a propensity of outcomes to some distribution sounds very metaphysical. Furthermore, the issue of how that propensity might be observed and quantified soon comes to the forefront. One way of grounding the concept is to adopt what has come to be known as the "frequentist" perspective in statistics. By running a series of trials, it is possible to count the frequency with which the outcome occurs. In the long run, the frequency of occurrence will converge with the actual value of things. Again, the classical example is that of a fair coin.

Given enough flips, the long-run probability of getting either heads or tails will be 1/2 or .5. Let us take another example. Assume for a moment that 10% of humanity truly is left-handed. To test this proposition, one might conduct a survey by drawing a small, simple random sample of, say, 200 people. The outcome of that sample may be an estimate that could range anywhere from 0% to 100%. If we draw enough such samples, say 1000, the proportion of left-handed persons will tend toward the actual proportion of 10%, or 10 out of every 100 people surveyed. This statistic may be interpreted as a probability based on frequency in the long run.

On the other hand, a "large number" of researchers might decide to conduct identical surveys independently of one another but at the same time. This would not exactly be the same as in the long run, but the idea is the same: over a large number of trials, we can expect the estimated proportion of left-handed people to equate to the actual proportion in the population. While the frequentist approach to estimating probability is a reasonable strategy for estimating some probabilities and their associated distribution, it is just one mechanism for operationalizing the inherent chance distribution of any particular outcome.

Hacking, then, defines chance as a property of the designated chance setup and,

> *A chance set-up is* a device or part of the world on which might be conducted one or more *trials*, experiments, or observations; each trial must have a unique *result* which is a member of a *class of possible results.*

By viewing the matter in this context, we can take a broader perspective on probability and speak of the outcome chance or probability of unique events. For example; we might wish to consider the probability of rain later in the day as we set out to work i in the morning. This day and its unique rain experience cannot be repeated; thus, the frequentist approach of observing today over many trials is not possible. However, we still consider the specific "trial" to have a probability associated with it.

It is on that basis that we decide whether taking an umbrella with us in the morning is worthwhile. It is for this reason—that we can subjectively assign probabilities to unique events—that many statisticians perceive the frequentist approach to be too restrictive. Still, the frequentist approach covers a wide range of practical situations and offers one of the easiest mechanisms for estimating probabilities. As will be shown in a later section, however, some statisticians have been successful in exploiting the ability of people to generate subjective probabilities.

Pearson-Neyman and a priori testing

The Pearson-Neyman approach to hypothesis testing is based on two fundamental conditions. First, the hypothesis to be tested is stated (in null form) a priori, or before the trial (survey, experiment, etc.) is conducted. Second, the decision concerning the outcome of that trial is a binary one, resulting in either the rejection or nonrejection of the null hypothesis.

Powerful in its simplicity, the PN approach has an elegance that is best seen when the issue can be truly and unequivocally expressed in either/or terms and a clear line of demarcation for either accepting or rejecting the null hypothesis can be identified. For example, we may posit a working hypothesis that income is related to level of formal education. The null hypothesis is that no relationship exists. In operational terms, this means that after taking a random survey, we would expect the sample correlation between income and education to be zero ($r = 0$) if the null hypothesis, H_0 were "true." If the data did not support the null hypothesis (i.e., $r > 0$, or $r < 0$), then we would assume that the alternative, or working hypothesis, H_a, is "true."

The crucial role of statistics is to recognize that even if the null hypothesis were true, we would not expect *r* to equal zero exactly. Measurement and other sources of error would serve to give us a sample estimate that might be slightly different from the true population parameter. Thus, the practical question is: How far away from zero can a correlation be and still be considered zero?

If H_0 were the true state of affairs, we could repeat the survey many times and observe how the individual sample estimates of r distribute themselves about the true population value of 0. Clearly, sample values close to 0 would occur more frequently; values far from 0 would occur less frequently. Some surveys might even generate estimates at the extreme values of + 1.0 or—1.0, although their likelihood would be infinitesimally small. At this point, we can decide to draw a line beyond which, say' only 5% of all values fall by chance when the true population value is 0.

This "critical value" helps us to decide whether any particular sample *r* is truly 0 (thus supporting the null hypothesis) or is not equal to 0 (thus negating the null hypothesis and leading us to give credence to the working hypothesis). Unfortunately, given some hypothesis A, rejecting the null hypothesis, or not-A, does not always increase our credence in A because there may be many reasonable competing alternates to not-A, (B, C, D, . . . , etc.). This is particularly the case when the hypothesis A is sufficient but not necessary. Similarly, many situations are not resolved convincingly by setting a cutoff point of 5%—that is, allowing only one chance in 20 of rejecting a true null hypothesis. In fact, repeated, independent trials may lead to the rejection of several different null hypotheses (e.g., null-B, null-C, null-D), thereby raising the specter of several working hypotheses that have "statistical" if not substantive credibility.

Thus, as Hacking says,

> It would be wrong to expect an absolutely sharp line between those hypotheses which should be rejected on some data, and those which should not. One can draw such a line for no hypothesis whatsoever, statistical or otherwise. One may only compare the stringency with which different hypotheses have been rejected.

Because of such insights, testing statistical hypotheses has grown beyond the a priori model first espoused by PN and has developed schools of procedures to sort among several credible competing hypotheses. While several such approaches exist, one of the more common is that attributed to the Reverend Bayes.

Bayesian approach based on prior probabilities

Most of us follow some form of Bayesian decision making at some point in our lives. Consider, if you will, the instance of parimutuel betting. Bettors who frequent race tracks and see eight horses or six dogs in a lineup are rarely willing to assume that all the horses have an equal .125 chance of winning, or all the dogs have an equal. 167 chance of winning.

Instead, prior knowledge is used to justify the assumption that track conditions and the individual physiological and experiential differences among the animals will combine to make some contenders more likely to win than others. Bayesians argue that we rarely enter a trial with complete indifference or ignorance among competing hypotheses. Instead, we do have some prior information or beliefs that can be brought to bear. Bayesian statistics is based on a theorem identified by the Reverend Thomas Bayes and published after his death.

The theorem is a simple explication of conditional and unconditional probabilities about which both classical and Bayesian statisticians essentially agree. The difference between these schools of statistics lies in the *interpretation* placed upon the formula. Consider the following hypothetical example. Assume that in a particular community, 30% of criminals carry weapons while the remaining 70% do not. This information is known as the *prior distribution.* When the police are about to make an arrest, however, they must decide whether the suspect has a weapon. From the arresting officer's point of view, the crucial element is being able to make a correct prediction in the face of uncertainty. Further research into this problem indicates that when arrestees in fact have weapons, the police are correct in 70% of their judgments that a weapon is present. On the other hand, when a person is not carrying a weapon, the police assume he is carrying one 20% of the time.

The question we raise is, can we improve upon the probabilities listed in prior distribution by taking into account the judgment of the police? Bayes's theorem suggests that by combining information-in this case, the prior distribution with the beliefs of the police about whether a person is carrying' a weapon—an improvement can be made. This improvement is termed the *posterior distribution* and the probabilities associated with it are called *posterior probabilities.* The mechanics of how prior probabilities are turned into posterior probabilities are as follows. First, the prior probabilities associated with the event space are listed according to a standard format:

Prior probabilities, $p(\theta_i)$

State θ_i	$p(\theta_i)$
θ_1, suspect has weapon	.30
θ_2, suspect has no weapon	.70

Second, the beliefs of the police officers are listed based on the states in the prior distribution. These beliefs are operationalized as conditional probabilities—the probability judgments of the police as to whether a suspect is carrying a weapon broken down by the actual state of affairs, θ. In this example, the conditional probabilities may be listed as follows:

Conditional probabilities, $p(X_j \mid \theta)$

state θ_i	X_1, *officer predicts weapon*	X_2, *officer predicts no weapon*
θ_1, suspect has weapon	.70	.30
θ_2, suspect has no weapon	.20	.80

Consider now the situation of the officer who believes that a suspect is carrying a weapon and the suspect actually has one. That joint probability is

$$P(\theta_1, X_1 = p(X_1 \mid \theta_1)\, p(\theta_1)$$
$$= (.7)(.3) = .21$$

When the officer's prediction that the suspect has a weapon is *wrong,* we write

$$P(\theta_2, X_{1)} = p(X_1 \mid \theta_2)\, p(\theta_2)$$

$$= (.2)\,(.7) = .14$$

The total predicted probability that the suspect is carrying a weapon is $p_{(weapon)}$ .21 + .14 = .35.

Based on this information, the posterior probabilities as to whether the suspect carrying a weapon become

$$p(\theta_1 \mid X_1) = \frac{p(\theta_1 X_1)}{p(X_1)}$$

$$= \frac{.21}{.35} = .60$$

and

$$p(\theta_2 \mid X_1) = \frac{p(\theta_2 X_1)}{p(X_1)}$$

$$= \frac{.14}{.35} = .40$$

To summarize, we can now list these posterior probabilities as

Posterior probabilities, $p(\theta_i)$

state θ_i	$p(\theta_i \mid X_1)$
θ_1, suspect has weapon	.60
θ_2, suspect has no weapon	.40

What, then, is the overall likelihood that a given suspect is carrying a weapon? When the officer believes the person is carrying a weapon, the probability is raised from the .30 given by the prior probability, to the posterior probability .60 that the suspect actually has one.

Summarizing the equations above for the posterior probabilities, we may write

$$p(\theta_i \mid X_1) = \frac{p(\theta_i X_1)}{p(X_1)}$$

and by writing out in full the joint probability, $p(\theta_i \mid X_i)$, we get what is traditionally termed the Bayes theorem:

$$p(\theta_i \mid X_1) = \frac{p(X_1 \mid \theta_i)\, p(\theta_i)}{p(X_1)}$$

The denominator component, $p(X_1)$, is a constant and, as the total of the joint probabilities, serves only to ensure that the individual posterior probabilities sum to one. On the other hand, the conditional probability, $p(X_1 \mid \theta_i)$, is an important element that appears in many applications. Most commonly, it is termed the *likelihood function.*

Neither classical nor Bayesian statisticians would have difficulty with the problem we analysed as it was stated. Ultimately, however, what separates Bayesian statisticians from others is their use of $p(\theta_i)$. Classical statistics does not include the prior probability distribution into the decision-making process; decisions are derived only from the information at hand. Bayesians, however, view the information in the prior distribution to be crucial to the inferential process. Most classical statisticians do not disagree with this approach in principle, since the essential logic underlying. Bayes's theorem is unassailable.

The major point of contention, however, is that in most applications, the $p(\theta_i)$ do not have a firm empirical estimate. Under these circumstances, the Bayesians Substitute "judgment" or subjective knowledge for known probabilities. It is this "guesstimation" process that irks the opposition. The Bayesians argue that this subjectivity is no different from the subjectivity that goes into deciding what is an appropriate alpha level. Further, they note that to be used fairly, the $p(\theta_i)$ need to be specified beforehand instead of after the fact. Where the $p(\theta_i)$ can be stated with some level of precision, the Bayesian approach often has the advantage of producing smaller standard errors and narrower confidence intervals than its classical counterpart.

Where the $p(\theta_i)$ are difficult to specify precisely, Bayesian analyses often differ very little from their classical counterparts. Unfortunately, in many circumstances a misspecification of the prior distribution call generate grossly misleading results. Throughout this book we will discuss situations in which the Bayesian approach is clearly superior to that provided by classical statistics. One particularly effective application is that involving the analysis of missing data, where the ability of the researcher to bring prior knowledge to bear can result in substantial improvements in our estimates.

Likelihood ratio tests

Another approach to the problem of competing hypotheses that has gained many adherents in recent years is what may be termed the *likelihood* approach. This method is again referred to as an posteriori model because the judgment of acceptability is usually made after the data have been viewed rather than beforehand. Unlike the Bayesians, who focus on $p(\theta_i)$, the primary concern for likelihood theorist, is the conditional probability $p(X \mid \theta_i)$.

The likelihood approach starts with the assumption that while several hypotheses may be credible, in that their null forms have been rejected, some are more credible than others. For example, a criminologist may start with two "competing" working hypotheses concerning the relationship between economic circumstance and crime. Practically, the first hypothesis is based on the argument of necessity (that people steal because they are in need); the second hypotheses is based on the argument of want (that people steal because they feel unjustly deprived in comparison to others).

The criminological literature contains studies in which the null forms of both' these hypotheses have been rejected. Thus, the logical conclusion is that both working hypotheses are true. Ignoring the thorny problem of contextual or interacting variables, we will assume that the researcher has to decide whether need or want is the more likely cause of crime. Under these circumstances, the researcher would probably look at the amount of variation explained by each hypothesis and assume that, while the null forms of both hypotheses have been rejected, the one that explains the most variation is most likely the correct explanation.

Thus, based on some appropriate statistic, the argument is made that one explanation has a greater likelihood of being correct than another. The likelihood approach can be extended to deal with any number of unsupported nulls and is able to provide a quantifiable assessment of relative credibility among the working hypotheses by comparing their relative likelihoods. Within statistics, the *law of likelihood* formally states that "it *h* and *i* are simple joint propositions included in the joint proposition *e*, then *e* supports *h* better than *i* if the likelihood ratio of *h* to *i* exceeds 1". Or put in more direct terms, "*d* supports *h* better than *i* whenever the likelihood ratio of' *h* to *i* given *d* exceeds 1." Likelihood ratio tests are most commonly found in applications of model building, where one explanation or model can often be subsumed by another.

For example, when a researcher is comparing a series of logistic or log-linear models, many Subsets of' the model are statistically significant. The researcher, however, usually chooses to go with" the model that generates the highest likelihood ratio in comparison to some base model. The use of both likelihood and Bayesian approaches has increased substantially in the last 30 years and will undoubtedly become more prominent ill the future. Many researchers currently see the likelihood ratio approach as ail extension of the classical PN model.

The Bayesian perspective has been slower to make inroads but has a great deal of intuitive appeal. One major problem with many Bayesian analyses is the lack of available software. For those not versed in Bayesian analysis, however, there is no immediate cause for alarm. Except where the various H_k can be specified with a high level of precision, the results of Bayesian and classical analyses tend not to differ by very much. Thus, while the theoretical differences are profound, the practical ones tend not to be.

Statistical decision making

Despite the critical problems associated with classical statistics, we will pursue the discussion of hypothesis testing within the PN approach throughout the rest of this chapter. We do this for many reasons. The pragmatic one noted *lit* the last paragraph is probably sufficient, but there are further considerations.

The primary purpose of this chapter is to explore the fundamentals of hypothesis testing, and all a priori approach is a good starting point. Besides, where one is totally ignorant of the prior probability distribution, the Bayesian approach clearly reduces to the classical one. Second, the classical approach has become the received way of doing things in most circles, and where it has not, it is the starting point for the discussion of other models. Third, this approach is congruent with the simple binary decision-making process of accepting or rejecting a hypothesis and as such, simplifies the discussion of error types and statistical power. Under the classical approach, we assume that some population parameter, θ, is given.

Thus, the question becomes one of whether the sample data are drawn from the population defined by θ. Once a particular null hypothesis has been formulated it is necessary to decide whether this hypothesis is "true" or "false." Obviously, when we its researchers are faced with the available evidence, out- goal is to accept true null hypotheses and reject false null hypotheses. Often, however, the wrong decision is made, and true null hypotheses are rejected and false ones accepted.

The situation faced by the researcher may be depicted as follows:

	Researcher's decision	
H_0 (Actual)	Reject H_0	Accept H_0
True	Type I or α- error	
False	1—β or power of the test	Typr II or β -error

The rejection of a true null hypothesis by the researcher leads to a Type I or α-error, while the acceptance of a false null hypothesis results in a Type II or β-error. The α-error is directly under the control of the experimenter and is set a priori—before the analysis. This is the standard *p*-level for the statistical test. Since α is under direct control, so is 1—α. The β or Type II error, on the other hand, is much more complicated, since β varies with a, the sample size, the specific statistical test used, the experimental design, and the magnitude of the effect.

For a fixed sample size, as α is increased, β decreases, although the relationship is not linear or monotonic. While it is commonplace to put some thought into how small α should be, many researchers fail to realize that a very small α may have dire practical consequences. In medical research, for example, committing a Type II error may lead to failure to accept a valid treatment (H_0: the treatment has no effect), with unnecessarily high morbidity or mortality rates as a result. This could be especially worrisome for a treatment that is otherwise benign (i.e., has few or no side effects), since the practical cost of an α-error would be quite low.

Within the social sciences, concerns involving power became a majors issue after Cohen surveyed the articles published in the 1960 issue of the *Journal of Abnormal and Social Psychology.* The average power for the studies that appeared in that issue of the journal was estimated to be .48. This is an abysmally low figure, implying that if all the studies were replicated using the same procedures, only about half would result in the detection of an identifiable effect. Armed with this fact, we are not surprised by the observation that few replications are achieved in the social sciences. Interestingly, Sedlmeier and Gigerenzer examined the same journal in 1984 and estimated the average power to be roughly.50. Although these findings are based on studies published in a leading psychology journal, nonpsychology readers should not feel smug. Similar results have been found in surveys of published studies in sociology and evaluation research.

Other factors that influence the β-error are the sample size, the choice of test statistic, and the experimental design. Large *N*s increase the accuracy of test statistics (ceteris paribus), thus increasing the power of the test. Parametric statistics are generally more powerful than nonparametric statistics because of the extra assumptions made about the sampling distribution of the error terms. Finally, the experimental design has a profound influence on power because it call (it) increase the accuracy of' treatment effect estimates (through blocking or stratification), and (b) control tor various biases affecting the internal and external validity of' the study.

Statistical power

The consideration of statistical power is not simply an academic exercise. There are profound practical implications. Geoffrey Keppel notes:

> Another reason for conducting a power analysis *is* to avoid wasting resources by performing experiments with too much power. Not only does all experiment with an excessively large sample size cost more in time and money than one with a more appropriate sample size, but also the conclusions drawn are often misleading.

As our decision table shows, the null hypothesis (H_0) may be either intrinsically true or false. Depending upon its condition in nature, a specific sample will belong to either the sampling distribution associated with a "true" H_0 or a "true" alternate, H_a. Unfortunately, the researcher has no prior way of knowing the distribution from which the sample is drawn.

The symbol α which appears in the left-hand tail of the distribution of μ_0 represents one half the α-level, or the Type I error. The symbol β which appears in the left-hand tail of the distribution of μ_0 represents the other half the Type I error. It also represents the cumulative probability of committing a Type II error, with the Type II error probability being the area to the left of this point under the curve centered about μ_a. The area under the μ_a curve to the right of β represents the power of the statistical test. Clearly if β is shifted to the right, the Type I or α-error will diminish but the magnitude of the Type II error will increase.

Correspondingly, the power of the statistical test (assuming μ_a is true) will diminish. We can also see that the distribution under the normal curve is not constant over the entire range of X, since as the Type I error decreases (as β is moved more to the right) the Type II error I increases disproportionately. To look at this from another perspective, by backing off from small α–levels in the extreme tails, disproportionate increases in the power of the test can be achieved. As the distance between μ_0 and μ_a increases, the overlap between the two curves will decrease. Clearly, as μ_a moves away from β the probability of a Type II error will decrease and the power will increase.

Ultimately, if the spread between μ_0 and μ_a is sufficiently great, the use of statistical tests becomes moot. On the other hand, where effect magnitudes are small, more sophisticated or "powerful" statistical procedures are required to detect them. Estimating statistical power or the required sample size for a given situation generally requires either specialized software or a series of published tables. These tables present values for what are termed "noncentral" distributions (e.g., noncentral *t*, X^2, or *F*). The noncentrality parameter (usually signified by λ) represents the distance that the center of distribution under H_a (i.e.,μ_a) is shifted away from μ_0. For those without access to the appropriate software, detailed tables for power analysis can be found in Cohen and Kraemer and Thiemann. In some respect, power analysis is in its infancy. Most discussions are tailored to designs in which the independent variables are fixed and the dependent variables are free, as is the case with designed experiments. Furthermore, it is generally assumed that the designs are reasonably balanced; that is, there are equal numbers of elements or subjects assigned to each condition.

Situations of dependent variables that are allowed to vary (e.g., surveys) and considerable covariation among the independent variables have not been explored in significant detail. These latter situations typify research in sociology and economics. Fortunately, most sociologists and economists generally use sufficiently large sample sizes in their surveys to make the issue moot. This is not always the case, however, since even moderately complex designs can require samples in the tens if not hundreds of thousands to achieve a modicum of power. For practical purposes, the power of a statistical test can be seen to depend on four items:

— the magnitude of the effect: that is, the difference between the value of the alternate hypothesis Ha (which is assumed to be true if H_0 is false) and the value of H_0

— the Type I, or α-error, level chosen by the researcher

— the variability in the population

— the size of, the sample

The normal distribution

The estimation of statistical power is perhaps best exemplified by the one-sample test. Assume, for a moment, that all instructor has given a similar introductory exam to classes of first-year students for several years. In the long run, it is noted that the mean score for this exam, μ, is 66, with a standard deviation, σ, of 12. Owing to the large number of students examined and the lengthy period covered by the exams, both quantities call be considered to be population values. The exam is now given to a group of students who have not taken the course and wish to obtain advances standing by challenging the course.

Advanced standing will be given to students who pass the test. A group 64 students writes the exam, and the mean score, $\overline{X}$ turns out to be 62. the instructor has two questions. Is this difference statistically significant, given a 5% chance of a Type I error ? and What is the power of the statistical test?

Estimating sample size

In the preceding example, the issue was one of estimating the power of the test for a given α-level and sample size. We may also turn the question around and ask: For a given α-level and power, how large a sample do I need to detect a difference of a given magnitude? Thus, the course instructor in the preceding example might hypothesize that students who challenge a course will score an average of 4 points lower than the broader population of students. Again, it is assumed that the parameters It and a are known. The instructor selects an α-level (say .05) and for convenience sake, is willing to accept a power level of .85. Since power is 1— β, the β-level is .15. Based on μ = 66, the instructor wants to be able to detect an effect magnitude of at least 4 points; thus, the expected value for $\overline{X}$ is 62. Previously, we defined β as:

$$z_\beta = \frac{\overline{X}_L - \mu}{\sigma / \sqrt{n}}$$

where

$$\overline{X}_L = \overline{X} + z_\alpha\left[SE(\overline{X})\right]$$
$$= \overline{X} + z_\alpha\left[\sigma / \sqrt{n}\right]$$

Combining these two equations, we get:

$$z_\beta = \frac{\overline{X} + z_\alpha(\sigma / \sqrt{n}) - \mu}{\sigma / \sqrt{n}}$$

Applying some basic algebra and rearranging a few terms, it is now an easy matter to find the required sample size, since:

$$n = \left[\frac{\sigma(z_\alpha - z_\beta)}{\overline{X} - \mu}\right]^2$$

The formula above also helps us to see the relative influence of different components on either the power of the test, or the sample size. The first thing we might look at is the denominator, or the difference between $\overline{X}$ and μ. This difference is usually called the *magnitude* of the effect. All else being equal, the larger this difference (hence, the larger the magnitude), the smaller the required sample size needed to attain a given level of power. Conversely, small differences require large samples in order for us to be able to detect them. Another factor to be considered is the alpha or Type I error level chosen by the researcher. Small α-levels translate into large z-values; larger α-levels relate to small z-values.

A small z-value (i.e., a large α-level) reduces the size of the numerator, thus again allowing for a smaller sample size for a given power level. The same functional relationship holds for the z-value corresponding to the Type II error. Small β errors, or large power requirements, generate large corresponding z-values. Again, with all else being equal, when a large z_β is added to the numerator, the sample size will increase.

The* t*-distribution

The preceding section dealt with power estimation based on the normal distribution. The same general issues apply to other distributions such as the t-distribution. Unfortunately, the estimate of power under the t-distribution is more complicated than under the normal distribution. The difficulty arises because if H_a is true rather than H_0 the t-distribution will be centered over H_0 rather than H_a. This shifting of the center oft requires that we use the *noncentral t-distribution. Because* of the shift in the anchor point of this distribution, another parameter is required to identify the location of the distribution, and this is the noncentrality parameter, λ. Formally, λ is the standardized difference between the expected means μ_a, and μ_0 under the alternate and null hypotheses respectively. That is:

$$\lambda = \left|\frac{\mu_a - \mu_0}{\sigma}\right|$$

Estimating the points for the noncentral *t*-distribution is reasonably complex; however, there are many statistical programs available, plus sources of printed tables. Where the degrees of freedom associated with the test are not too small (usually more than 10), it is possible to use a transformation of *t* based on the normal distribution to estimate the power of the *t*-test. Specifically, β is associated with the *z*-value found by:

$$z = \frac{t_c - \lambda}{\sqrt{1 + t_c^2 / 2v}}$$

Here, λ is the noncentrality parameter as defined above; t_c, is the *t*-value of the central or standard *t*-distribution (the "critical value") with v degrees of freedom for the specified α-level.

Organizing material and exam outcomes

Fifty college students were randomly assigned to two groups of 25. One group was exposed to the "organizer"; the other group was asked to read an essay on Euler and Riemann. Each group was asked to answer several questions after having read the essay on topology. The dependent variable was the number of correct answers given to the questions. Briefly, the results were as follows:

	Group 1 (Experimental)	Group 2 (Control)
n	25	25
$\overline{X}$	7.65	6.00
s^2	6.50	5.90

Given the small sample size, this question is clearly amenable to analysis through a two-sample *t*-test. Formally, we may state the null hypothesis as H_0: μ_1-μ_2 = 0. Selecting an α-level of .05, the test may be constructed as follows:

$$t = \frac{(\overline{X}_1 - \overline{X}_2) - (\mu_1 - \mu_2)}{\sigma_{diff}}$$

$$= \frac{7.65 - 6.00}{\sqrt{\frac{24\,(6.5) + 24\,(5.90)}{25 + 25 - 2}\left(\frac{1}{25} + \frac{1}{25}\right)}}$$

$$= \frac{1.65}{.704}$$

$$= 2.34$$

This value is compared with $|t_{48.05}|$ = 1.68 for a one-tailed test and $|t_{48.05/2}|$ = 2.01 for a two-tailed test. Since the calculated *t*-value is greater than the absolute critical *t* value, we reject the null hypothesis and assume that the difference between the two groups is a consequence of exposure to the treatment.

To estimate the power of this test, we must first estimate the noncentrality parameter, λ Specifically,

$$\lambda = \left|\frac{(\overline{X}_1 - \overline{X}_2) - (\mu_1 - \mu_2)}{\sigma_{diff}}\right|$$

Again, using α = .05 (one-tail), we can calculate the z-value for the β-error by:

$$z = \frac{t_c - \lambda}{\sqrt{1 + t_c^2 / 2v}}$$

$$= \frac{1.68 - 2.34}{\sqrt{1 + (1.68)^2 / 96}}$$

$$= \frac{-66}{\sqrt{1.03}}$$

$$= --.65$$

The area to the left of $z = -.65$ is the β area, .26. Since the power of the test is 1- β, the power in this instance is approximately .74. If we wished to estimate the power based on a two-tailed test, the value of t_c, would become 2.01 above rather than 1.68. This would produce a power estimate of .63.

Estimating sample size

Estimating the required sample size for a given effect magnitude, power, and α-level can he done by working backward front the preceding solution. Specifically,

$$\therefore z = \frac{t_c - \lambda}{\sqrt{1 + t_c^2 / 2v}}$$

$$\therefore v = \frac{t_c^2 z^2}{2\left[z^2 - (\lambda - t_c)^2\right]}$$

Since v (the degrees of freedom) was defined as $n_1 + n_2 -$ 2, the estimated sample size should be v + 2. While estimating sample size by hand is possible, one is best advised to use a statistical program designed for the Purpose. The main reason for this (besides reducing the likelihood of arithmetic error) is that most published tables for t and z have limited precision. Inaccurate estimates of t and z can result in relatively large errors in the estimated sample size.

The F-distribution

Few practical research problems involve simple situations

in which the research merely compares a sample mean against a population mean or two sample means. More often, we are concerned with multivariate cases, where several means simultaneously, are to be compared or we wish to consider several independent variables. Analyses of this type are most often conducted with reference to the *F*-distribution. Two "typical" cases are discussed in this section, the first being a one-way ANOVA with four groups the second, a regression equation with four independent variables.

One-Way ANOVA

Generally, the first statistical problem one faces in power analysis is obtaining an estimate of the magnitude of the effect. This is generally best done by examining similar research or by conducting a pilot study. Since scale makes a difference, it is generally necessary to standardize differences by dividing by the standard error of the estimate (square root of the MSE). Following Cohen's notation, (where m is used for $\overline{X}$) for the two-category situation, we may calculate the standardized difference between two means as:

$$d = \frac{m_1 - m_2}{\sigma}$$

It is clear from this formula that the value d is a z-score. The σ in the denominator is the common within group standard deviation.

In the more generalized situation with k treatment groups, where $k \geq 2$, the spread in group means is represented not by a range across means but by the variation among the means. Cohen defines this magnitude statistic as f, where:

$$f = \frac{\sigma_m}{\sigma}$$

where for equal n in the groups,

$$\sigma_m = \sqrt{\frac{\sum_{i=1}^{k}(m_i - m)^2}{k}}$$

Here the m_i are the category means and m is the grand mean, or for equal *ns*, the mean of the means.

One advantage of using f is that it is closely related to the noncentrality parameter, λ, which defines the anchor point for the anchor point for the noncentral *F*-distribution. That is λ is the expected population value about which the sampling distribution is distributed when H_a is true. The relationship between f and λ is given by:

$$f = \frac{\lambda}{\sqrt{n}} \text{ and } \lambda = f\sqrt{n}$$

An Anova analysis of four exam types

Here we have four test groups, G1 through G4. The groups may re present one of four exam types to which students are randomly assigned. G1 might be a multiple choice exam, G2 a short-answer exam, G3 an essay-type exam, and G4 a "mixed" exam containing elements of the other types. The null hypothesis is that there is no difference in the students performance across exam type the working hypothesis is that differcnces will exist, although at this time we are not sure of the exact outcome pattern.

Each group has 8 observations; therefore, we have a simple, balanced, one-way ANOVA. A priori, it is decided to use an alpha level of .05. These data may be analysed in the standard fashion, with the results reported in Table 2. Clearly, the *F*-ratio is significant the specified alpha level therefore, we reject the null hypothesis of no difference across the means. We might be interested, however, in assessing the statistical power of this experiment.

The proportion of variance explained. η^2, is 114.375/429.875 or approximately 0.226. η is approximately 0.516. The effect magnitude, *f*, can be estimated from the group means and the summary ANOVA table. The numerator, σ_m becomes $[(22.75 - 25.44)^2 + (28.00 - 25.44)^2 + (26.00 - 25.44)^2 + (25.00 - 25.44)^2]^{1/2} = -1.89$.

Table 1

Data on four exam types

	G1	G2	G3	G4
	25	28	29	28
	21	29	26	24
	22	30	30	27
	20	26	20	27
	26	25	25	17
	26	28	20	21
	19	30	30	30
	23	28	28	26
Mean	22.75	28.0	26.0	25.0
Grand mean	25.44			

The denominator, σ, is simply the square root of the mean squared error, or $\sqrt{11.268} = 3.36$' Thus, $f = 1.89/3.36$ -.56. By using either a set of tables (e.g., Cohen) or an appropriate computer program, we discover that for α = .05; degrees of freedom = 3, 28, in f =.56; the power level is approximately .70. In our original ANOVA example, the value for η^2 was estimated at 0.226; therefore, f = .60. Again, this value off is similar to our estimate of *f* based on σ_m/σ and f_2. With α = .05; degrees of freedom = 3, *28*, and f = .60, the power level is estimated to be approximately .77.

Table 2.

Summary ANOVA table for four-exam problem

Source	*Sum-of-squares*	*DF*	*Mean-square*	*F-ratio*	*P-value*
Treatment	114.375	3.	38.125	3.384	0.032
Error	315.500	28.	11.268		
Total	429.875	31			

Distribution of effects

The value σ_m represents the square root of the *mean Squared difference of* the column means about the grand mean m. For a particular situation, it may not make sense to use the mean deviations about the grand mean. Instead, we may wish to focus on different patterns of distributions for the m_i. Let us return to the simple case of two categories. Here, the statistic, d, was defined as:

$$d = \frac{m_1 - m_2}{\sigma}$$

For any group of k means, the values m_1 and m_2 may be replaced by the minimum and maximum values among the m_i. Thus, we may write:

$$d = \frac{m_{max} - m_{min}}{\sigma}$$

Within that range of d, however, the other means may be distributed in any number of patterns.

Cohen presents three situations that he identifies as minimum, intermediate, and maximum variability. Specifically, he defines these patterns as:

— *Minimum variability*: one mean at each end of d the remaining k—2 means .01 at the midpoint.

— *Intermediate variability*: the k means are equally spaced over d.

— *Maximum variability*: the means are all at the end points of d.

For the first scenario (minimum variability) f relates to d as:

$$f_1 = d\sqrt{\frac{1}{2k}}$$

For the second scenario (intermediate variability) f relates to d as:

$$f_2 = \frac{d}{2}\sqrt{\frac{k+1}{3(k-1)}}$$

Finally, for the third scenario (maximum variability) f relates to d differentially according to whether k is even or odd. When k is even, we have:

$$f_3 = \frac{d}{2}$$

but when k is odd:

$$f_3 = d\,\frac{\sqrt{k^2 - 1}}{2k}$$

The distributions underlying these three patterns of variability are somewhat easier to Understand in a graphic format. In Figure 1, the three ideal types are presented with minimum variability showing a clustering of the means around the grand mean, medium variability showing a fairly even dispersion of the means, and maximum variability illustrated by a clustering of means at the ends of the distribution.

Thus, using the preceding example, where k = 4, for differing sample means, we obtain, first, for minimum variability,

$$f_1 = d\frac{\sqrt{1}}{2k}d$$

$$= \sqrt{\frac{1}{8}}$$

$$= .55$$

and for medium variability,

$$f_2 = \frac{d}{2}\sqrt{\frac{k+1}{3(k-1)}}$$

$$= \frac{d}{2}\sqrt{\frac{5}{9}}$$

$$= \mathrm{d}(.037)$$

whereas for maximum variability,

$$f_3 = d, \text{ since } k \text{ is even}$$

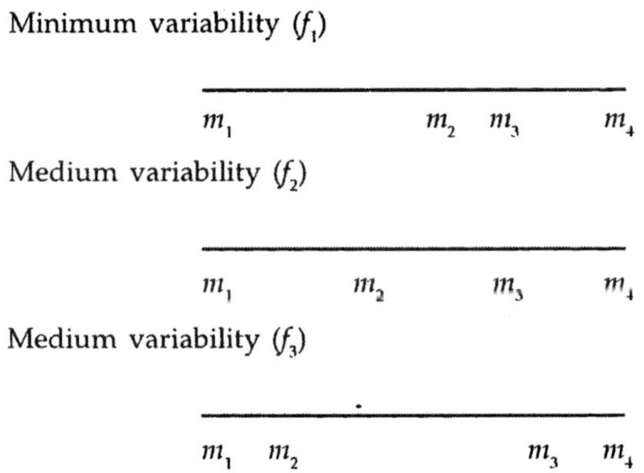

Fig. 1. Illustrations of three classes of variability (f)

In this situation the group means of 22.75, 25, 26, and 28 appear to be reasonably evenly distributed across the entire range. Thus, f_2 would appear most appropriate. For this situation,

$$d = \frac{m_{\max} - m_{\min}}{\sigma}$$

$$= \frac{28 - 22.75}{3.36}$$

$$= 1.56$$

thus, f_2 = (1.56)(0.037) = 58. This value is only slightly higher than the original effect magnitude of .56.

Regression

For both the traditional ANOVA situation and the regression approach to the GLM; the proportion of variance explained can be estimated. In ANOVA, this term is usually identified as eta-squared, η^2 ; *in* the regression approach, we refer to R^2. It call be shown that for the general case:

$$f = \sqrt{\frac{\eta^2}{1 - \eta^2}}$$

$$f = \sqrt{\frac{R^2}{1 - R^2}}$$

Estimating sample size

Calculating estimated sample sizes under the noncentral *F*-distribution is quite complex and generally involves some form of iterative procedure. There are, however, several excellent statistical programs that call do these estimations.

Final considerations

Different statistical tests have different power functions. Some tests are relatively powerful with small *Ns*; others are most powerful compared with other tests with large samples. The relative power of one test to another is termed power *efficiency*. The power efficiency of a test is the power of a test compared with its most powerful alternative. In concrete terms, this implies that a test with a 90% power efficiency would require a sample of 100 cases to achieve the power level of the most powerful test with 90 cases. Excepting broad generalities, it is difficult to rank-order tests as to their power efficiency because the power curves for a particular test can change radically with different magnitudes or sample sizes.

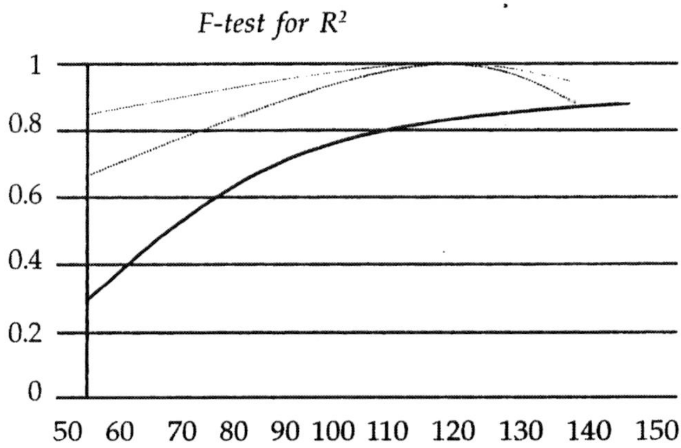

Fig. 2. Power vs. sample size under the F-distribution

Thus, it is possible for one test to be more powerful than another for small samples but not for large samples. Also in specific circumstances, nonparametric tests can be more powerful than parametric tests. When considering the issue of power in planning a research design, the best strategy is to obtain a good power analysis program and explore several scenarios based on different tests, sample sizes, alpha levels, and other factors that affect power. The text by Kraemer and Thiemann is a good starting point for comparing many tests, particularly nonparametric tests. Kraemer and Thiemann's approach, however, is to take advantage of normal approximations For many tests they consider. It is also possible to approach the power issue through simulation. While simulation procedures may be very computer intensive, the wholesale availability of powerful microcomputers removes many practical impediments that limited the usefulness of this procedure in the past. As Noreen has clearly shown, simulation procedures can be relatively easy to cary out, are immensely flexible, and are ideal solutions for dealing with tests for which the sampling distribution is unknown. Generally, pure or academic research is conservative with respect to rejecting the null hypothesis.

This institutionalized conservativism is designed to limit the generation of incorrect and spurious explanations. On the other hand, it must be recognized that both society and the individual researcher expend considerable resources on social science research. Structuring a research project where a true working hypothesis has almost no chance of being considered is a tragic waste of effort. The obverse side of the coin is also true. Studies that entail too much power are a waste of resources. Too much power usually means more subjects than necessary, which incurs extra expenses and unnecessarily inconveniences people. Ultimately, the question that might be asked is: What is a reasonable level of power? Just as with setting α-levels, setting a β-level involves many issues, not the least of which are the resources available to the researcher, the inconvenience accorded the subjects involved and the practical implications of errors of both types.

Sadly, α-levels of .05 and .0 1 have become ritual practice throughout the social sciences, and journal editors and reviewers are often loath to accept studies with more liberal Type I error potentials—even if they do enhance the power of the study. Setting a rule of thumb for an acceptable power level is fraught with similar threats. Still, it would be encouraging to see most studies striving for a power level of .80 or greater. Research into statistical power is expanding dramatically. Given our present understanding of the phenomenon, there is one significant stumbling block in extending power analysis to complex multivariate procedures. That stumbling block is the necessity of estimating σ^2 and the magnitude of the effect(s) a priori. In any complex design, multiple estimates of the magnitudes of the effects will exist, and likely significant difficulties will arise in estimating or σ^2.

10

Validity and Reliability

The language of science also contains *theoretical* terms (better called "hypothetical terms") that are not defined operationally, for example, "utility" in economics and "reinforcement" in psychology. The place of theoretical terms is a hotly debated issue in the philosophy of science. Later these terms will be discussed as they affect the empirical research work. Each term that actually enters into the *empirical* work, however, *must* be defined operationally.

Another example: Assume, that you are a psychologist and you wish to write to another psychologist to tell him what colour stimulus card you used in an animal training experiment, so that he can duplicate ("replicate") the experiment. The word "green" alone might be dangerously imprecise. There are many shades and intensities of green, and your correspondent might choose a colour that would lead to different experimental results.

You could ensure that he uses exactly the same colour if you send him the stimulus card you actually used. Your operational definition would then be "Use the enclosed colour card." But if it is impractical to send out samples—as it is when you are writing up the experiment for publication—this simple solution will not work. You could improve the chances that another researcher would use the same colour if you compared your stimulus card to an interior decorator's colour chart, then wrote down the name and number of the matching colour and the firm that puts out the colour chart. Comparing the stimulus card against the colour chart is the *operation* that *defines* the colour in question. Now some actual examples. Army Research Branch scientists in World War II wanted to study "how personal adjustment varied in the army."

The key theoretical (hypothetical) term, "personal adjustment," was operationally defined this way: With respect to verbal behaviour, it is assumed that, on the average, men who said that they were in good spirits, that they were more useful in the Army than as civilians, that they were satisfied with their Army jobs and status, and that in general they liked the Army, were better adjusted to the Army than men who were negative in several of these expressions. Notice the words "who said that they were in good spirits . . ." A questionnaire is an essential part of this particular operational definition.

Men who answered the questions in one fashion are operationally defined as well adjusted; others are ill adjusted, by *definition.* Happiness is a concept related to personal adjustment but even more difficult to define satisfactorily. Happiness is perhaps as elusive it concept to define perfectly as it is to achieve. N. M. Bradburn tackles head-on the problem of operational definition: "One way to find out whether people are happy is to ask them.

Respondents were asked to answer this question: 'Taking all things together, how would you say things are these days-would you say you are very happy, pretty happy, or not too happy?' ". Now that operational definitions have been exemplified, a formal operational definition of "operational definition" may be appropriate. "A definition is an operational definition to the extent that the definer (a) specifies the procedure (including materials used) for identifying or generating the definiendum and (b) finds high reliability for [consistency in application of] his definition". A. J. Bachrach adds that "the operational definition of a dish . . . is its recipe". P. W. Bridgman, the inventor of operational definitions, put it that "the proper definition of a concept is not in terms of its properties but in terms of actual operations."

He believed that definitions in terms of properties had held physics back until Albert Einstein and constituted the barrier that it took Einstein to crack. Psychologists have thought more deeply about operational definitions than have other social scientists because psychology tries to connect what can be observed to what is unobservable inside people's minds.

The foregoing definition of "personal adjustment" is an example of what they have done. By contrast, creating satisfactory operational definitions is seldom a problem in economics, for the theoretical concept ill economics often points clearly to the empirical variable that should be used. Of course even a concept like "money" is not automatically defined operationally; in some cases the economist includes savings deposits along with cash and checking accounts in the operational definition of money, in other cases not. And the concept "economic backwardness" bristles with such definitional problems as whether a country's present income level or its rate of growth is the more appropriate proxy.

Furthermore, putting values on a country's output is a very tricky procedure that affects the relative backwardness of the country and makes one scholar ask "Is [backwardness] an operational term ?". But seldom is the relationship between theoretical and empirical variables as arguable in economics as is the relationship between, say, the theoretical (hypothetical) concept of love and its operational definition.

Operational definitions are to be distinguished from

property or *attribute* definitions, in which something is defined by saying what it *consists* of. For example, a crude attribute definition of a college might be "An organization containing faculty and students, teaching a variety of subjects beyond the, high-school level." An operational definition of university might, be "An organization found in *The World Almanac's* listing of Colleges and Universities. Operational definitions also differ sharply from dictionary definitions. A dictionary definition of "green" is "la: of the colour green (~jade) b: having the colour of growing fresh grass or of the emerald (~lawns)" *(Webster's Third New International Dictionary*.

The dictionary definition often gives you synonyms, which help you translate the word you do not know into words you already know, or *examples* of the word that help you to learn how it is used. But for many words the dictionary definition could not *guide the actions* of one person to correspond exactly to what someone else wanted. A dictionary definition of "New York" would not be at all helpful to your friend who wants to drive there from Urbana.

A dictionary definition of "apple strudel" will not guide your grand mother to make exactly the dish that you enjoy so much. A dictionary definition of "green" will not guide another experimenter to use exactly the same colour you did. The dictionary definition of "consumer price index" will not tell you how to reproduce the consumer index used by the United States. The subtleties of these and other nonoperational definitions are discussed later when we define "causality." There have been heated philosophic arguments about operational definitions and their place in science.

In these lines, the poet catches the essence of empirical science, even though he denounces its effects, With ingenious empirical research designs and instruments, meteorologists actually do measure spring. But notice that the researcher must specify which readings on the instruments he will consider to denote spring. That specification is his operational definition. Cummings would have been disturbed if he had known that scientists also measure love—sometimes with the very kisses that he mentioned. "Love" call mean many things, of course, and the operations for measuring any facet of it are far from obvious.

Consider, for example, measuring the amount of love between mother and child by the number of times the mother kisses the child. In this case, we certainly have established ail operational definition of *something* when we specify counting the number of kisses. But few of us would believe that the number of kisses is a perfect and true index of the amount of "love"; in fact, there may be cases in which number of kisses and amount of love may be inversely related. But for some purposes it might be a useful index. Dispute has arisen because some scientists have taken a position implying that love is the kiss count and that the word "love" can have no meaning apart from the description of ail operation.

Whether or not this general position is wise, a less extreme position is possible, that is, that hypothetical (or theoretical) concepts can certainly be useful in science (and in common language) even though they are not operationally defined. The very fact that one can have in mind a concept that is not yet defined operationally but toward which one reaches with an operational definition is proof that concepts call have meaning even though they are not operationally defined.

For example, you and we probably can have some meaningful conversation about happiness even though it is a many-sided and imprecise concept to us both. And, when introducing an operational definition of happiness, I may talk about the concept in general terms. That general discussion is a "hypothetical" concept of happiness or, as B. Underwood calls it, a "literary definition". When you come to execute a piece of empirical research, all the concepts in the research and all the important words used in the write-up must be defined in terms of operations. About this point there should be no argument: If, for example, you are to study love empirically, there must be something that you can count or measure that will stand for love; otherwise you simply cannot do any empirical research. What is the relationship between the operationally defined kiss count and love? Is there a logical relationship between the two? Does "love" mean something apart from a kiss count? Is "happiness" only the answer to a question on a questionnaire? Troublesome disagreement can be avoided by saying that the kiss count stands for love in at least a partial way and that the questionnaire answer is a partial proxy for happiness.

We need not assert that the kiss count is love or that it *is all* there is to the concept of love. We can agree that there may be other measures that stand for other aspects of love, while still making good use of the operational definition. "Basically, an operational definition asserts only that a phenomenon has been reliably measured". Whenever you complete the sentence " I measured it by . . . ," referring to a variable, you have provided an operational definition of the variable. The relationship between the operationally defined kiss count concept and the hypothetical concept "love" can never be pinned down logically. Rather, the relationship is one of good judgment and scientific artistry. A wise scientist develops operationally defined concepts that are good " proxies" (that is, that stand for the hypothetical concept). But a proxy can never be perfect and complete; it cannot represent all aspects of the hypothetical term.

Repeatability (replicability) is a major characteristic of

scientific research. And operational definitions help make it possible for other researchers to repeat exactly what one researcher has done. This is the key property of operational definitions.

Numbers and operational definitions

Now let us talk about numbers. Such a suggestion has the unfortunate effect of frightening some of you nearly out of your wits. Relax; this discussion will not trouble you. "How far is it to New York?" the travelling man asks you next. He is again annoyed when you answer, "a long way," because what is a long way to you might be a short way to him or vice versa. But just putting the distance into numbers is not enough. He will still be confused if you tell him "three short ways." You might do a little better if you told him it was 3,382,000 cubits to New York—provided he has studied his Bible carefully.

The Bible, however, is not clear about the length of a cubit, so describing the distance in cubits might still be confusing. And if the travelling man has never read the Bible he has even less information than if you said, " a long way. " "About 950 miles, or 860 miles on the old road if you want to go that way," is a very satisfactory answer. The travelling man will know what you mean, and be will be able to figure how much time and how much gas it will take him to get there.

Stating quantities in common numerical measurements is *so* important that a very good book is entitled *Number: The Language of Science* Behind every numerical measurement lies an operational definition. A very precise interpretation of "three feet long" is "put three foot rulers end to end, and the distance in question is from one end of the foot rulers to the other." Many years ago, the operational definition of "three feet long" was cruder. It was "Put the heel of your left foot on a mark on the, ground, put your right foot directly in front of your left foot, and then your left foot in front of your right foot. Then compare the thing you ate measuring against the distance between the mark on the ground and the toe of your left foot." Now an example. Assume you must determine what proportion of the children in Lincoln County live on farms. How should you go about it? Your first impulse is to answer "Go and look at all the farms." Or if you are slightly wiser you might say, "Look at a sample of the farms." But those are bad answers, as we shall see.

For convenience in discussion let us narrow the problem to determining how many children live on just a *single* farm, say the old Mintz place. You send a boy to look at it, and he comes back with the answer, "two children." But then you wonder—did he count *all* the children and *only* the children? You had never told him whom he should consider a child, that is, at what age a child stops being a child, and you have never told him whether or not to count infants as children.

Now you must make those decisions. You send him out again and he returns and says, "Well, there are two children playing on the road near the house but not on the farm land itself." Should you count them or not? You must give your "enumerator," as the U.S. Bureau of the Census calls such data collectors, a rule for deciding whether children live or do not live on a farm, in order to cover children visiting on the farm or visiting away from the farm.

Then you must instruct him about whether or not a particular place is to be considered a farm (does the land have to be farmed in order for the place to be a farm?) and so on. You must give him instructions that will cover almost every possible situation in which he may have doubt, plus the important general instruction to ask you for further instructions about any situation that his rules do not cover. Notice that each of your instructions tells him how *to perform an operation.* "Ask 'do you live here?' " is in instruction to perform the operation of asking. The operation to determine whether or not a farm is being farmed is not obvious; for example, does a small patch of vegetable garden make it a farm? Other language need not always be as precise as the language of science.

The glory of poetry and biblical language is often that many meanings are possible, and the reader may find the meaning that satisfies his heart. Legal decisions are often purposely ambiguous; sometimes a judge writes a decision that will not bind future generations or reduce their flexibility, using "words that trail rainbows but disguise his meaning," in Oliver Wendell Holmes' lovely description. It is easier to be vague than to be specific or numerical, as you know if you have ever tried to evade a difficult examination question. Vague and empty language, which Jacques Barzun calls "hokum," may go undetected elsewhere but is fatal in research.

> Hokum is the counterfeit of true intellectual currency. It is words with- out meaning, verbal filler, artificial apples of knowledge. . . . Words should point to things, seen or unseen. But they can also be used to wrap up emptiness of heart and lack of thought. As a test of precision, state your research procedure as a written set of instructions to a *layman*. If he can follow your instructions and then return to you with the correct data you want to gather, then you have stated your research design well. A class exercise dramatizes how difficult it is to write even the simplest set of instructions in unambiguous language. Students work in pairs.

Each student leaves the classroom for five minutes and counts any set of objects in the rest of the building-perhaps the number of chandeliers on the first floor, the number of doors to the building, the number of stairs in the north staircase, or anything of which there is more, than one. Then each student writes a set of instructions for his partner that he hopes will lead his partner to count exactly what he did and to arrive at the same answer. The partners then exchange instructions and carry them out. The results are often funny. One person counts five statues on the first floor, the partner counts none. Why ? The instructions said "black statues," and the partner did not think the statues were exactly black.

One person counts fifteen chandeliers on the first floor; the partner counts none. Why? What one partner called the first floor the other called the basement. One person counts eight staircases, and the partner counts two staircases. Why? One person counts the stairs between each floor as a staircase; the other counts the stairs from top floor to bottom floor as a staircase. And so it goes, showing how difficult it is to write *any* set of instructions, that is, an operational definition, that will really be satisfactory. The language of empirical science has much similarity to the language that a witness is permitted to use in court: no hearsay, no speculation, what the witness himself observed and only what he observed.

The empirical researcher must transform the vague, the unspecified, the abstract, into the specified and concrete, even though precision is hard work and all of us, are lazy. Trouble with scientific language also arises because of wrong notions about the relationship of words and things. Most people assume that, if there is a word, there is also a thing that corresponds to the, word. If that were so, finding the right word would be a matter of searching through dictionaries and rule books until you found the right word for any thing or vice versa.

This attitude is fostered by our laws and by the rules that parents must make for children as they are growing up. The state and city ordinances tell you, as they must, exactly what "speeding" is. And our immigration laws are precise about what makes a person "American." But, if you are doing a research study on speeding, the legal definition will probably not help you. Instead, you will have to make your own definition, a definition that is operational, so that you can work with it and communicate it to others. And the definition must fit your particular research needs.

And, if you are studying Mexican musicians, you will have to decide whether a pianist born and brought up in Russia but who now holds Mexican citizenship is a Mexican musician. The legal definition will not suffice. Nor can you use an operational definition that someone used in a study of Mexican exports. The crucial idea is that *you must create your own definitions*—no one can do it for you. And the words do not have meaning—at least for the purpose of your study—until you give them meaning.

On the other hand, one must try to use words in a manner that other people can understand. It is seldom sensible to coin words or to use familiar words in unfamiliar ways, and whenever possible you should use *exactly* the same operational definitions as previous writers in the field so that your work may be compared with theirs. In applied research for clients, one often has trouble getting the client to be specific about what he wants to find out. If the client says, "Find out how to improve our advertising operation," the researcher cannot answer him as a researcher. (He may act in the role of consultant, but that is not research).

The researcher must find out whether the client wants to know the optimum amount of advertising or the best type of advertising, or what. The same is true in applied research for government agencies. It should be a policy decision whether the City of Los Angeles, say, orders research done on how disadvantaged a minority group is in housing, employment, or both, though the researcher may advise on which of the research projects would be most fruitful and feasible.

Every piece of research aims to produce ail answer to a scientific question. And it is reasonable to ask just how good an answer the research provides, This section is about concepts that may be used in judging how good the answer is. Validity is the over-all concept used to refer to how good an answer the study yields. If the answer given by the research is likely to be sound, the research is said to be valid.

The concept of validity may be applied to the investigation as a whole, or it may be applied to one or another aspect of the study. The rest of this section and much discussion throughout the book should help you to judge whether or not a study is valid and its conclusions sound. Reliability is one of the constituent elements of validity. Reliability is the extent of random variation in the results of the study. Wildly unreliable results cause a study to be invalid.

A subconcept of validity that applies to the research as a whole is *construct validity* or *external validity. No* matter how accurate and error-free the research, the study may be quite inapplicable to the original question. For a study may also be invalid because its *internal* procedures are invalid. For example, a study of the effects of early stair-climbing training on a group of infants is invalid unless the results are compared with those from a group of infants who received no training.

The results of such a "control group" will indeed reveal that the training has no long-run effect; the untrained group soon catches up with the trained group. An important cause of overall unreliability—and therefore a cause of invalidity—is a too-small sample. For example, a sample of tell people, no matter how representative, will give unreliable results for a Presidential election poll, because different samples of size ten will give different answers on such a close issue.

The constituent elements of a study may also be described as "valid" or "invalid," "reliable" or "unreliable." Let us concentrate on operational definitions and measuring devices. A specified set of conditions, that is, a definition or a measuring device, is reliable if the same input always leads to the same output. Reliability is roughly the same as *consistency* or *repeatability.*

The concept applies to *either* operational definitions or to measuring devices. A good operational definition is very reliable; that is, applying the definition produces the same result every time. And a weighing scale is reliable if it shows exactly the same reading every time a given iron bar is placed upon it. An I.Q. test is reliable if people get the same score when they are tested twice. Good operational definitions of "children," "live," and "farm" will lead *any* person to count the same number of children at a sample of dwelling places. It is easy enough to check the reliability of a merchant's scale with repeated weighings of the same iron bar. But checking the reliability of ail I.Q. test is more difficult.

For example, most people do better the second time they take a given test. One of many ways to check the reliability of the I.Q. test is to split the test into two halves and examine whether or not the scores on the halves are similar. An operational definition or measurement can be very reliable but still be worthless. For example, if the weighing scale always reads 10 per cent higher than a fair scale, the readings are no good. And if ail I.Q. test has excellent split-half reliability but does not give higher scores to the students who later do better in school, the test is not useful. Another example: A thoroughly reliable operational definition for "love" is "Add the weights of a boy and a girl. If their combined weights total over 322 pounds, they will be said to be in love." But this measurement does not correspond at all to the hypothetical concept of love you are trying to measure, and therefore it has no meaning. All these worthless operational definitions are said to "lack validity." A definition (or a classification or measurement) is valid if it really classifies or measures what you want it to classify or measure. An I.Q. test is valid if it really does measure the future school success of students, because that is what it is intended to measure.

A scale weighs validly if its weights agree with the commonly accepted weights of the U.S. Bureau of Standards in Washington. A pre-election Presidential poll is valid if it accurately picks the election winner. A count of the gold bars in Fort Knox is valid if it reveals how many bars there "really" are there. (The best answer we can get might be off by $20 million in either direction, according to O. Morgenstern.) An operational definition of love is valid if all those people who fit it seem to the experts in the field to be in love. There is no simple rule for deciding whether or not an operational definition is valid. Rather, the decision calls upon your judgment and scientific wisdom.

Often a good test is whether or not you can persuade other scientists that the definition is valid. And of course the validity must depend upon the purpose of the study. For example, it is easy to make up a very reliable operational definition of "tile faculty of the University of Illinois." You could use any of these definitions: the full professors listed in the staff directory; all assistant, associate, and full professors in the directory; all members of the faculty club; all buildings-and-grounds employees listed ill the directory; or any other easily defined group. But if your purpose is to survey "faculty" opinion about all important campus issue it is not so clear which definition to use. Should you include teaching assistants? research associates? retired professors? and so on.

A bad choice will give you all invalid definition. But

what is the criterion of validity? The most valid definition in this case probably includes *those people whom your listener or reader will have in mind when you tell him what the faculty opinion is.* Another example of how validity depends upon purpose. Often there are several possible ways to validate an operational definition, and the validating method is best that gets "closest" to what the definition is intended to define or measure. One can think of a hierarchy among various validating methods.

For example, no one would disagree that the *ultimate* validation of an I.Q. test is that it predicts well which students do well in school and which students do poorly. But another approach to validating an I.Q. test is to compare its results to those of well-established I.Q. tests. The latter validation is less powerful than the school-success validation, for it is less direct and therefore more subject to flaw; the well-established tests themselves may not be very valid. One method may be said to provide stronger validation than another method in a given situation, in another situation the relative validation power of the same two methods might be the reverse.

Writing scientific reports

The "mere" writing up of results may strike you as a minor part of the research process. But do not skip this section; the subject is not trivial at all. The written description of research is part of the very warp and woof of the research itself. For example, in some kinds of research—especially experimental and survey tests of sharply stated hypotheses—you can often write up the report of the research before the data are collected, except for the actual results. This exercise helps you to think through a study and often uncovers difficulties in theory and design that would otherwise appear later and cause trouble.

If you write up the report early and if you write it up

well, you have done much of the research job. Research reports, and research proposals too, must follow the specifications that we have set forth for scientific language. Scientific communication must be *objective,* rather than *subjective,* in both the words and the concepts used. "Subjective" here means the thoughts that are inside one man's head and that are unavailable for checking by other people.

"Objective" here means those statements that are public and checkable. ("Public knowledge" and "private knowledge" may be better terms respectively than "objective" and "subjective.") Amateur researchers often neglect this requirement of objective checkability. Recently I found an old account by two men who showed a batch of advertisements to groups of advertising men and tested whether or not the advertising men could distinguish the "good" ads from the "bad" ads.

The authors used mail-order advertisements in which the index of "goodness" was how many orders the advertisements had pulled in. The reported results of the study were fascinating but ambiguous, because the report gave only percentages and did not give sample sizes or data for individual advertisements. One cannot know exactly what the authors did, and therefore one cannot reexamine the interpretation of their results or repeat the study to check the data. This limitation reduces the value of the study. We will not give you a set of step-by-step instructions on how to write up a research project.

Such a set of procedures might force all your write-ups into that format whether or not it fits the needs of a particular project. And no format will fit *all* research. When preparing to write up a piece of research, read well-done pieces of research in your field, and choose as models one or more that resemble your .project. Notice that no one format is used by all writers, even within a single restricted journal in a branch of psychology, say. There may be some very general similarities of format, but the organization of each report is tailored to the particular needs of each research project. An important issue in many write-ups is how much to generalize from the data or how much to qualify the conclusions. Some researchers are supercautious about drawing inferences about their work or about hazarding the inferences in print. For example, to report a finding that men have more dreams of violence than women do but to claim that, because the sample all came from Illinois, the results can not therefore be generalized beyond Illinois is ridiculous.

Or a biologist who finds that cigarette tars cause cancer in rats may refuse to suggest that cigarette tars may well have the same effect in humans. By so doing he may protect himself from criticism, but he may also lessen the importance of his work by failing to make it relevant to researchers who are interested in cancer in humans. (Furthermore, there is ail unattractive hypocrisy in the overcautious position. We all know damn well that the only reason he ever studied the effect of cigarette smoking in rats is because of the possible implications for human beings.)

Later, and particularly in the section on experiments, there is further discussion of when it is and when it is not reasonable to draw general inferences front samples. On the other hand, the researcher also has an obligation to keep his reader front jumping the rails and drawing unfounded inferences. A. Kinsey, *et al.*, devoted much of their long explanation of method to limitations of data and method. But the officially appointed statisticians who reviewed the work gently chided them for not repeating the cautious regularly in the rest of the book so that the casual reader would not be misled.

Sometimes when you have a great many data you must decide how much to include in your report. Err on the side of reporting too much rather than too little, especially in appendixes. You can always cut out the excess. A word about style in scientific writing. One of the purposes of the founding of the great Royal Society of London in 1660 was to encourage writers on scientific matters not to write special-pleading polemics full of loaded adjectives but rather to use unemotional and unbiased language. This purpose is indeed admirable, but it has had some unintended and unfortunate consequences. For example, many scientists now refuse to write in the first person, which means that they must often forgo the active voice in their sentences.

The passive voice often leads to tortured and ludicrous sentences that resemble a mail's contortions when he tries to hide his face from a spotlight; the movement is not graceful. Furthermore, if a writer is artificially restricted from using such linguistic constructions as "I," he has fewer options and fewer tools, and his precision must diminish. Scientific caution and the desire to avoid criticism also make scientific, writing more complicated and sap its vigour and pleasantness. But, when we must make a choice, it is unhappily true that vigour and stylistic grace are the less important of the virtues.

Communicating with yourself

Being precise, specific, and concrete in communicating with *yourself is* also important. To fail to make detailed plans is unwittingly to make important decisions by postponing or ignoring them. Not deciding may mean not doing, and what is not done flow may not be possible at a later stage. Specify as much as you call in advance. Draw up the tables for which you wish to collect data; you will be surprised how hard it is to do this, a sure tip-off that your thinking is too vague. When possible, it is wise to write up the research report prior to collecting data as ail aid to good design planning. I cannot overemphasize the importance of these and similar exercises *early* in your research work. One's self -communication is improved by subjecting oneself to the same discipline and requiring the same precision as for communication with someone else. Make liberal use of pencil and paper. Write down what you think you are thinking. You will constantly be surprised at how this method helps to clarify your thinking.

It also helps to ask and answer such questions as "What do I really want to know?" and "What am I really trying to find out?" Returning to these fundamentals when you get stuck often clears up confusions magically. Your jottings in the course of the work serve as a better record of your research than your memory does. For example, when you make a decision to exclude or include a subject or datum in the sample, write down why. Later you will need this note when you write up the research.

11

Reasons of Research Analysis

Causality is not a simple idea for science. It is inextricably caught up in a web of metaphysical debate that transcends time and culture. For some scientists and philosophers, the difficulties surrounding the concept are such that they have ceased to view it as a viable entity within the framework of the scientific method. Perhaps the most notable proponent of this position was Bertrand Russell, who viewed causality as a relic of a bygone age, surviving, like the British monarchy, only because of its supposed benign nature. Among contemporary scientific disciplines, the rejection of causal frameworks remains strongest in physics.

Athearn, for example, espouses a framework of *scientific nihilism* for physics that incorporates the tenets of antirealism and acausality as its primary building blocks. Yet others, such as Michael Scriven, see causality as one of the most important elements in the methodology of applied science. Whereas Russell asserted that causal thinking offers little to modem physics, to Scriven believes that causality continues to be a fruitful framework. The disutility of causal imagery may be related to physicists' transcending what philosophers call the narrative basis of causal models. At the leading edge, much of what constitutes modern physics is best defined in functional or mathematical terms. There is no longer a need for the semantic discourse found in other disciplines, filling out caveats and assumptions that are not, or cannot be, expressed in functional format. As Athearn states. Most of the social sciences, it might be argued, are nowhere near the stage at which the narrative can be abandoned. Instead, the best we can generate are simple functional models that rely upon a narrative background to provide context and to fill a multitude of conditions not explicitly incorporated into the functional model. Although the problems surrounding causality are many, it would appear that the importance of the difficulties varies, depending upon whether one takes a realist or an instrumentalist approach to the issue.

An instrumentalist approach "only" needs to identify a set of criteria that may be agreed upon as defining a *caused relationship*. These criteria may be arbitrary in the sense that they need not reflect some inherent aspect of nature. On the other hand, the criteria must be consistent with the theoretical model or framework within which causality is defined.

From in instrumentalist perspective then, causal relationships are not "true" or "natural" but are relationships that behave *as* if *they were causal,* where causality is defined by a set of theoretical assumptions. For instrumentalists, the ontological issue of what causality really is, is not an issue of the first degree. Realists, on the other hand, see causality as something much more than whether empirical data meet a set of arbitrary theoretical assumptions.

While not explicitly speaking within this context, Kevin Hoover succinctly expresses the realist view when he states: "Causal order is not a property of the statistically observed relations between variables. Rather it is a property of the underlying and not directly observed data-generating process." From the realist's perspective, one starts with the difficulty of coming to grips with what the term *cause* truly means. Conventional thinking often associates cause with some type of physical linking or producing mechanism, such that causes "create" effects. The notion of causality as a physical mechanism is so ingrained in our language that some observers do not believe it can be transcended unless we abandon a semantic framework.

Thus, as Athearn concludes, researchers are faced with "the stark options of *mechanistic* causal models or the abandonment of narrative explanation." The difficulty for realists is further compounded with the necessity of determining what properties identify real causal relations. For most of us, causal thinking is so culturally ingrained that treating it in instrumentalist terms makes us feel queasy. However, we think it is best dealt in this manner for several reasons. First, causality is indeed a product of human ways of organizing the world, just as any other theory might be.

Thus, imposing an ontological meaning to the concept beyond this is just another instance of reification. Second, asserting "realness" to the concept almost invariably leads to the problem of infinite reduction. That is, one soon starts on the search for the "ultimate cause" underlying the relationship of interest. Within the instrumentalist framework, it is much easier to define boundaries and to distinguish those elements that are of interest to the model at hand (endogenous relationships) from those that are outside the domain of the immediate model (exogenous relationships).

Third, the instrumentalist approach allows one to avoid some unsolved (and perhaps unsolvable) philosophical problems surrounding whether causality really exists and to propose causal models of different types (e.g., strong causality, weak causality) depending upon whether some or all of one's criteria for causality are met. This view of causation is similar to that espoused by Mario Bunge, who notes that causation is but one form of determinacy. Determinacy can also be expressed in other forms, such as statistical determinacy and teleological determinacy. Regardless, the value of the causal principle is that it provides an easy way of organizing the empirical world through a familiar logical framework. Most discussions of the fundamental properties of causality propose three identifying conditions: regularity of occurrence or covariance between causes and effects, asymmetry between causes and effects, and nonspuriousness within the cause-effect relationship. It is on those conditions that we now focus our attention.

Covariance

A fundamental aspect of causal imagery is that regularities exit in the relationship between purported causes and effects. This assumption was so deftly argued by both Hume and Mill that it has become a basic axiom underlying nearly all current conceptualizations of causality. Identifying regularity should be a relatively easy, empirical issue to resolve. After the appropriate observations have been recorded, standard statistical techniques can be used to assess the level of empirical association between two or more variables.

Pearson's *r*, the product moment correlation coefficient, is a prime example of a covariance measure, although many other parametric and nonparametric statistics are possible (Kendall's tau, tetrachoric *r*, phi, etc.). In all empirical research, however, measurement error is a problem and, as we will see in a later chapter, substantial measurement error can lead most empirical estimates of association to be biased toward zero.

Asymmetry

Inherent in causal imagery is the notion of asymmetry: causes result in effects; effects do not result in causes. Conventionally, this asymmetry has been described as temporal precedence. Causes are believed to precede effects. This simple criterion of asymmetry works for many causal models; however, it soon reaches breaking points in both theory and operationalization. Because of the ubiquity of temporal precedence as a definition of asymmetry, exploring the issue in significant detail is worthwhile. As we have stated, it is commonly proposed that for *X* to be considered the cause of *Y*, *X* must precede *Y* in time. While conceptually simple, this requirement can be problematic when the relationship between *X* and *Y* is reciprocal or near instantaneous.

The first condition creates a "chicken and egg" situation that can sometimes be unravelled through the use of lag correlations (time series analysis). However, we must be aware that the simple but common fallacy of *post hoc, ergo propter hoc* (after this, therefore caused by this) often leads to the confusion of causes with effects. And, contrary to popular belief, simply extending the period of observation will not necessarily allow us to disentangle the relationship. For example, it is a virtual truism in criminology that slums cause delinquency. Yet, a little thought soon suggests that delinquency may, in fact, cause slums.

Therefore, the relationship may be one of reciprocal causation. To date, the ultimate starting point in this model has not been identified. One further caveat must be kept in mind: even when a temporal dimension is explicitly called for in a causal model, *temporal precedence is impossible to determine from purely cross -sectional data. This* creates significant problems for much sociological research that is based on single point in time surveys. Practically, the issue of temporal precedence is not always easy to tease out even when reliance on it is warranted. Often our observations cover a period that is too wide to allow us to see which variable comes first.

Hence, observations may appear simultaneous when,

in fact, they are not. A good example here is official statistics that are often available only annually, whereas the phenomena of interest may operate daily or monthly. In other instances, ongoing relationships may have achieved a state of *equilibrium* or *stationarity*, thus again assigning the issue of temporal precedence to the realm of theory rather than the realm of observation. A second, and especially difficult issue for the requirement of temporal precedence, is embedded in the need to decide what we ought to do with *simultaneous* relationships.

Formally, from a temporalist conception of causality, simultaneous relationships cannot be causal relationships. That is either the relationships we term simultaneous must be temporally related in a time duration shorter than our observation period (thus, only appearing simultaneous), or the two factors must be related through a common antecedent variable. Excluding simultaneous relationships within the causal framework would exclude a wide range of nonrecursive structural equation models in which simultaneous reciprocal causation can easily be specified and estimated. Yet another difficulty with temporal precedence is found in the task of making sense of *lead* indicators. We fully expect in empirical research to observe significant lag relationships. That is, we expect to see situations where X or Y at some time, t, are the outcomes of changes in X or Y at $t - 1$.

Still, what if the reverse is true? This may be counterintuitive for many, but it is empirically viable. The situation occurs so often in economics that the concept of *rational expectations* has been introduced to explain the phenomenon. In its simplest states (A and not-A) simultaneously. Since a given element cannot be in treatment and control simultaneously, we can never be certain that our results are nonspurious. Thus, while experimentation may be one step up on survey research as a framework for exploring causal relationships, it is not the ultimate solution. At present, the most sophisticated theoretical analysis of causation and spuriousness is attributable to Mackie. From the point of view of practical methodology, Mackie's most significant contribution is the observation that traditional experimental designs, while adequate in theory, pose considerable practical difficulties. Specifically, Mackie sees traditional experiments as bordering on naive because they focus almost exclusively on main effects.

Mackie's world is far more complex. Considerable higher order interactions exist that are difficult to isolate in standard designs, and much of what passes for causal knowledge is what he terms "gappy." Mackie's exposition is presented within a deterministic framework. While the assumption of determinism is highly restrictive in most social science settings, it is sufficient for introducing the vocabulary and for gaining a basic understanding of the logic behind Mackie's argument.

For those who are interested in pursuing this matter in greater detail, Cartwright has clearly shown that Mackie's discussion can be readily generalized to probabilistic models that incorporate nonexperimental procedures. Consider the nontrivial case of some outcome *P*, which results from a situation with elements *A*, *B*, and C, where only the complete set *{ABC}* is sufficient for *P*. Furthermore, it is assumed that any given subset (e.g., *{A B})* is not sufficient to result in *P*. Thus, *P* will follow only when all of *A*, *B*, and C are present. Now, let us assume there is a plurality of causes such that any of *{ABC}* or *{DGH}* or *{JKL}* is sufficient for P.

Again, the condition holds that P will not follow from any lesser subset (e.g., *{AC}*, *{DG}*, *{J}*, etc.) of the elements listed. On the other hand, if *P* will result only from the situations *{ABC}* or *{DGH}* or *{JKL}* and none other, then these are also necessary conditions for *P*. Thus to summarize the sets, *{ABC}* or *{DGH}* or *{JKL}* are both sufficient and necessary conditions for *P*. Therefore, all *[{ABC}* or *{DGH}* or *{JKL}]* are followed by *P* and all *P* are preceded by *({ABC}* or *{DGH}* or *{JKL})*. Mackie defines as a *minimal* sufficient condition the fact that all elements of, say, the set *{ABC}* are required to be a sufficient condition for *P* to occur. Thus, in elaboration:

> *ABC* is a *minimal* sufficient condition: none of its conjuncts is redundant: no part of it, such as *AB*, is itself sufficient for *P*. But each single factor, such as *A*, is neither a necessary nor a sufficient condition for *P*. Yet it is clearly related to *P* in an important way: it is an *insufficient* but *non-redundant* part of an *unnecessary* but *sufficient* condition: it *will* be consentient to call this ... an *inus* condition.

It is the elaboration of the "inus" condition that forms the unique basis of Mackie's contribution. If the three sets, {ABC}, *{DGH}*, and *{JKL}* are a complete enumeration of the causes of P, then they are collectively called the full *cause*. As Mackie and others have pointed out, however, it is rare for us to be able to enumerate all the elements in the full cause.

Theoretical and empirical limitations often reduce both our knowledge and our interest to only parts of the full cause. Thus, as Mackie remarks, "what is typically called a cause is an inus condition or an individual instance of an inus condition". How, then, does this discourse advance our formal understanding of what it means for a relationship to be spurious within a causal model? Consider the situation in which *{A BC}* may be an inus condition for two separate effects *P* and *E*. Under this circumstance we might be misled into believing that *E* is the cause of *P* for both *E* and P will be evident when *{ABC} is* evident.

Granger causality

To continue working within the framework of causal

imagery while trying to avoid the deeper philosophical pitfalls, some researchers have proposed limited or operational forms of causality. This gambit of proposing models of weak causality has found particular favour in disciplines characterized by a greater reliance on survey as opposed to experimental data. An example of one such approach is that outlined by Granger. Granger's is essentially an operational definition of causality based on two conditions.

First, it is assumed that causality is asymmetrical; only the past can affect the present or future and not vice versa. Thus, any observed asymmetry must be of the form of a standard, temporally evolving feedback loop. Second, Granger causality is limited to discussions of stochastic variables. Practically speaking, Granger causality is an attempt to justify standard regression models as a sufficient mechanism for assessing causal models. Within the regression framework, X is assumed to be a cause of Y if past and present observations of X allow for better forecasts of the Y variable, ceteris paribus. To test Granger causality, a number of hypotheses need to be specified.

First, there is the substantive hypothesis that the outcome variable Y_t is a function of some previous or current manifestations of Y and a set of causal variables, X_i. Stated more formally, it is posited that $Y_t = f$, (any Y_{t-j}, $X_{i,t-k}$, where $j = 1, 2, \ldots$, and $k = 0, 1, 2\ldots.$). If the null of this hypothesis cannot be rejected, then the specified Y_{t-j} and $X_{i,\,t-k}$ cannot be considered to be candidates for causality. Second, for Granger causality to hold, it must also be shown that the null hypothesis that Y does not have a significant effect on past and future X_i cannot be rejected.

Since tests for Granger causality invariably involve time series data, the statistical procedures for testing the appropriate hypotheses can become complex, particularly when correlated error terms are involved. Succinct reviews of appropriate statistical testing procedures can be found, however, in most standard econometrics texts.

Practical issues

Having explored some conceptual issues surrounding causality, we will now focus our attention on some practical issues of working within a causal framework.

General vs. individual causes

Carl Hempel makes a distinction between what he terms general and individual causes. General causes are those that follow specific laws. Thus, for example, when paper is exposed to a sufficient source of heat (451°F) along with several other coextensive conditions, (e.g., presence of oxygen), it will ignite. This process follows a general rule that can be reproduced under a variety of specific circumstances.

This rule constitutes the general cause. Specific or individual causes are of the variety that consider unique factors. Thus, for example, who put a match to the paper, and why? By making this distinction, Hempel is recognizing two situations. First, scientific explanation relies on our ability to replicate similar events (i.e., events of a given class). Second, there may be some processes (individual causes) so unique that they are not amenable to standard analysis.

Is experimentation a necessary condition for science?

It is often argued that the classical experiment is the ideal approach in the scientific method, and some researchers, such as Holland, argue that it is only through experimentation that any degree of causality can be imputed. We must ask ourselves, however, whether this is really a necessary condition for the advancement of scientific knowledge or merely a sufficient condition. For, as Holland himself has shown, there are ultimate limits to the cause-inferential viability of experiments. In principle, the answer is that the controlled experiment is only one possible approach. As Nagel states:

> It is in consequence beyond dispute that many sciences have contributed, and continue to contribute, to the advancement of generalized knowledge despite severely limited opportunities for instituting controlled experiments.

What is needed, however, is what this author terms *controlled investigation.*

> Controlled investigation consists in a deliberate search for contrasting occasions in which the phenomenon is either uniformly manifested (whether identical or differing modes) or manifested in some cases but not in others, and in the subsequent examination of certain factors discriminated in those occasions in order to ascertain whether variations in these factors are related to differences in the phenomena—where these factors as well as the different manifestations of the phenomenon are selected for careful observation because they are assumed to be relevantly related.

A nonexperimental approach is probably a necessity, even with the possibility of controlled experimentation. This is likely the case for several reasons. First, the very act of modifying social conditions artificially (the experiment) can affect the subjects involved in the experiment. This process is akin to the phenomenon known as the Heisenberg principle in physics.

Second, introducing a change in social conditions might produce irreversible changes in the relevant variables, thereby disabling our ability to replicate the situation by returning to the initial conditions. Third, it is well known that many results found in the social laboratory are difficult, if not impossible, to replicate in the field. Thus, especially for policy purposes, it is often necessary to test for complex interaction effects in the field before presuming to make firm instrumental conclusions. Unfortunately, achieving any degree of control over the relevant variables in field experiments is often difficult. Returning to our earlier discussion, it would appear that Nagel is asserting that a science can progress even when it meets only what we have termed the *weak* assumptions of causality. If this is the case, then what is the final arbiter of a theory's validity? Ultimately, it is the ability of a theory to make correct predictions.

As Nagel points out, astronomy is a physical science that defies classical experimentation, yet has advanced because its models are able to make consistent and adequate predictions about the future state of the universe. Sadly, most of the social sciences have yet to produce predictive models on par with those of astronomy. Still, as all utopians would argue, it is the principle we are examining here and not necessarily its inadequate implementation.

Suggestions for the improvement of controlled inquiry

Since controlled observation is likely the best we can aspire to in many social sciences, what can we do to improve the situation? There are some general procedures that can help.

Variance maximization

Traditional statistical techniques and experimental designs assume that the independent variable is under the control of the researcher. The researcher attempts to provide as wide a range of values as possible to extend the external validity of his conclusions. Conclusions concerning the relationship outside this range are made at one's own risk. For example, a consumer survey of automobile ownership that focuses on consumers with family incomes of less than $ 100,000 per year may show that there is a positive relationship between income and the "newness" of the family automobile(s). It may be, however, that those earning more than $ 100,000 per year (who were not surveyed) tend to purchase automobiles with long life expectancies; therefore, their automobiles often are older than those of the middle class.

Thus, anyone extrapolating the demand for new cars to the very wealthy may be disappointed in seeing a market much smaller than expected. Generally, ex post facto research does not allow for a valid determination of the range of *X*. Therefore, attempts should be made to survey situations with as much variance (and as great a range) in *X* as possible. Practically, this often requires the oversampling of the tails of the distribution through stratification.

A priori positing of hypotheses

ex post facto research conducted without the prior statement of hypotheses is of utmost danger. Conversely, this leads to the traditional "fishing expedition," where researchers dredge data for significant relationships. As classical statistics teaches us, for a given alpha level say $\alpha = .05$, 1/20th of all true null hypotheses will be rejected by chance alone. After-the-fact explanations should be considered totally suspect, since new interpretations can always be found to fit the facts. In essence, such explanations are scientifically invalid because nullifying them is impossible. A good example is psychotherapy, which molds the explanation to fit whatever "facts" manifest themselves. It is *only* by positing the hypothesis a priori that the researcher has any chance whatsoever of *not* being able to reject a null hypothesis.

Distinguishing proximal from contextual causes

It is often easy to confuse the impact of what might be termed proximal variables with contextual variables. The educational example is that of "school effects." In demography, we often note a tension between contextual factors that influence fertility decisions, such as economic or cultural conditions, and proximal factors Such as expectations and pressures from other family members. In general sociology, one must distinguish between "structural" and proximal effects and decide (a) what is it that one wishes to focus upon, and (b) what is the most important factor? One published example of asking whether it makes sense to ask what factors predict exam performance when the grade distribution is set a priori is a good issue.

The debate has raged between "radical" and "conservative" theorists for some time about whether the real issue of analysis is the social system itself, or how people behave within that system. For example, does it make sense to ask what motivates some to become criminals when the system itself constrains opportunities such that criminal behaviour is the only "rational" response?

Conceptual clarity in variables

Some variables are clearly not as subject to selection bias as others. Examples of more resistant variables include age, gender, race, and marital status. The distinction here is between what Talcott Parsons termed "achieved" and "ascribed" characteristics. Ascribed characteristics are generally those immutable factors, or at least the factors outside one's personal control, that described an individual. Age is a good example. Achieved characteristics, on the other hand, result from one's volition.

Unfortunately, most ascribed characteristics are what we might term proxy variables. For example, chronological age is an irrelevant characteristic by itself. Chronological age is often used as a proxy for many biological, psychological, and sociological factors. So too are sex, race, or any number of other "basic" dimensions. Often these factors stand in stead for such things as experience, learned culture, or social role acquisition. Even the relationship between age and mortality is really a relationship between physical decay and mortality, and exposure to risk (disease, accidents) and mortality. Thus, anything that increases the rate of exposure to a given disease (besides mere time) will increase or decrease the relationship.

Appropriate design

Survey researchers often spend considerable time analysing sampling questions without exploring many of the more subtle issues of design. For example, cross-sectional designs can often be combined into what we term "multiple panel" designs. This lends a longitudinal component to our research that provides one way of operationalizing the asymmetry requirement. Once a panel approach has been chosen, it is necessary to address the issue of whether a "true" panel or "pseudo" panel design should be used.

True panel studies follow the same individuals over time. These designs are often expensive to execute, since subject mortality can often be very high. Pseudopanels consist of multiple cross-sectional samples drawn independently from the same population. They are often less expensive to execute, but loss of information must be factored into the savings achieved. A primary distinction between true and pseudopanel designs is the general inability to estimate prevalence over incidence. The distinction between these two concepts is aptly illustrated by Gottfredson and Hirschi, who speak of the problem of measuring participation in criminal activity.

> The crime rate is a function of both the number of persons in the population committing crimes (the prevalence of crime) and the number of crimes they commit. When the denominator of the rate consists of the total number of people in the population, the first rate is traditionally called the prevalence rate and the second the incidence rate.

A second example can be drawn from labour force participation. From a cross-sectional survey, we may learn that 50% of all women participate in the labour force. However, we do not know whether the same sample of women are consistently in the labour force, or more women work but only 50% are in the labour force at one point in time. It is very possible for the incidence of female labour force participation to be 50%, yet the prevalence may be close to 85%. To address both the problems of sample mortality and differing panel samples, some surveys engage in a compromise.

The Canadian monthly Labour Force Survey, for example, commences with an initial sample and proceeds to drop one-sixth of the sample each month, while picking up a new sixth at random. Thus, any one individual is sampled for a maximum of 6 months; simultaneously, the costs of finding a mobile sample are limited, since the same person has to be tracked down only for a maximum of 6 surveys.

Identifying where our interests lie

In his short methodological treatise, *Making it Count*, Stanley Lieberson states: "Explanations of variation are not substitutes for explanation of the existence of the phenomenon itself." At first glance, this appears obvious. Further thought, however, suggests that the statement is very misleading. The issue is one of measurement—the difference between nominal and ratio measurement, and how a phenomenon manifests itself. Most scientists recognize that phenomena can be measured nominally (presence/absence) and, if present, in degrees of presence (ratio).

Lieberson suggests that the issue of presence/absence is more important than levels of presence. This may or may not be the case, given substantive considerations. However, the two types of explanation are not exclusive by any means, and a priori, deciding purely on issues of measurement is difficult. Furthermore, there is no conceptual reason dictating why one should be exclusive of the other. Many situations may be considered the outcome of a "two-stage" decision process. For example, how much I decide to spend on a house comes second to my decision to purchase a house in the first instance. Some factors that contribute to the first decision also contribute to the second (e.g., how much I have for a down payment; presence of a stable job; my monthly income).

On the other hand, certain factors that relate to the "purchase" decision may be independent of the "how much" decision. For example, the likelihood of being transferred to another city may contribute to the "purchase" decision, not to the "how much"; the number of people in the household may determine how much can and is to be spent on the purchase price. One example of the type of analysis that can be used to handle both existence and variance is Tobit analysis, so named after J. Tobin, an economist who looked into similar problems in the mid-1950s. Tobin's immediate problem was to determine how much people spend on automotive repairs. In this instance, Tobin realized, the question of how much is spent is determined by the presence or absence of mechanical breakdowns.

Simply ignoring those who did not have repairs, however, would severely bias the parameter estimates, causing an overestimation of the amount spent in the population.

Another threshold phenomenon is illustrated in Figure 1. This diagram represents the phenomenon known as *catastrophe theory*. Here we have two separate functions defined in the diagram as Level 1 and Level 2. At low levels of *X*, Level 1 defines the function relating *X* and *Y*. The function follows Level 2 for higher values of *X*. For part of the range, however, there is an overlap in the two functions. When the phenomenon enters the overlap range, it is assumed to be capable of making a quantum leap from one level to the other. Where that leap will take place is not determined, but often the leap from Level 1 to Level 2 (as indicated by the line segment *AB*) takes place at higher levels of *X* than the drop from Level 2 to Level 1 (as indicated by the line segment *CD*).

The typical substantive example presented by catastrophe theorists is that of a frustrated dog. At low levels of frustration, the dog exhibits varying degrees of aggressiveness, usually in the form of snarling. At some point, however, increasing the dog's frustration level will lead to a change in the type of aggressive behaviour from snarling and baring of teeth to a physical attack. The viciousness of attack, *y*, is determined by *X* along the trajectory outlined by Level 2. Ultimately, the dog will "cool down," will retreat from his attack, and return to snarling. Word has it that frustrated parents and teachers follow similar patterns of behaviour.

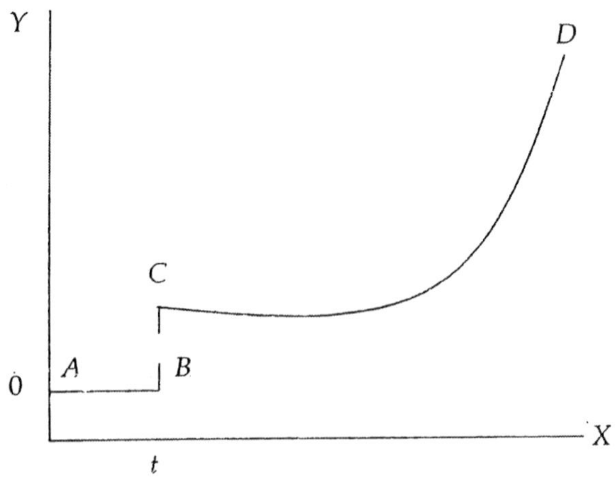

Fig. 1. Example of a threshold effect.

Causality and correlation: An elaboration

As we have already noted, correlation is a necessary but not a sufficient condition for causality. At some level, the identification of correlation is a simple matter: observe two variables (X and Y) over some domain of X and calculate a correlation coefficient. Unfortunately, X and Y rarely occur in isolation. Other variables may mediate the relationship in a theoretically meaningful way (in which case we call them endogenous), or they may influence the relationship outside the immediate theoretical model (in which case we call them exogenous).

In most *real* research, there are often many mediating variables to consider. The single biggest problem for empirical scientists working within a causal model framework is that several competing models can be consistent with the same data. It is the role of the methodologist to try to create test situations or procedures that can result in data that distinguish between competing models. Still, one can never be sure whether all competing models have been accounted for. To quote Mackie on the matter:

> And even with any one cause, we do not know all the possible counteracting causes, all the factors the negations of which would have to be conjoined with our positive factors to make up just one minimal sufficient condition. Causal knowledge progresses gradually towards the formulation of such regularities, but it hardly ever gets there. Causal regularities *as known* are typically incomplete....

Thus, again we are reminded that the inability to disprove a model does not necessarily confirm that model. Many basic problems underlying the determination of correlation can be illustrated with the simplest scenario: that of three variables. Let us assume that the key relationship of interest is that between X and Y, and that Z is the (potentially) mediating or spurious variable. Thus both X and Z conform to Mackie's inns conditions, but from a theoretical standpoint, Z is not considered to be a genuine cause. The issue of spurious relationships is particularly problematic when we engage in empirical fishing expeditions without strong theoretical guidance. It is also a primary pitfall underlying raw empiricism when we let "reality" alone guide our explanatory models. Put in other terms, statements that "everybody knows" or "it is self-evident" that X causes Y do not mean that X truly causes Y.

Most of what we now identify as superstitious or magical thinking likely had its origins in spurious relationships. The relationship depicted in Figure 3.3b, on the other hand, is that of a *confounding* relationship. Depending upon the magnitudes of the correlations among the three variables, Z may act as either a suppressor variable or an augmenting variable. If the presence of Z reduces (attenuates) the absolute empirical correlation between X and Y, we call it a suppressor; if it increases the absolute empirical correlation between X and Y, it is an augmenter.

In the extreme, the unknown impact of a suppressor variable can fool us into believing that there is little or no relationship between X and Y. The unknown impact of an augmenter, however, leads to an inflated estimate of the impact between X and Y. Exactly how r_{ZX} and r_{ZY} influence our perception of r_{XY} depends on the signs of the three correlations. Without getting into covariance algebra to my great extent, we can see this relationship if we take a close look at the familiar formula for the partial correlation coefficient. By definition,

$$r_{XY.Z} = \frac{r_{XY} - r_{XZ} r_{YZ}}{\sqrt{1 - r_{XZ}^2}\sqrt{1 - r_{YZ}^2}}$$

The denominator values will always be positive, and for our purposes can be ignored. Let its consider the relationship in greater detail. The component $r_{XY,Z}$ can be seen as an estimate of r_{XY}, or the true relationship between X and Y. The correlation, r_{XY}, is what we observe. Thus, the observed correlation consists of the true correlation plus the product of the correlations between X and Z, and Y and Z. That is,

$$\mathrm{r}_{xy} = \mathrm{r}_{xz}\mathrm{r}_{yz} + \mathrm{r}_{xy.z}\left[\sqrt{1-r_{XZ}^{2}}\,\sqrt{1-r_{YZ}^{2}}\right]$$

The observed covariance between X and Y, therefore, is a consequence of the product ($r_{XZ}r_{YZ}$). Following through with this line of reasoning, it becomes apparent that if one or both of r_{XZ} or r_{YZ} equals 0, then $r_{XY} = \mathrm{r}_{XY} = 0$. If the product of r_{XZ} and r_{YZ} is positive, r_{XY} will be positive; if the product is negative, r_{XY} will be negative. The same reasoning can shed some light onto the confounding relationship between X, Y, and Z. If the product of r_{XZ} and r_{YZ} is positive, then Z becomes an *augmenting* variable that produces an observed $r_{XY} > \rho_{XY}$. By calculating $r_{XY,Z}$ we will obtain a reduced estimate of the causal link between X and Y.

On the other hand, if the product of r_{XZ} and r_{YZ} is negative, Z will be a suppressor variable that leads to an observed $r_{XY} < r_{XY}$. Thus, $r_{XY,Z}$ will be larger than the observed r_{XY}. The remaining relationships in Figure 3.3 consist of theoretically meaningful relationships between X, Y, and Z that are both nonspurious and nonconfounding. That is, Z is an endogenous variable of substantive interest.

X has both a direct effect on Y and an indirect effect through Z. Sometimes this is called an interactive model, since X and Z not only have main effects on Y, but also an interactive effect based on r_{XZ}. Exactly how Z moderates the impact of X on Y depends upon the signs of the three zero-order correlations involved in the relationship. Instead of discussing the impact of the permutations of the signs of the correlations on the relationships between X and Y for each of the diagrams, we will simply have a quick look at the structural form of the relationships. A more general and detailed approach for examining the relationships and estimating the magnitudes of the effects is presented in the next section on path analysis.

Z is an antecedent variable that has an impact on Y but only through X. Empirically, then, it is only necessary to observe variations in X to predict the behaviour of Y. X is a sufficient condition but not a necessary condition for Y, since Z can also affect the behaviour of Y. In this instance, the behaviour of Y can be predicted 'only by including the two main effects of X and Z into the model.

Z is irrelevant to our understanding of the relationship between X and Y because in no case is Z a causal variable. Z acts as a *mediating* or intervening variable between X and Y. In the absence of Z (i.e., $Z = 0$), X has no impact on Y.

Path analysis

The technique was incorporated into the social science literature after its popularization by Otis Dudley Duncan in the 1960s. As a pedagogical procedure for delving into the intricacies of causal modelling, it is an excellent starting point. Unfortunately, as presented by Wright and Duncan, the procedure imposes constraints that are difficult to achieve empirically. Specifically, classical path analysis requires the same assumptions as ordinary least squares regression analysis. That is, for some structural equation, say $Y_i = \beta_0 + \beta_1 X_{i1} + \ldots + \beta_n X_{in} + \varepsilon_i$, we assume that the error terms, e_i, are normally and independently distributed (of each other and the Xi_j), with a mean of zero and some constant variance, σ^2. We also assume that the independent, or X variables, are measured without error.

The reason for these OLS assumptions is that the

path coefficients are essentially standardized *b*-values. Most independent variables as operationalized in the social sciences, we would argue, are highly subject to measurement error. Furthermore, those error terms are often correlated with one another. From a statistical point of view, then, path analysis allows for the analysis of a *structural* model, but not of a *measurement* model. That is, where we know, or have good reason to believe that these assumptions are violated, we have significant difficulties identifying and accounting for those violations within the framework of the model.

This limitation has been overcome in recent years with the theoretical development of generalized structural equation modelling (e.g., Joreskog, Bollen) and the availability of software designed to estimate those models. Still, making those restrictive assumptions about measurement to explore the issues surrounding the structural or causal model is worthwhile.

Path diagrams

For many of us, the great utility of path analysis is the graphical interface it provides between verbalizations of theory statements and the mathematical representations of those statements. This interface is known as the path diagram. Path diagrams consist of the proverbial "circles and arrows" that help us organize the relationships between our theory components visually. While researchers have undoubtedly used ad hoc graphical procedures for generations, path diagrams follow a set of rules that allow for the systematic depiction and interpretation of our theory statements.

The variables are connected to each other through a series of arrows. Boxes and circles linked through arrows are assumed to influence one another either causally or otherwise. Boxes and circles not linked to one another are assumed to be theoretically independent. The *causal direction* implied in the theory statements is represented by the direction of the straight arrows, with the variables at the head of the arrow being considered the effects, and those at the base, the causes. The double-headed, curved arrows assume association but not necessarily causation. In the terminology of econometrics, the curved arrows represent exogenous relationships, while the straight arrows represent endogenous relationships. Boxes and circles connected by arrows that go in both directions are assumed to be reciprocal in their causation.

Path coefficients

Path coefficients are equivalent to beta coefficients or standardized b—values obtained from an ordinary regression model. Starting with a matrix of correlations, R, it is possible to estimate the standardized b—values. Let us assume that a correlation matrix has been partitioned into two submatrices: R_{xx}, which consists of the $m \times m$ intercorrelations among the independent variables; and R_{xy} which is an $m \times 1$ matrix of correlations between the independent variables and the dependent variable, An $m \times 1$ matrix of standardized b—values or path coefficients, b^*, may be estimated as:

$$b^* = R_{xx}^{-1} R_{xy}$$

Although there are several formulations, the squared multiple correlation, R^2, is Most easily determined by

$$R^2 = b^* / R_{xy}$$

From this, we may estimate the standard errors for each of the j path coefficients, b^*_j as approximately:

$$\mathrm{SE}(b_j^*) = s_{b_j^*} = \frac{\sqrt{1-R^2}}{\sqrt{r_{ij}(n-k-1)}}$$

The r_{ij} constitute the inverse of the jth diagonal elements of the R^{-1}_{xx} matrix; n is the number of cases; and k is the number of slopes (independent variables) in the regression model. Individual path coefficients can be tested for statistical significance by comparing the ratio of the b^*_j s to their standard errors [i.e., b^*_i /SE(b^*_j)]. This ratio can be compared with the t-distribution with $n - k - 1$ degrees of freedom (df).

Example: Estimating Path Parameters

Assume that a survey is conducted in which three observations, X_1, X_2, and Y are taken on each of 50 people. Intercorrelations arc calculated among the three variables resulting in:

$$R_{XX} = \begin{bmatrix} 1.0 & .40 \\ .50 & 1.0 \end{bmatrix}, \quad R_{XY} = \begin{bmatrix} .35 \\ .25 \end{bmatrix}$$

From this, the coefficients can be estimated as:

$$R^{-1}_{XX} \; R_{XY} = b^*$$

$$\begin{bmatrix} 1.0 & .40 \\ .50 & 1.0 \end{bmatrix}^{-1} \begin{bmatrix} .35 \\ .25 \end{bmatrix} = b^*$$

$$\begin{bmatrix} 1.25 & -.5 \\ -.625 & 1.25 \end{bmatrix} \begin{bmatrix} .35 \\ .25 \end{bmatrix} = \begin{bmatrix} .31 \\ .09 \end{bmatrix}$$

Thus, the betas or path coefficients estimated within this model are .31 and .09. The proportion of overall variance explained, R^2, becomes $(.31 \times .35) + (.09 \times .25) = .13$. Since the diagonal elements of R^{-1}_{XX} are both 1.25, each r_{ij} is equal to 1/1.25 or .80. Thus, both estimates of the standard errors of the betas are given by:

$$\text{SE}(\text{b}^*_1) = \frac{\sqrt{(1-R^2)}}{\sqrt{r_{11}(n-k-1)}}$$

$$= \frac{\sqrt{1-.13}}{\sqrt{.80(50-2-1)}}$$

$$= .15$$

A 95% confidence interval may be determined as approximately $b_j^* \pm 1.96\ (.15)$ or $b_j^* \pm .29$. This would imply that only b_1 *is* statistically significant, since the confidence interval around b_2^* (.09) encompasses 0 but that around b_1^* (.31) does not. The best estimate of b_1^*, therefore, is r_{XY} or .35.

Example: A Path model of Fertility in Developing Countries

The model is designed to test a substantive hypothesis currently of interest in demography: that is, whether economic development has a greater impact on a country's total fertility rate than rates of female literacy. From the data set, five variables have been chosen: total fertility rate (TFR), log gross national product per capita (Log-GNP), percentage of population in agriculture (Agriculture), percent female literacy (Literacy), and the difference between the mean age of marriage between men and women (Difference). Ultimately, TFR is what we want to explain.

Log-GNP and Literacy are the primary explanatory variables, and Agriculture and Difference are subsidiary causal variables. Agriculture is believed to influence TFR and Literacy, while Difference is considered an indicator of relative status. Where the difference between the average age at marriage is great, we assume that there is a large gender status differential. We also assume that this status differential is influenced by literacy among women. It is further assumed that Log-GNP and Agriculture are also correlated although not causally. Together, these relationships are outlined in Figure 2.

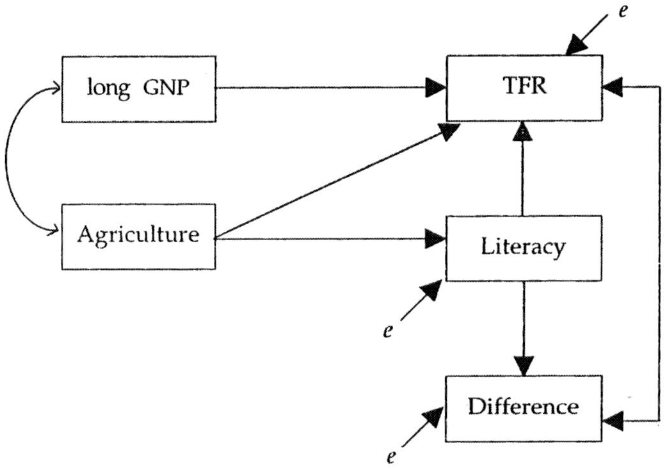

Fig. 2. A path meodel of ferility

A correlation matrix was generated from the data set. Since there are values missing from the data, it was decided to estimate the correlation matrix by deleting cases that had at least one missing element. This resulted in the matrix based on a sample of 68 nations. The correlation matrix is reproduced in Table 1.

To estimate the paths, three equations must be set up:

TFR=Log-GNP + Agriculture + Literacy + Difference (1)

Literacy = Agriculture (2)

Difference = Literacy (3)

Table 1
Correlation matrix of variables in fertility path model

	TFR	*Log-GNP*	*Literacy*	*Agriculture*
TFR	1.0			
Log-GNP	–666	1.0		
Literacy	–.742	.604	1.0	
Agriculture	.698	–.772	–.677	1.0
Difference	.579	–.442	–.611	.461

For equation (1) we can obtain the betas or path coefficients by solving:

$$R_{XX}^{-1} \quad R_{XY}' = b^*$$

$$\begin{bmatrix} 1.0 & .604 & -.772 & -.442 \\ .604 & 1.0 & -.677 & -.611 \\ -.772 & -.677 & 1.0 & .461 \\ -.442 & -.611 & .461 & 1.0 \end{bmatrix}^{-1} \begin{bmatrix} -.662 \\ -.742 \\ .698 \\ .579 \end{bmatrix} = b'$$

Since equations (2) and (3) involve only one independent variable, the estimated path coefficient or standardized b-value is equivalent to the correlation coefficient, r. Solving the equations (1)-(3), we obtain the results presented in Table 2. While the parameters and standard errors can be estimated either by hand or by almost any general regression routine, we chose to conduct the analysis using LISREL8. One advantages of using a generalized structural equation package such as LISREL8 is that it will provide overall indicators of goodness of fit for the entire model.

One way of measuring the entire model is to assess the degree to which it reproduces the correlation matrix, R. Essentially, we are testing the null hypothesis that $\hat{R} = R$. In this instance, a chi-squared test can be used. The estimated chi-square is 2.97 with 3 df with an associated p-value of .40. These results suggest that we ought not to reject the null hypothesis, since the expected correlation matrix closely resembles R; thus, using this global assessment, the model provides a good overall fit. While the overall model appears statistically significant, an examination of the individual parameters in Table 2 suggests that the model is clearly not parsimonious.

In particular, the paths flowing front Agriculture to TFR and Difference to TFR and not statistically significant. Since the Difference to TFR path is not significant, it also does not make sense to retain the path from Literacy to Difference. The path from Log-GNP to TFR is also not significant; however, we will retain this path for the moment, since it does have crucial theoretical significance. Reestimating this model, we note changes in some parameter values. Specifically, the path from Log-GNP to TFR changes from –.20 to –.34 and that from Literacy to TFR changes from –.38 to –.53, since the relationship between these variables is no longer modified by either Agriculture or Difference.

The error term relating to TFR also changes slightly, from .34 to .37. The path between Agriculture and Literacy remains unchanged, since no other path led to Literacy. Similarly, the correlation between Log-GNP and Agriculture remains constant at –.77. Standard tests suggest that this model still replicates the correlation matrix reasonably well: the calculated chi-squared statistic is 4.82 with 2 df.

Table 2

Regression results for fertility path model

TFR *Variable*	*Coefficient*	*Standard Error*	*T-value*
Literacy	–.38	.11	–3.33
Difference	.16	.09	1.75
Log-GNP	–.20	.11	–1.79
Agriculture	.21	.13	1.59
R^2 = .65			
Literacy			
Agriculture	–.68	.09	–7.42
R^2 = .46			
Difference			
Literacy	–.61	.10	–6.22
R^2 = .37			

Just as importantly, all the individual parameter values can be judged as statistically significant, including the path from Log-GNP to TFR. Details of the path coefficients and their standard errors are presented in Table 3.

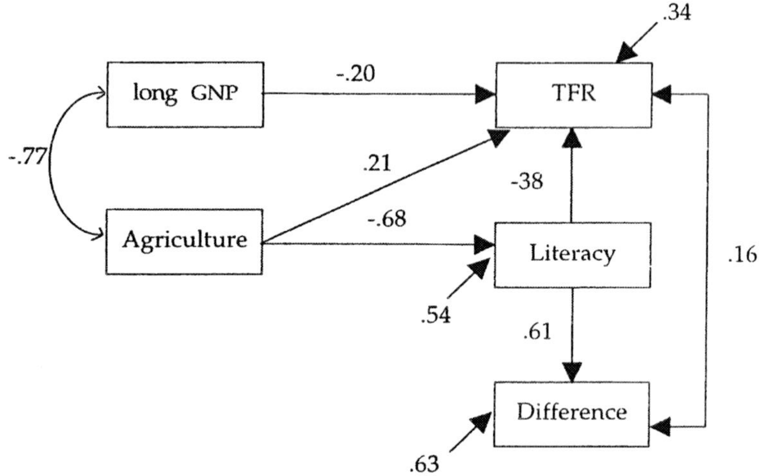

Fig. 3. Path diagram with estimates of path coefficients for fertility model.

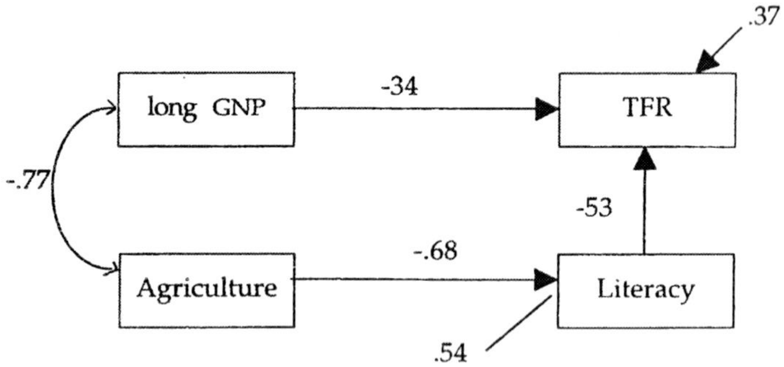

Fig. 4. Path diagram with estimates of statistically significant path coefficients for reduced ferility model.

Causal path models

The preceding example is typical of much research that

appears in the professional journals. We posited the model within a causal framework and directional arrows suggest the direction of the influences. Formally, however, the model is one of weak as opposed to strong causation because the data are not temporally asymmetrical.

The data are essentially measured at one point in time. More properly, the causal variables should be time lagged with respect to the outcome variables for the model to fulfil all the traditional requirements for "causality." As given, the example simply describes the relationships as they exist: it gives little insight into how they "got there."Path models can be used, however, to illustrate simple processes in time. Figure 5 presents one such example. For more complex models, the path framework loses its parsimony of expression and often obscures the underlying processes. Complex time-series models (typically of the econometric variety) generally use standard mathematical or statistical notation instead of path imagery.

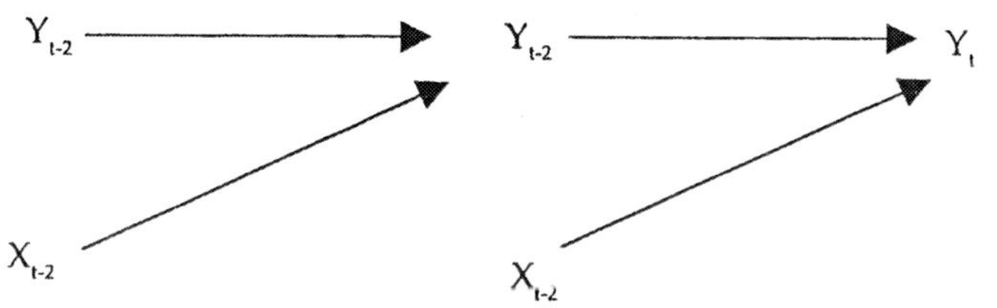

Fig. 5. Examples of time-series path diagram

Exploratory causal models

The primary focus of science as a method is that of hypothesis testing. Substantive science also involves the context of discovery. In practice, it is likely that scientists spend more time in the discovery phase than in the justification phase. This is nowhere more evident than in the enterprise of causal modelling.

Few scientists are fortunate enough to have a well-specified causal model simply waiting for empirical assessment. Typically, we have a vague model with clear a priori linkages among some variables but not others. Typically, we have also put together a data set that reflects an operationalization of those variables. The crucial problem, then, becomes one of specifying the exact linkages that we believe are important within the model. There are many mindless and atheoretical techniques that allow for the determination of the "best fitting" model (e.g., stepwise regression; all possible regressions), but those approaches generally lead to capitalization on chance.

12

Quantitative Techniques

The quantitative methods comprise mainly mathematical and statistical methods, the latter ecompassing econometric tools also. The purpose of this note is to discuss the use and limitations of some of the statistical tools which a researcher may employ in the analysis of an economic problem.

If one referes to any learned journal on economics, he would invariably come across research articles in which quantitative methods, simple or sophisticated are used either to derive a set of consistent conclusions or to empirically test a given hypothesis or theory. It is believed that the level of applications of quantitative techniques in any discipline is indicative of the degree of its exactness. Viewed in this way, economics can be regarded as a scientific discipline more exact than perhaps some other social sciences in as much as wide ranging applications of qualitative methods are possible in the analysis of various economic phenomena.

Mathematical methods

Before turning our attention to statistical tools, it may be deemed proper to understand the nature of mathematical methods of analysis, which are of great use to an economist. Since economics concerns itself with the study of relationships among different variables/concepts and also deals with drawing a set of conclusions and hypotheses from given a set of definitions, axioms and assumptions via the process of logical reasoning, the role of mathematical analysis in this task is immensely important.

The advantages of using mathematical approach in economics are that it enables an economist (a) to be precise iii defining relevant variables and concepts; (b) to state clearly and precisely the assumptions made and (c) tone logical in developing the analysis and (d) to consider a large number of variables that might be feasible verbally. Prof. Chang mentions four advantages of mathematical approach as follows :

1) The language used is more concise and precise.
2) There exists a wealth of mathematical theorems at our service.
3) In forcing us to state explicitly all our assumptions as a pre-requisite to the use of mathematical theorems, it keeps us from the pitfall of a unintentional adoption of unwanted implicit assumptions and
4) It allows us to treat the general n - Variable case.

Mathematical analysis, which is based on powerful deductive logic, enables an economist to draw a set of consistent conclusions or hypotheses, given the definitions axioms and assumptions stated precisely in terms of symbols and equations. It may be noted here that mathematical method of analysis does not ensure accuracy of conclusions with respect to observed facts or data. It only ensures consistency of the conclusions in relation to the definitions, assumptions and axioms with which the inquiry starts. If the conclusions/hypotheses are not empirically valid, then mathematical analysis is not at fault but the fault lies in the definitions adopted and assumptions made.

Hence if conclusions/hypothesis are not correct with respect to empirical observations, the researcher has to re-examine the definitions and assumptions for their accuracy and completeness rather blame mathematical analysis which as mentioned earlier only ensures consistency of conclusions. Thus, it is clear that mathematical methods have a crucial role in developing consistent economic theories/hypotheses. While *mathematical methods, deductive in nature,* help in the formulation of economic theories/hypotheses, statistical tools which are *largely* based on *inductive logic,* help in empirically testing and verifying the economic theories/hypotheses.

Statistics as we all know, is a science, embodying tools and techniques which are invariably used in almost all branches of knowledge including economics. Keeping this in view, it has been said that statistics is a science without a subject matter of its own. Statistical tools and techniques like the methods of any other discipline have their own limitation and underlying assumptions. For example, when it is stated that simple random sampling gives a representative sample, the underlying assumption is that the universe, from which the sample is drawn, is fairly homogeneous. Similarly other statistical methods have their limitations and assumptions.

Therefore user of these techniques whether he is an economist, political scientist or any analyst, belonging to any other discipline, should first acquire thorough knowledge of these techniques, their relevance, purpose, assumptions and limitations. On the other hand if the techniques are used regardless of their relevance and limitations, dangerous results causing greater damage to social welfare would follow. In the pages that follow, examples of certain statistical techniques, the use of which requires adequate caution and care, are given.

Statistics techniques

One of the most popular and fundamental measures of

statistics is the *arithmetic mean.* This measure, along with similar other averages, does not tell us about the degree of variation or dispersion. A story is told to illustrate the misuse of this measure.

A professor of mathematics, in order to cross a river with his family members, chose a point on the bank of the river, at which average depth of the river is less than the average height of the members of the family. This is a clear example of the misuse of the tool average. Instead of choosing the *average,* the professor should have used a *measure of dispersion,* i.e., range. He should have chosen a point on the river bank where the maximum depth of the river is less than the *minimum* height of the members of the family.

Growth rate is also an important tool, used invariably by researchers in analysing economic problems. As is well-known, there are many formulae of growth rates, which have their relative advantages and disadvantages. Some growth rates take 'into account only the initial and terminal values and therefore depending upon the choice of the initial and terminal years the growth rate differs.

Thus the researcher should select the period careful and properly on the basis of objective considerations, and not on the basis of his own to prove his point, i.e., high growth rate or low growth rate. It may also be borne in mind that equal growth rates do not necessarily imply equal magnitude of effort, or achievement. A given rate of growth say 5% over larger base means a larger magnitude of progress or achievement than the same rate of growth over a smaller base. That is why it is easier to attain high rate of growth in the earlier five year plans, i.e., first and second plans etc., than to achieve the same high rate of growth in later five year plans.

One should also be very careful In using

percentages, particularly when absolute numbers are very small. The following example may be cited to show how the percentages alone would be somewhat misleading. "Johns Hopkins University some decades ago permitted women to enter classes, thus breaking a precedent. Shortly thereafter it was reported that 33 1/3% of women students at Johns Hopkins had married members of the faculty. This looked like a sizeable number until it was discovered that there were only three women students enrolled there at the time and one had married a faculty member." This example clearly illustrates that reliance on percentages alone is not proper. When absolute numbers are small, percentages have to be given along with actual figures. In the use of *correlation* technique necessary care and caution have to be exercised.

The coefficient of correlation, as we all know, does not necessarily indicate causation. Causation implies correlation is a measure which can be calculated for any two series of data. It can be used to measure the Co-variation of two series. But before using this technique, the economist or any other social scientist should know on the basis of theoretical considerations whether there can be a logical relationship between the variables X and Y under consideration. In certain situations a Linear correlation may be found to exist only within limits.

If the yield of the crop is larger, higher is the rainfall, it does not mean that the output of the crop goes on increasing as we have more and more rainfall. This is because too much rainfall may ruin the crop. Thus instead of positive linear correction, we have in this case a curvilinear correlation with positive relationship upto a certain limit and a negative relationship setting in after that point.. Hence this technique should not be applied mechanically. Sometimes there is a danger of wrong policy prescriptions based on improper interpretation of the Co-efficient of correlation. In a simple *regression analysis,* there are two regression equations; one for regressing Y and X and the other one for regressing X on Y: The choice of a particular regression equation depends upon whether X is regressed on Y or Y is regressed on X. In other words one has to know which of these variables is an independent one.

The science of statistics tells that if X is an dependent variable, regression equation of Y on X is to be used. On the other hand if Y is the independent variable, regression equation of X on Y is to be chosen. Thus which one of them is an independent variable depends on the nature and type of causation between them. It is the theory that tells us about the nature of causation rather than the technique of regression. Therefore, knowledge of theory is essential before applying the proper tool of analysis. From the above illustrations it becomes clear that statistical techniques have to be applied in their proper context with great care and caution.

An economist who wishes to apply these techniques should not only possess complete knowledge about various statistical tools including their assumptions and limitations but should also possess sound knowledge of economic theory and the problems under investigation. While inappropriate use of the techniques may lead to faulty conclusions forming the basis of wrong policy prescriptions their proper use would undoubtedly result in better understanding of the problems and their remedies. In this context the statement by P.C. Mahalonobis about the importance of statistical approach is worth-mentioning. "The statistical approach is so fundamental to the modern way of looking at things—the affairs of every day life as well as scientific theories and experiments—that it should form part of mental equipment of the educated man which is not at present."

Dummy variable technique

Economic discipline in recent years has witnessed a phenomenal growth in empirical research work. The availability of huge mass of macro-economic data collected by various government departments and agencies either for running day-to-day administration or for plan formulation has facilitated empirical research works. The development of Econometrics, where mathematical and statistical tools are adopted to suit economic analysis, has given a boost to empirical research work. Appearance of personal computers and the development of user friendly computer packages has also promoted empirical research work.

As a result of these developments a research scholar in his survey work is bound to come across many statistical techniques about which he may not have efficient understanding. Consequently, the scholar either may fail to appreciate a good research piece of work or may misinterpret the results. The general textbooks on econometrics do not come to the rescue of the scholars, as these books concentrate more on statistical properties and computational aspects. At the other extreme, the books on research methodology concentrate more on philosophical aspects of research and very briefly touch upon statistical tools.

Therefore, there is a need to fill this void. In this context, the present paper intends to introduce a very widely used technique—technique of dummy variable and discuss its usefulness and limitation. Dummy Variable Technique is very widely used technique in economic research. It has been used for various purposes. Most often, it is used to incorporate qualitative variables like season, caste, religion, region, sex etc., in economic analysis. In the present paper, the technique of dummy variable is explained with the help of an illustration dealing with regional disparities.

Dummy variable is a special type of variable which takes, only two values either one or zero. "One" indicates the presence of the variable while "zero" indicates the absence of the variable.

Suppose, it is proposed to estimate the influence of the level of capital on the level of industrial output using time-series regional-level data for Andhra Pradesh. We shall start with a simple hypothesis that there is a linear relationship between the level of fixed capital employed (X) and the level of output (Y), i.e.,

$$Y = a + bx + U \ldots \quad (1)$$

'a' and 'b' are the parameters of the equation to be estimated. U is a random variable introduced basically to represent the influence of the variables excluded from the analysis.

'a' is called the intercept of the regression line and

'b' is called the slope of the regression line.

'b' represents the addition to the output level in response to employment of an additional unit of capital. Suppose it is felt that one of the regions is distinct from rest of the state and therefore the relationship between X and Y is different in that region.

$$Y = a + bx + U \ \ldots \ 2(a) \textit{ for the rest of the state.}$$

$$Y = a + a_1 + bx + U \ldots \ 2(b) \textit{ for Region } 1.$$

It is assumed that there is a difference only in intercept 'terms'. This assumption is made only to keep the matter's simple. One can assume that there is a difference in slope or in both slope and intercept.

The equations 2(a) and 2(b) can be clubbed into a single equation with the help on a dummy variable (D_1) which takes values one for region 1 and 0 for other regions: The equation with dummy variable will be

$$Y = a + a_1 d_1 + bx + U \ldots \quad (2)$$

If we take $D_1 = 0$ we obtain equation 2(a) and if we take $D_1 = 1$ we obtain equation 2(b).

Suppose, instead of the region 1 it is felt that the region 2 different from rest of the state, i.e.,

$$Y = a + bx + u \ldots \textit{ 3(a) for rest of the state}$$

$$Y = a + a_2 + bx + u \ldots \textit{ 3(b) for 2nd Region of the state}$$

The two equations, viz., 3(a) and 3(b) can be clubbed into a single equation with the help of another dummy variable D_2 which takes value 'one' for the region 2 and 'zero' for the rest of the state. The equation with dummy variable D_2 will be $Y = a + a_2D_2 + bx + u \ldots$ (3)

If we take $D_2 = 0$, we obtain equation 3(a) and if we take $D_2 = 1$, we obtain equation 3(b).

Suppose it is felt that all the three regions of the state are distinct from one another i.e.,

$$Y = a + bx + U \ldots \textit{ 4(a) region 3}$$

$$Y = a + a_1 + bx + U \ldots \textit{ 4(b) region 1}$$

$$Y = a + a_2 + bx + U \ldots \textit{ 4(c) region 2}$$

The above three equations can be clubbed into 'one' equation with the help of two dummy variables, viz., D_1 and D_2. The equation with two dummy variables would be

$$Y = a + a_1 D_1 + a_2 D_2 + U \ldots \quad (4)$$

If we take $D_1 = 0$ and $D_2 = 0$, we obtain equation 4(a)

If we take $D_1 = 1$ and $D_2 = 0$, we obtain equation 4(b)

If we take $D_1 = 0$ and $D_2 = 1$, we obtain equation 4(c)

Estimations

The equation (1) is estimated by regressing Y on X. The

equation (2) is estimated by regressing Y on X and dummy variable D_1. The statistical significance of the estimated coefficient of dummy variable is examined by comparing the magnitude of the coefficient with its standard error. If the coefficient of dummy variable D_1 is statistically significant then it implies that the region 1 is distinct from rest of the state. Equation (3) is estimated by regressing Y on X and D_2. Statistically significant coefficient for D_2 implies that the region 2 is distinct from rest of the state. Equation (4) is estimated by regression Y on X, D_1 and D_2. Statistically significant coefficient for D_1 implies that the region 1 is distinct from the region 3. Likewise, statistically significant coefficient for D_2 implies that the region 2 is distinct from region 3.

Data

Regional level data on industrial output Y and fixed capital employed (X) for ten-year period, 1980-81 to 1989-90 has been collected from Directorate of Economics and Statistics (AP). Coastal Andhra is taken as Region 1, Rayalseema as Region 2 and Telangana as region 3. For each region we have ten data observations. Therefore, in all we have 30 data observations.

Index